Building Distributed Systems

Designing scalable architectures with microservices, event-driven patterns, and robust deployment strategies

Ranjit Aneesh

bpb

www.bpbonline.com

First Edition 2025

Copyright © BPB Publications, India

ISBN: 978-93-65898-514

To View Complete
BPB Publications Catalogue
Scan the QR Code:

Dedicated to

My Parents,
*my wife **Sonal** and*
*my son **Ritvik***

About the Author

Ranjit Aneesh is an engineering leader with two decades of experience building large scale distributed systems. He currently leads teams at Capital One building systems to support the future of banking. Ranjit has previously managed serverless services at AWS Lambda where he led programs to increase the developer friendliness, feature set and scale of the service. He also built Capital One's fraud resolution systems which handles millions of transactions. Ranjit specializes in high-scale architecture design, microservices, and event-driven systems that power critical financial services. Ranjit has previously built a startup that specialized in digital media and online payments for digital publishers.

About the Reviewers

❖ **Jagadish Kamisetti** is a technology leader with over 15 years of experience in large-scale distributed systems design and development. As a technical lead at Zoom Video Communications Inc., he currently leads the Zoom Local Survivability solution, which ensures secure and reliable communication during network disruptions. His expertise has been crucial in advancing Zoom's enterprise-grade solutions.

Previously, Jagadish worked as a technical lead at Rockwell Collins, where he managed the components for Airbus A350 information management system, developing mission-critical communication systems for inflight and ground operations. An IEEE senior member and Sigma Xi research society member, Jagadish has significantly contributed to secure communications. He holds multiple patents in high-availability and security-driven communication technologies, demonstrating his innovation in unified communications and survivability solutions. His diverse experience spans scientific computing, aerospace, telecommunications, and unified communications, establishing him as a recognized leader in secure and scalable system architectures

❖ **Murugan Lakshmanan** is a recognized expert in cloud-native data streaming and real-time analytics, known for pioneering work that has significantly elevated operational efficiency and enhanced customer experiences at Fortune 100 financial institutions. With over 17 years of experience designing and implementing event-driven architectures, microservices, and cloud solutions, he empowers organizations to handle massive data volumes and transform digital services at scale.

His passion for continuous innovation drives him to mentor emerging technologists, review cutting edge research, and provide strategic insights that modernize data pipelines. By aligning robust engineering practices with core business objectives, Murugan guides enterprises toward data-driven decision-making and future-proof technology ecosystems. His expertise spans large-scale data integration, advanced security measures, and real-time analytics enabling organizations to automate complex workflows, optimize customer journeys, and remain agile in a constantly evolving digital landscape.

A dedicated proponent of thought leadership, Murugan actively contributes to conferences, technical book reviews, and global hackathons. His commitment to sharing knowledge underscores his mission to reshape how industries harness data and build transformative digital platforms.

Acknowledgement

I would like to express my sincere gratitude to all those who guided me with their suggestions in helping me complete the book

First and foremost, I would extend my heartfelt appreciation to my wife Sonal for her support and motivation that helped me keep chugging along and get the initial manuscript completed.

I am grateful to BPB Publications for their guidance and expertise in bringing this book to fruition. Their patience and flexibility to accommodate my timeline, working on multiple review sessions and thoroughness have helped shape the book immensely.

I would like to acknowledge the reviewers, technical experts, and editors who provided valuable feedback and contributed to the refinement of this manuscript. Their insights and suggestions have significantly enhanced the quality of the book.

Last but not the least, I want to express my gratitude to the readers who have shown interest in the book. I hope you enjoy the book and it helps you appreciate the subject as you increase your depth of knowledge.

Preface

In today's technological landscape, distributed systems have evolved from specialized architectures to fundamental building blocks that power the services we interact with daily. Whether you are ordering a product online, streaming content, or using a social media platform, you are relying on distributed systems designed to operate at scale while maintaining reliability and performance.

This book aims to provide a comprehensive guide to understanding, designing, and implementing distributed systems. The book starts with foundational concepts, we explore how these systems have evolved from traditional monolithic architectures to flexible microservices. We examine the crucial trade-offs between consistency and availability, investigate various strategies for managing traffic, and delve into practical approaches for ensuring speed and efficiency.

Throughout these pages, you will find practical insights drawn from real-world scenarios. The book uses an e-commerce platform as our primary example to illustrate how distributed systems principles apply in practice. This approach helps ground abstract concepts into tangible applications, making them more accessible whether you are a seasoned architect or a developer new to distributed systems.

The book is structured to build your knowledge progressively. It begins with the fundamentals and architectural patterns before moving to more complex topics like event-driven systems, data storage strategies, and observability. Each chapter builds upon previous concepts while introducing new techniques and considerations that will expand your toolkit for addressing distributed systems challenges.

The book is designed with resources to be both theoretical and practical. While we explore important concepts like the CAP theorem, we will also provide concrete implementation strategies and examples of how these ideas develop in production environments. The goal is to equip the reader with the knowledge to make informed architectural decisions based on their specific requirements and constraints.

Distributed systems present unique challenges, from ensuring data consistency across multiple nodes to managing network partitions and handling failures gracefully. Rather than avoiding these difficulties, we confront them directly, offering proven strategies for building resilient, scalable systems that can withstand the demands of modern applications.

As you progress through this book, you will develop a deeper understanding of not just how distributed systems work, but why certain approaches are favored in particular situations. This knowledge will empower you to design systems that balance competing concerns like performance, reliability, and maintainability.

Whether you are building a new distributed system from scratch or evolving an existing application, I hope this book serves as a valuable companion on your journey.

Chapter 1: Distributed System Fundamentals- In this chapter, we will look into the evoulution of computing from both the hardware and software side. We will identify the big ideas that changed how we design and build highly scalable systems. We will explore what are the key characteristics of such systems. We will further try to categorize different distributed systems and understand how they achieve scale. We will also learn from some examples of such systems.

Chapter 2: Monoliths and Microservices- In this chapter, we will look at what monoliths are and how their constraints led to the evolution of microservices. We will identify strengths of microservices and their challenges. We will also look at how services that leverage could follow various design constructs namely orchestrated or choreographed.

Chapter 3: Architecture of Distributed Systems- In this chapter, we will look at certain components, design constructs and technologies that enable these systems like API gateways, request/response processing cycle. We will learn more about containers and how they have helped resolved theworks on my machine issues that many software professionals are quite familiar with. We will also try to understand the containerization technology itself and how it facilitates building on top of microservice arhictecture. we will further look at security aspects and explore identity and access management. Finally, we will take a look at off the shelf distributed systems technology offerings-cloud based serverless systems.

Chapter 4: Consistency and Availability- In this chapter, we will explore the CAP theorem and how it has helped bring into the realization that every systems needs to make certain tradeoffs, the more we understand this, the better we get at designing software optimized for the use case we would like to address. We will look at different consistency models and data locking strategies. We will explore how availability of distributed systesm can be achieved by focusing on identifying important factors for a specific use case. We will also look at real world systems and try to learn how they are optimized for certain tasks. Finally, we will look at some emerging trends in this space.

Chapter 5: Design for Speed and Efficiency- In this chapter, we will explore the twelve factor app design principles and try to understand them better. We will look at understanding best practices around setting up codebase, dependencies and associated configuration. We will look at continuous integration and continuous delivery methodology of building software iteratively. We will learn design principles like stateless applications and ways of simplifying execution. We will look into concurrency and scaling systems horizontally and try to understand how stateless systems and ephemeral proceeses and displosability go hand in hand. Further, we will understand the SOLID design principles.

Chapter 6: Event-driven Systems- In this chapter, we will look at synchoronous and asynchronous system to understand best approaches to effectively design systems based on the specific use case at hand. We will then go further in learning publish and subscribe models to understand how these models help event-driven systems facilitate decoupling in systems. We will look deeper into message queues and how message identifiers, correlation identifiers help us design systems with effective tracing capability. We will dive into streaming systems like Kafka to understand how such systems are able to achive massive scales needed for internet based applications.

Chapter 7: Traffic Routing Strategies- In this chapter, we will try to learn how to handle traffic and considerations that should go into helping one design traffic routing. We will explore how to setup failover traffic routing, routing based on the geographic location of the users. We will learn how to manage external as well as internal load and the role of load balancers. We will look at how massive scale distributed systems use consistent hashing to not only manage the load but at the same time minimize the fallout when servers handling the load fail for some reason. We will further explore how cloud providers and in particular AWS's off the shelf solutions can help manage request traffic load.

Chapter 8: Building Resilient Systems- In this chapter, we will explore ways in which a large systems can be divided into different subsystems based on their traffic pattern. We will further understand a common architectural pattern called CQRS. We will lead about the role of observability and setting internal standards within the organization that help create guidelines to ensure SLAs are met based on expectations of consumers of a service with service level objectives.

Chapter 9: Data Storage Strategies- In this chapter, we will learn about different storage models and architectures. We will explore the evolution of data storage and how distributed systems may have different storage needs based on their use case. We will learn when to use RDBMS or No-SQL and understand tradeoffs with both systems. Similarly, we will try to understand transactional systems and learn if eventually consistent systems are acceptable for some use cases. We will further dive deeper to understand data partitioning and sharding. We will finally see how replication of data impacts consistency and resiliency model for the overall system.

Chapter 10: Observability and Operational Readiness- In this chapter, we will learn about the main pillars of observability such as logs, metrics and tracing. We will look at best practices around them and ways to leverage them effectively. We will also explore different technologies available and compare them for their strengths. For operational readiness we will learn how to ensure effective release management. Once in production, how to ensure critical metrics are derived and their monitoring done effectively.

Chapter 11: Distributed Caching- In this chapter, we will learn about different caching strategies in distributed systems and building caching hierarchy in systems. We will look at specific caching features like eviction methods and learn how to select one based on various use cases. We will further dive into ensuring consistency when using cache. We will try to understand common pitfalls when using cache and ways to avoid them. We finally look at a real world application to understand how to effectively design by leveraging cache.

Chapter 12: Choosing Platform and Technologies- This chapter guides architects through the complex task of selecting platforms and technologies for distributed systems, focusing on e-commerce applications. It examines runtime platforms, data storage options, message brokers, and serverless architectures, helping readers make informed decisions that balance performance, scalability, maintenance, and cost considerations while avoiding common pitfalls of technology selection.

Chapter 13: Deployment Strategies and Production Readiness- This chapter explores modern deployment strategies for distributed systems, detailing how to deliver software safely while maintaining availability. It covers feature flags for controlled rollouts, progressive deployment patterns like blue-green and canary releases, comprehensive testing frameworks, automated safety mechanisms, and container orchestration. Readers learn practical approaches to balance rapid deployment with system stability through continuous validation and intelligent rollback capabilities.

Code Bundle and Coloured Images

Please follow the link to download the
Code Bundle and the *Coloured Images* of the book:

https://rebrand.ly/8b4f46

The code bundle for the book is also hosted on GitHub at
https://github.com/bpbpublications/Building-Distributed-Systems.
In case there's an update to the code, it will be updated on the existing GitHub repository.

We have code bundles from our rich catalogue of books and videos available at
https://github.com/bpbpublications. Check them out!

Errata

We take immense pride in our work at BPB Publications and follow best practices to ensure the accuracy of our content to provide with an indulging reading experience to our subscribers. Our readers are our mirrors, and we use their inputs to reflect and improve upon human errors, if any, that may have occurred during the publishing processes involved. To let us maintain the quality and help us reach out to any readers who might be having difficulties due to any unforeseen errors, please write to us at :

errata@bpbonline.com

Your support, suggestions and feedbacks are highly appreciated by the BPB Publications' Family.

Did you know that BPB offers eBook versions of every book published, with PDF and ePub files available? You can upgrade to the eBook version at www.bpbonline. com and as a print book customer, you are entitled to a discount on the eBook copy. Get in touch with us at :

business@bpbonline.com for more details.

At **www.bpbonline.com**, you can also read a collection of free technical articles, sign up for a range of free newsletters, and receive exclusive discounts and offers on BPB books and eBooks.

Piracy

If you come across any illegal copies of our works in any form on the internet, we would be grateful if you would provide us with the location address or website name. Please contact us at **business@bpbonline.com** with a link to the material.

If you are interested in becoming an author

If there is a topic that you have expertise in, and you are interested in either writing or contributing to a book, please visit **www.bpbonline.com**. We have worked with thousands of developers and tech professionals, just like you, to help them share their insights with the global tech community. You can make a general application, apply for a specific hot topic that we are recruiting an author for, or submit your own idea.

Reviews

Please leave a review. Once you have read and used this book, why not leave a review on the site that you purchased it from? Potential readers can then see and use your unbiased opinion to make purchase decisions. We at BPB can understand what you think about our products, and our authors can see your feedback on their book. Thank you!

For more information about BPB, please visit **www.bpbonline.com**.

Join our book's Discord space

Join the book's Discord Workspace for Latest updates, Offers, Tech happenings around the world, New Release and Sessions with the Authors:

https://discord.bpbonline.com

Table of Contents

CHAPTER 1
Distributed Systems Fundamentals

Introduction

Today, our mobile devices act as an extension of ourselves helping us stay connected with each other, helping us consume digital content. The largest social media platforms have billions of daily users. Handling large amounts of digital content where every user can randomly view any content and also post their pictures or videos for others to view instantly requires a sophisticated system to work together. In this book, we will understand the fundamentals of how these systems work and help be your guide to design and build one yourself.

In the field of computer science and information technology, a paradigm shift has quietly revolutionized the way we process, store, and disseminate information. This shift is towards distributed systems, a complex and fascinating domain where multiple computer systems work together to achieve a common goal.

Distributed systems are networks of independent computers that work together. These systems are foundational to modern computing, enabling functionalities a single machine cannot efficiently or feasibly handle. Understanding the various types of distributed systems is essential for designing and implementing effective solutions across different application domains.

A distributed system appears as a single system, to the outside world. A google search page is just a single page. However, behind this system that is serving billions of queries every day are systems that have evolved over time and have hundreds of thousands of servers in data centers across the world. Social media platforms like *Facebook, Instagram, YouTube,* streaming platforms like *Netflix* and *Prime* are all examples of applications that rely on distributed systems.

The history of computing is marked by a continual evolution, from the era of large, centralized mainframes to the present-day landscape dominated by decentralized, commodity hardware. This journey reflects not just technological advancements but also a fundamental shift in the approach to data processing and system design.

It is important to consider what are the technical requirements in terms of scale, availability and storage to make design decisions. Diving deep into the design will help us to find bottleneck in the system and then address individual bottlenecks with the right solution.

At its core, any computer system has three domains to make it functional, that is, a processing system where requests are serviced, a data storage system to store and retrieve information from, and finally a way to access the overall system. We want to ensure the system works with thousands and sometimes millions of requests every second while also having the capacity to store data that may not just be in gigabytes or terabytes but petabytes and exabytes as well. We also want to ensure the system keeps working even if there is an outage or disaster in one physical location, we should still have an accessible copy of the data. When we have this copy, we also want it to be up-to-date with what we lost so that we can start using this copy like nothing ever happened. We will also understand tradeoffs and how to make an informed choice. You will learn that designing the system become more and more challenging when you start storing copies of data at multiple places to not lose them. As your system's capabilities grow, the system's complexity grows with it. This is the exciting world of distributed systems!

Structure

The following topics are covered in the chapter:

- Evolution of computing
- Turning point in distributed systems
- Key characteristics of distributed systems
- Components of distributed systems
- Types of distributed systems
- Challenges in distributed systems
- Achieving scale
- Techniques used to Scale
- Popular distributed systems

Objectives

By the end of this chapter, readers will have an in-depth exploration of distributed systems, outlining their fundamental principles, historical evolution, and key components. It begins with an introduction to distributed systems, highlighting their significance in modern computing and the complexity involved when multiple computer systems work collaboratively. The chapter investigates historical perspectives, illustrating the transition from mainframes to decentralized computing, and discusses the impact of significant technological innovations like the **Google File System** (**GFS**) and MapReduce on the field. It also covers various types of distributed systems, including cluster, grid, and peer-to-peer systems, and introduces concepts like microservices architecture, containerization, and serverless computing as modern approaches to scaling in distributed environments. Through real-world examples like Amazon, Netflix, and YouTube, the chapter illustrates how distributed systems underpin the operations of major digital platforms, highlighting the challenges and strategies in data management, scalability, and system design. This foundation sets the stage for further discussion on distributed systems' complexities and their important role in advancing digital infrastructure.

Evolution of computing

In the early days of computing, mainframes were the cornerstone of business and government operations. These gigantic machines, housed in large, temperature conditioned rooms, were revered for their processing power and ability to handle substantial computational tasks. IBM, with its series of mainframes, was synonymous with computing during this period. Mainframes excelled in reliability and centralized control, making them ideal for the batch processing tasks, prevalent at the time.

However, mainframes had significant limitations. They were expensive, consumed vast amounts of energy, and required specialized personnel for operation and maintenance. Moreover, their centralized nature led to bottlenecks in processing and a lack of flexibility.

The 1970s and 1980s witnessed the rise of minicomputers and personal computers. Companies like DEC with its PDP series and later VAX systems, brought computing power to a broader audience. The introduction of PCs, most notably by IBM and later by Apple, marked a pivotal moment. These smaller, more affordable machines democratized computing, making it accessible to individuals and small businesses.

This shift was not just about size and cost; it represented a move towards decentralized computing. PCs allowed users to process data locally, reducing reliance on centralized mainframes.

The proliferation of PCs set the stage for the next significant shift, networking. The development of LAN technologies in the 1980s and the expansion of the internet in the 1990s transformed isolated computers into interconnected nodes in a vast network. This networking revolution paved the way for distributed computing, where tasks could be shared across multiple machines.

The turn of the millennium saw the rise of commodity hardware which is, affordable, standardized, and interchangeable components that could be easily scaled and replaced. This trend was driven by the increasing power and decreasing cost of microprocessors, following *Moore's Law.*

Moore's Law, put forward by Intel co-founder Gordon Moore in 1965, observes that the number of transistors on a microchip-doubles approximately every two years, while the cost of computers halves. This principle has guided the semiconductor industry, signifying rapid technological progress with increased computing power, reduced device size, and lower costs. However, as technological advancements approach physical and material limitations, maintaining this exponential growth is increasingly challenging, leading to discussions on the future applicability of Moore's Law in the era of advanced computing and miniaturization

Simultaneously, the concept of cloud computing emerged. First Amazon and then Microsoft, Google and others began offering cloud services. This allowed users to access computing resources over the internet. The cloud was built on the backbone of commodity hardware, leveraging its scalability and cost-effectiveness to provide flexible, on-demand computing services.

Today, the landscape of computing is vastly different from the era of mainframes. Commodity hardware, combined with advanced networking and cloud technologies, has enabled a distributed computing revolution. This paradigm shift is characterized by decentralization, scalability and flexibility, dramatically altering how we process, store, and access information.

As we advance, the lessons learned from this evolution guides us to address modern computing challenges, particularly in designing and managing distributed systems at scale. The journey from mainframes to commodity hardware is not just a showcase of technological progress; it is evidence of the ever-changing nature of computing and the relentless pursuit towards efficiency and accessibility.

Turning point in distributed systems

Today's technologies have compounded on the technological innovations of yesterday that led to the next set of innovations. This is the virtuous cycle that has led to the current state of computing world. Two papers written two decades earlier provided developers and architects a way to help organize and process large amounts of data. There groundbreaking papers from Google were the GFS and MapReduce. These are not just any academic papers but the kind of text that reshapes how we think about storing and processing massive amounts of data. So, let us dive into why these papers were significant for distributed systems.

Google File System

GFS was Google's answer to a big question about *how do you store and access vast amounts of data across multiple computers without overwhelming complexity*. They came up with a system that is like a massive, super-resilient library to use an analogy. In this library, you can find and check out books (data) quickly, no matter how many people are using it. Even if a section of the library is destroyed, you can still access your books because there are backup copies stashed. The GFS solved several challenges related to large-scale data processing, especially for applications requiring rapid access to extensive amounts of data. It addressed the need for high throughput and reliability in the face of frequent hardware failures. GFS also provided a scalable and efficient file storage system capable of handling massive amounts of data distributed across many machines, ensuring data integrity and availability even when individual components failed. This made it particularly suitable for the storage needs of Google's large-scale computing tasks. Google's search works by consuming document across the internet. This technology helped google store and organize such large amounts of data and make it searchable for end users.

MapReduce

MapReduce took on another big question on *how do you make sense of all that data spread across your computers?* Imagine you have a jigsaw puzzle spread out over several tables. MapReduce is like having a bunch of friends come over, each working on pieces of the puzzle at their table, and then bringing it all together to see the big picture. It made processing huge datasets not only possible but also efficient. MapReduce solved this problem by processing vast amounts of data across many machines in a reliable and fault-tolerant manner. It simplified the complexity of distributed computing by abstracting the processing over large datasets into two main functions: Map, which processes and transforms the data, and Reduce, which aggregates the results. This approach enabled efficient parallel processing, scalability, and the handling of failures, making it possible to analyze large datasets on commodity hardware.

Impact of the papers

Before these papers, the idea of working with data across many machines was pretty daunting. But GFS and MapReduce laid out a blueprint that said, *this is the recipe, anyone can do this!* This was huge because it opened up the possibilities for more people and organizations to start tackling big data problems without reinventing the wheel.

These papers triggered other open-source projects. Apache Hadoop, for example, is a big name in big data that got its inspiration from GFS and MapReduce.

Hadoop took the ideas from Google and turned them into something anyone could use. Now, businesses can sift through mountains of data to find the insights they need. It can be seen as a superpower where you can instantly find a needle in a haystack, but for data.

Ever wonder how services like Amazon S3 or Google Cloud Storage work so smoothly? You can thank GFS for that. They took the principles from the GFS paper and built their own massive, resilient libraries for data. Now, storing your files in the cloud is as easy as saving them on your computer, but with the bonus of being able to access them from anywhere.

While GFS and MapReduce were game-changers, technology does not stand still. We are now looking at new challenges like processing data in real-time or making sense of data for AI and machine learning. Tools like *Apache Spark* and *Google's BigQuery* are the next generation, building on what GFS and MapReduce started but pushing the boundaries even further.

So, what is the takeaway here? The GFS and MapReduce papers were more than just academic exercises. They laid the foundation for a revolution in how we store and process data. They solved a tough problem of managing large amounts of data, organize them and process them. This made data more accessible and inspired a wave of innovation, paving the way for the big data and cloud services we rely on today possible. As we move forward, the ideas from these papers will continue to influence how we tackle the ever-growing ocean of data in our digital world.

Key characteristics of distributed systems

In the exploration of distributed systems, understanding their key characteristics is essential. These systems, which consist of multiple components located on different networked computers, communicate and coordinate their actions by passing messages. These systems have some core fundamentals that can be broken down into decentralization of processing away from a single server, provide scalability, build fault tolerance, provide concurrency, work with heterogeneous systems and security considerations.

In distributed systems, control and resources are decentralized. Unlike centralized systems where a single node handles multiple tasks, distributed systems spread these tasks across multiple nodes. This decentralization reduces the risk of a single point of failure and allows for more resilience and flexibility in handling workloads.

Scalability is a fundamental attribute of distributed systems. They are designed to efficiently handle an increasing load, either by scaling up (adding more resources to existing nodes) or scaling out (adding more nodes). Effective scalability involves not only handling more users or transactions but also maintaining performance and manageability at larger scales.

Distributed systems are inherently more robust in terms of fault tolerance. The failure of a single component often does not lead to system-wide failure. Techniques such as redundancy, replication, and failover mechanisms are employed to ensure high availability and reliability, even in the face of hardware or software failures.

Concurrency is inherent in distributed systems due to the presence of multiple nodes working simultaneously. Managing concurrency is crucial to ensure data consistency and system integrity. This involves complex coordination and synchronization, often necessitating specialized algorithms to handle concurrent operations effectively.

Distributed systems often involve a mix of different types of hardware, operating systems, and network technologies. Heterogeneity is a challenge and a characteristic of these systems, requiring interoperable protocols and middleware to enable different systems to work together seamlessly.

Security in distributed systems is complex due to the multiple nodes and network connections involved. Challenges include ensuring secure communication across the network, authentication, authorization, and maintaining data integrity and privacy.

Components of distributed systems

To understand distributed systems let us look at various components and how they interact. These systems consist of multiple elements, each playing a distinct role in ensuring the system's functionality, efficiency, and reliability. The four overarching parts of any distributed system are the hardware, software, communication between different components and the data they operate on. In today's day and age, developers and software architects work with cloud service providers, so, while we will touch upon some hardware aspects, our primary focus will be on the other three aspects.

Hardware components can be divided into servers, storage systems and network infrastructure. Servers are the backbone of distributed systems; servers perform the bulk of the processing work. They range from powerful central servers to a network of simpler, interconnected nodes in distributed architectures. Storage systems are essential for data management, storage systems in distributed environments include traditional databases, distributed file systems, and newer technologies like object storage. Amazon's Simple Storage Service is an example of object storage. The network infrastructure includes routers, switches, load balancers, and the physical network connections. The network infrastructure is critical for facilitating communication between the different nodes of the system. Most applications are built on cloud in the current day and age, so, we will focus on their counterparts in cloud service providers as we discuss in later chapters in this book.

Communication in distributed systems

The current state of communication between components off late, has evolved with the advancements and changes in the field of computing. As networks, hardware, operating systems and programming languages evolved, each of them changed the pattern of communication. It begins with the client-server model, a fundamental concept where dedicated servers respond to requests from multiple clients. This model laid the groundwork for distributed computing, but as systems grew more complex and larger no of clients were served via a single server, new protocols were invented. One such protocol was the HTTP protocol. It was stateless and connectionless i.e. it did not maintain any information between each request response cycles and once a response was sent for a request, the connection would be broken, freeing up server resources to serve other clients.

The HTTP protocol emerged as a critical evolution, marking a shift towards more interoperable and manageable systems. This was not just about ensuring different machines could talk to each other; it was about creating a common language and set of rules that would facilitate smoother, more reliable interactions across diverse computing environments.

Into this evolving domain stepped **Remote Procedure Call (RPC)**, **Common Object Request Broker Architecture (CORBA)** and **Remote Method Invocation (RMI)**. These represented a leap forward in distributed computing. RPC allowed functions to be executed on a remote system with equal east as a local invocation. This simplified the process of building distributed applications. CORBA and RMI extended this concept into the object-oriented realm and enabled objects and structures written in one language to interact with structures written in another language. This enabled seamless bridging of the gap between local and remote execution by making the process transparent. It encapsulated the underlying complexity of network calls, dealing with different languages and runtimes.

Then came the **Simple Object Access Protocol (SOAP)** protocol for exchanging structured information in the implementation of web services in computer networks. SOAP worked on top of the HTTP protocol and was pivotal in supporting operations over networks, offering a standards-based method for sending XML messages between client and server applications in a decentralized and distributed environment.

Building on these advancements, **Service-Oriented Architecture (SOA)** and **Representational State Transfer (REST)** further transformed inter-service communication. SOA provided a framework for building applications that could easily communicate and exchange data, regardless of the underlying platform or language. REST, leveraging the HTTP protocol, simplified interactions even further, using standard web protocols and methods to access and manipulate web resources. Its lightweight, stateless nature made it particularly suited to the modern web, driving the development of scalable, performant web services.

This evolution, from the client-server model to sophisticated protocols like SOAP, through architectural patterns like SOA, to the simplicity and efficiency of REST, reflects the computing community's ongoing quest for more robust, scalable, and flexible ways to facilitate inter-service communication.

The components of distributed systems are diverse and interconnected, each playing a pivotal role in the system's overall functionality. Understanding these components and how they interplay is essential for any professional dealing with the design, implementation, and maintenance of distributed systems. This knowledge forms the basis for addressing the challenges inherent in distributed computing and leveraging its full potential.

Types of distributed systems

Distributed systems are categorized based on their architecture, use cases, and the nature of the network and resources they use. Understanding the different types of distributed systems is important for architects, developers, and engineers to design solutions that align with specific operational requirements and challenges. This section outlines the primary types of distributed systems, each serving distinct purposes within the scope of distributed computing.

Cluster computing systems

These systems involve linking multiple computers (nodes) together to work as a single entity, often to perform complex computations or process large data sets. Clusters are typically located in close proximity to each other, often in the same data center, to minimize latency and maximize communication speed. They are used for tasks requiring high computing power, such as scientific simulations, data analysis, and rendering tasks. Their advantages are high performance, scalability, and cost-effectiveness while their challenges are their management complexity, especially as the cluster size increases. For example, a weather forecasting model might require the analysis of vast amounts of meteorological data to predict future weather patterns accurately. In this scenario, a cluster might consist of hundreds of individual computers, each contributing to the computation of complex algorithms that analyze and interpret the data. By dividing the workload among multiple nodes, the cluster can process the data more swiftly and efficiently than would be possible with a single computer, enabling researchers to obtain timely and accurate forecasts. This shows how cluster computing can harness the collective power of multiple machines to solve problems that are beyond the scope of individual computers.

Grid computing systems

Grid computing systems connect disparate computers, often geographically dispersed, to solve large-scale, complex problems that a single computer or local cluster cannot efficiently solve. Unlike cluster computing, grid computing leverages a more decentralized and heterogeneous architecture, making use of spare computing resources across different locations. They are effective in the use of underutilized resources and thus suitable for large-scale scientific problems which would be otherwise quite costly. Their challenge is managing the complexity across diverse systems and networks. One such example is the *SETI @ home* initiative that utilizes grid computing to analyze radio signals for signs of extraterrestrial intelligence. Volunteers share their computer's idle processing power over the internet, creating a highly distributed computing grid.

Peer-to-peer systems

There are decentralized networks where each participant (peer) shares a part of their resources, for example, processing power, disk storage, network bandwidth. These shared resources are available to other peers directly, without intermediary network hosts or servers. **Peer-to-peer** (**P2P**) systems are widely used for file sharing, distributed storage, and cryptocurrency networks. These systems are scalable, fault tolerant, and reduce dependency on centralized servers, however they can introduce security vulnerabilities if peers have open access across the network, data consistency can become an issue over unreliable networks, and management of peers as they connect and disconnect to the network. A widely used implementation of a P2P network is BitTorrent which is a file sharing protocol.

Multi-agent systems

A **multi-agent system** (**MAS**) is a network of agents that interact and collaborate to achieve common or individual goals. These agents are autonomous entities with the ability to perceive their environment, make decisions, and communicate with other agents. They can work in tandem or independently, adapting to changes in their environment to optimize outcomes.

Consider the example of a smart grid system in an urban setting, where multiple agents work together to optimize energy distribution and consumption. In this MAS, different types of agents represent various components of the grid: households, power plants, substations, and renewable energy sources. Each agent has specific roles and objectives household agents aim to minimize energy costs, power plants balance production to meet demand, and renewable sources adjust output based on available resources like wind or sunlight.

These agents continuously communicate and negotiate with each other, sharing information such as energy demand, supply availability, and market prices. Through this dynamic interaction, the system can efficiently balance energy distribution, reduce waste, and adapt to fluctuating demands or unexpected outages. For instance, if a substation detects a surge in demand, it can request additional power from nearby plants or even redistribute energy from areas with excess supply, ensuring a stable and efficient energy network. This MAS exemplifies how decentralized decision-making and cooperation can lead to optimized solutions in complex, dynamic environments.

Edge computing

Edge computing design brings computation and data storage closer to the location where it is needed, to improve response times and save bandwidth. By processing data near the edge of the network, closer to the source of data, edge computing supports real-time applications such as IoT devices, mobile computing, and autonomous vehicles. They help reduce latency, improve bandwidth usage, and enhance privacy.

For example, Netflix harnesses edge computing to enhance streaming quality and speed, bringing content closer to viewers worldwide. At the heart of this strategy is its **content delivery network** (**CDN**), Open Connect, a sophisticated array of servers distributed globally, designed to store, and deliver Netflix content efficiently. These servers, positioned near user locations, cache popular shows and movies based on local viewing preferences, ensuring quick access and reducing latency.

When you stream a Netflix show, it is likely coming from an Open Connect appliance within your local ISP's data center, not from a central server far away. This proximity minimizes data travel distance, reducing buffering and improving playback quality. Netflix's edge servers dynamically adjust video quality in real-time, based on your internet speed, enhancing viewing experiences without interruptions, thanks to adaptive streaming technology.

Moreover, Netflix's edge computing infrastructure supports load balancing and failover mechanisms. If one server faces issues, traffic is seamlessly redirected to another nearby server, maintaining uninterrupted service. This approach not only boosts streaming efficiency but also scales effectively as Netflix's audience grows, showcasing edge computing's impact on delivering content swiftly and reliably to millions of viewers globally.

The diversity of distributed systems offers a rich collection of solutions tailored to specific needs, from high-performance computing clusters to decentralized P2P networks. Each type of system presents unique advantages and challenges, necessitating careful consideration in their design and deployment. By leveraging the strengths of these systems, organizations can achieve unparalleled efficiency, scalability, and flexibility in their operations, paving the way for innovative applications and services in an increasingly interconnected world.

Challenges in distributed systems

Designing and managing distributed systems involves navigating a complex landscape of technical, operational, and conceptual challenges. These systems are characterized by their decentralized nature, geographical distribution, concurrent operations and present unique difficulties not encountered in centralized systems. Let us look into the key challenges faced by architects and developers when working with distributed systems, providing insights into the complexities of ensuring efficiency, reliability, and security in these environments.

Managing complexity

Distributed systems are inherently complex due to their multiple interacting components, diverse technologies, and varying network conditions. This complexity makes designing, implementing, and maintaining these systems challenging, requiring sophisticated coordination and management strategies. By adopting standardized protocols, leveraging middleware for abstraction, and employing automated management tools we can help reduce complexity. We will cover some of these topics like observability and identifying right communication depending on the use cases.

Ensuring consistency

Achieving data consistency across distributed nodes is a major challenge, especially in systems that allow concurrent access to shared resources. Ensuring that all nodes have a consistent view of data in the face of updates and failures is critical for system integrity. Implementing consistency models such as eventual consistency, strong consistency, or causal consistency, depending on the application requirements, can address this challenge. We will look into these aspects in more detail in later chapters.

Achieving scalability

As distributed systems grow in demand, they must scale efficiently without degradation in performance. Scalability challenges include managing resource allocation, balancing load effectively, and minimizing bottlenecks. Techniques such as horizontal scaling (adding more nodes) and vertical scaling (adding more resources like CPU/Memory/Storage per node), along with load balancing, throttling and partitioning, are essential for achieving scalability.

Handling partial failures

Distributed systems must contend with partial failures, where some components fail while others continue to operate. Detecting and recovering from such failures, without disrupting the entire system, is a significant challenge. Implementing robust fault tolerance mechanisms, such as redundancy, replication, and failover processes, can mitigate the impact of partial failures.

Securing distributed systems

Security in distributed systems is multifaceted, encompassing data security, network security, and access control. The distributed nature makes these systems particularly susceptible to various security threats and vulnerabilities. Employing comprehensive security measures, including encryption, secure communication protocols, authentication, and authorization techniques. The systems also need to consider mechanism to prevent DDoS attack and API abuse by implementing rate limiters to help protect distributed systems.

Dealing with latency

Network latency and varying data transmission speeds can significantly affect the performance of distributed systems. Minimizing latency is crucial for applications that require real-time responsiveness. Optimizing communication protocols, using caching and data replication closer to the user, and selecting appropriate data distribution strategies can help reduce latency.

Network and communication issues

Ensuring reliable and efficient communication between distributed components over potentially unreliable networks poses a challenge. Network issues can lead to data loss, delays, and miscommunication. Implementing reliable communication protocols, using message queuing systems, and employing techniques to detect and compensate for network failures are essential.

Synchronization

Coordinating actions and synchronizing state across distributed components, especially in the presence of concurrent operations and network delays, is challenging. Utilizing synchronization algorithms and time coordination protocols can help maintain system coherence and coordination.

The challenges in distributed systems are diverse and complex, stemming from their distributed, decentralized, and dynamic nature. Overcoming these challenges requires a deep understanding of distributed computing principles, innovative design strategies, and the judicious use of technology. By addressing these challenges effectively, developers and architects can harness the full potential of distributed systems, delivering scalable, reliable, and efficient solutions that meet the evolving demands of modern computing.

Achieving scale

Scaling is the ability of a system to accommodate increased loads by adjusting its resources. It ensures that the system can handle growth, whether in user traffic, data volume, or computational intensity, without compromising performance or availability. As digital applications become more integral to our daily lives, the ability to scale efficiently becomes critical for businesses and organizations.

Let us look at some of the ways that distributed systems achieve scaling.

Microservices architecture

One of the most significant trends is the shift from monolithic architectures to microservices. This approach breaks down applications into smaller, independently deployable services, each running in its own process and communicating through lightweight mechanisms. Microservices allow for easier scaling and faster development cycles, as teams can deploy updates to individual components without affecting the entire system.

Containerization and orchestration

Closely related to microservices is the adoption of containerization technologies like Docker and container orchestration tools like Kubernetes. Containers encapsulate microservices and their dependencies, making them portable across different environments. Orchestration tools manage these containers' deployment, scaling, and networking, facilitating efficient scaling and resource utilization in distributed systems.

Serverless computing

Serverless computing represents a paradigm shift, abstracting the server layer entirely from the application development process. It allows developers to build and deploy applications without managing the underlying infrastructure. The serverless model scales automatically based on the application's demand, offering cost-efficiency and operational flexibility, particularly for event-driven architectures.

Edge computing

Edge computing addresses the limitations of centralized data processing by bringing computation and data storage closer to the data source. This trend is particularly relevant in the **Internet of Things (IoT)**, where devices generate vast amounts of data. Edge computing reduces latency, conserves bandwidth, and enhances privacy, making it an essential scaling strategy for distributed systems.

Cloud-native technologies

The rise of cloud-native technologies, which are designed to exploit the flexibility and scalability of cloud computing, continues to shape scaling strategies. These technologies, including microservices, containers, and serverless functions, are built to scale seamlessly within cloud environments, supporting dynamic workloads and global distribution.

Autoscaling infrastructure

Autoscaling, a feature of many cloud services, automatically adjusts resources based on real-time demand, ensuring that applications maintain performance without over-provisioning. This trend towards elastic infrastructure is crucial for scaling in distributed systems, enabling efficient resource utilization and cost management.

Database scalability

Scaling databases in distributed systems has led to the adoption of NoSQL databases and NewSQL databases that offer scalability, flexibility, and high availability. Techniques such as sharding, replication, and database partitioning are increasingly important for managing large, distributed datasets.

Decentralization with blockchain

Blockchain technology introduces a decentralized model for data management and transactions, offering a novel approach to scalability, security, and trust. Distributed ledger technologies are being explored beyond cryptocurrencies, in areas such as supply chain management, healthcare, and finance, for secure and scalable solutions.

The trends in scaling within the software industry reflect a broader move towards more distributed, flexible, and efficient systems. As the volume of data and the scale of operations continue to grow, these trends will shape the future of software development, deployment, and management. The emphasis on scalability not only addresses current demands but also anticipates the future needs of the digital world, ensuring that distributed systems can adapt and thrive in an ever-changing technological landscape.

Techniques used to scale

Let us look at two broader techniques of scaling systems. We will also compare their pros and cons and also look at some architectural patterns for scaling.

Horizontally scaled systems

Horizontal scaling, also known as scaling out, involves adding more machines or nodes to a pool of resources to manage increased load. It contrasts with vertical scaling, which involves adding resources to a single machine. The process typically involves distributing the system's load across multiple machines to ensure no single machine is overwhelmed. This can be achieved through techniques like load balancing. Horizontal scaling helps systems scale to handle high loads by simply adding more machines. It can adjust capacity quickly in response to varying loads. There are a few challenges to horizontal scaling revolving around managing the complexity as it requires more sophisticated management and monitoring tools. As we add more notes, ensuring data consistency across nodes can be challenging. When systems scale, chances of nodes failing is also high. Consistent hashing enables horizontal scaling by distributing data across servers in a virtual ring, ensuring that adding or removing a server only redirects a small subset of data rather than requiring a full reshuffle. This minimizes disruption and keeps the system efficient, allowing it to scale smoothly as demand changes.

The ideal use cases of these systems are for applications with stateless operations, such as web servers, where each request is independent.

Vertically scaled systems

Vertical scaling, or scaling up, involves adding more power (CPU, RAM, storage) to an existing machine to increase its capabilities. This is relatively less complex in comparison to horizontal scaling. It provides for an immediate performance boost. However, there are physical and technological limits, CPUs are constrained by clock speeds, their architecture and amount of power they consume and heat they generate can create other challenges. Amount of storage on a single node has its own matrix of aspects to be considered. Suppose a node stores terabyte of data, if the storage hardware fails, one needs to account for its replica/backup to take control or spin up. The larger the storage, larger is the blast radius of impact for the system, if the storage is needed to be available at all time then one will need to keep a replica on standby at all times. We have not even dived to the consistency aspects of maintaining this replica. Apart from these considerations, sometimes, bulking up the hardware is more expensive than adding more of the same hardware and sharing load across multiple nodes, because hardware prices are not linearly proportional to their capabilities. Vertical scaling is best suited for applications with stateful operations, such as databases, where the data context is essential and spreading very frequent operations to multiple nodes will be impractical or when considering the tradeoffs, they are not worth the benefits.

Comparing horizontal and vertical scaling

Let us look into the performance, cost, scalability, and application suitability differences between horizontal and vertical scaling, providing an informed understanding of when and why one might be chosen over the other.

Refer to the following:

- **Application requirements**: The nature of the application (stateful vs. stateless) significantly influences the choice of scaling strategy. If the application is stateful or needs state to function to use its full potential, then moving to horizontal scaling becomes more challenging. This is one of the reasons we still find mainframe systems still in existence. AI training and inference systems also have similar challenges as distributing a neural network has large tradeoffs in processing speed.

- **Budget and resource availability**: The financial and physical resources available can limit options for scaling. As we discussed earlier, capabilities of physical resources do not increase linearly with their price. This is because companies developing them charge a premium for their latest and greatest systems than their older less capable hardware. This is true across CPUs, memory, and storage.

- **Long-term growth expectations**: Anticipated growth trends can dictate a more flexible scaling strategy to accommodate future demands.

- **Maintenance and operational support**: Vertical scaling may be a little less costly in terms of operational support as it is simpler to handle a single server than managing a fleet of servers. However, that does not mean that we will have to consider the total lifetime of the hardware considering the cost of wear and tear of hardware.

Impact of horizontal scaling on system design

The architectural considerations of distributed systems have been fundamentally transformed by the adoption of horizontal scaling. This method distributes workload across multiple machines or resources to enhance performance, reliability, and scalability. Unlike vertical scaling, which increases the capacity of a single node, horizontal scaling offers a scalable and flexible approach to system design, crucial for handling the dynamic and demanding workloads of modern applications.

Horizontal scaling, or scale-out architecture, is based on the principle of adding more nodes to a system to distribute the workload more evenly. Horizontal scaling's core advantage lies in its ability to scale beyond the physical limitations of a single machine, offering a path to virtually unlimited scalability.

When building a system using horizontal scaling, we need to keep the following core principles in mind:

- **Statelessness**: Systems are designed to ensure that individual nodes do not retain state information, facilitating easier scaling and redundancy. New nodes can come up any time and other nodes may terminate. The system keeps functioning without a hitch.

- **Distributed data management**: Essential techniques like sharding that is, data partitioning and replication are employed to manage data across a distributed system, ensuring data availability and consistency.

- **Load balancing**: A crucial component that distributes incoming network traffic across multiple servers to ensure no single server becomes a bottleneck, maintaining optimal service performance.

Architectural patterns for scalability

Adopting horizontal scaling requires architectural considerations to ensure systems are scalable, resilient, and maintainable. Here are some of the patterns we will discuss in more detail later in the chapter.

Event-driven architecture

Event-driven architecture (EDA) is a design paradigm that plays a pivotal role in enabling scalability in distributed systems. At its core, EDA is structured around the production, detection, consumption, and reaction to events. These events are significant occurrences or changes in state that are identified and processed asynchronously across various components of a system. EDA facilitates scalability by decoupling the components or services, allowing them to operate and scale independently. When a component generates an event, it does not need to know which other component will consume the event or how they will react, enabling a loose coupling that is inherently scalable. This decoupling allows system architects to add or remove components without disrupting the overall system, making it easier to scale out (add more nodes) or scale in (reduce nodes) based on the demand.

Command Query Responsibility Segregation

Command Query Responsibility Segregation (CQRS) is a design pattern in software architecture that separates the responsibilities of reading and updating data into distinct interfaces. This separation allows for more specialized, efficient, and scalable handling of operations in a system.

In traditional architectures, the same data model is used for both updates and reads, which can lead to complex models that are difficult to scale. CQRS tackles this by splitting the data operations into two paths: commands, which are responsible for updating data, and queries, which are responsible for reading data. This split allows each path to be optimized independently.

A real-life example of the CQRS pattern can be observed in e-commerce platforms like Amazon. In such platforms, the separation of commands (write operations) and queries (read operations) is vital for handling the massive scale of user interactions and data management.

In the case of Amazon, when a customer places an order, this action is a command. It updates the system's state, such as changing the inventory count and creating a new order record. This operation requires consistency and transactional integrity to ensure accurate processing of the order.

On the other hand, when users browse the Amazon website to view products, search for items, or read reviews, they are engaging in query operations. These read operations vastly outnumber the write operations, as millions of users may be browsing at any given time, while only a fraction simultaneously makes purchases.

To handle this, Amazon separates the read and write data stores. The write store processes all the transactional commands related to orders, user account updates, and inventory management. Meanwhile, the read store is optimized for fast data retrieval, supporting the high volume of users browsing the site. This store is updated asynchronously from the write store to ensure that the browsing experience is quick and efficient, even if it means showing data that is a few seconds or minutes behind the write store.

By using the CQRS pattern, Amazon can scale its read operations independently of its write operations, ensuring that user browsing remains fast and responsive even as the system processes complex transactions in the background. This separation not only enhances performance and user experience but also allows for more straightforward maintenance and scalability of each component within the system. *Figure 1.1* illustrates how the ecommerce platform may implement CQRS:

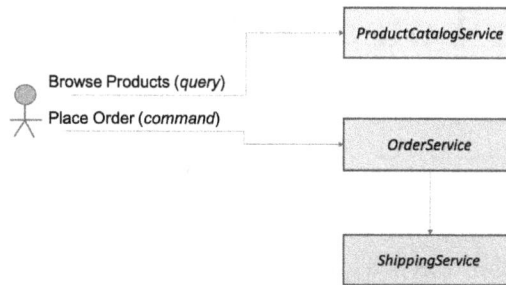

Figure 1.1: CQRS in action

Data management challenges

Scaling a system effectively often involves overcoming several database challenges, crucial for maintaining performance and reliability. As a system grows, databases must handle increased loads, more concurrent users, and larger data volumes, which can strain traditional database architectures.

One major challenge is ensuring database performance does not degrade as the amount of data and the number of queries increase. This might involve optimizing query performance, indexing, and considering more efficient data models. Additionally, as the system scales, the database must manage more connections and transactions, requiring robust concurrency control mechanisms to prevent data inconsistencies and conflicts.

Another significant challenge is maintaining data consistency across distributed databases. In distributed systems, data might be replicated across multiple nodes to improve availability and fault tolerance. Ensuring that all nodes are synchronized, especially in the face of network partitions or node failures, requires sophisticated synchronization and consensus algorithms.

Scalability also introduces complexities in database partitioning or sharding, where data is divided across multiple databases or tables to distribute the load. This can complicate query execution and transaction management, as operations may need to span multiple partitions with consistent and atomic execution.

Moreover, backup and recovery processes become more complex and resource-intensive in scaled environments, necessitating efficient strategies to ensure data durability without impacting system performance.

Addressing these challenges often involves a combination of advanced database technologies, fine-tuned configurations, and sometimes, re-architecting the system to leverage different database models or more scalable infrastructure solutions.

Developers and architect of systems should weigh whether they really need an RDBMS system or a NoSQL database will suffice. There are a lot of factors and variables to consider when assessing and analyzing one technology over the other. We will look at them in depth in a later chapter.

Popular distributed systems

This section discusses some examples of common distributed systems that many of us will be familiar with.

Amazon

Amazon's e-commerce platform is a great example of a distributed system, demonstrating how such architectures can handle vast scales of operations and data. At its core, Amazon's infrastructure is designed to support millions of users simultaneously, managing a colossal inventory, processing countless transactions, and providing a multitude of services worldwide.

In Amazon's ecosystem, distributed computing enables the platform to efficiently distribute loads across servers and data centers, ensuring high availability and resilience. For instance, when a customer searches for a product, the request is handled by a network of servers that distribute the workload, ensuring rapid response times despite the enormous volume of queries.

Moreover, Amazon employs sophisticated data storage solutions that distribute data across multiple locations, enhancing both reliability and access speed. This distributed data approach ensures that if one data center experiences an outage, the system can seamlessly shift operations to another, maintaining uninterrupted service for users.

Amazon's use of microservices architecture is another testament to its distributed nature. Each service, from payment processing to product recommendations, operates independently yet communicates effectively with others, enabling scalable and flexible system enhancements and maintenance.

Additionally, Amazon leverages distributed caching to reduce latency. By storing data in geographically distributed caches, Amazon ensures that users can access frequently requested information swiftly, enhancing the overall user experience.

In essence, Amazon's e-commerce platform exemplifies how distributed systems can achieve scalability, reliability, and efficiency, showcasing the power of distributed computing in handling the complexities and demands of modern digital commerce.

Netflix

Netflix, a global leader in streaming entertainment, epitomizes the prowess of distributed systems in delivering content at an unprecedented scale. With millions of users streaming content simultaneously around the globe, Netflix relies on a sophisticated distributed architecture to ensure seamless, high-quality viewing experiences.

At the heart of Netflix's success is its distributed content delivery network, which caches content in various locations worldwide. This strategy minimizes latency by serving content from a location nearest to the user, significantly enhancing streaming quality and speed. The CDN is a vital component of Netflix's distributed system, enabling it to efficiently manage the massive data throughput required for high-definition video streaming.

Furthermore, Netflix employs a microservices architecture, where different functionalities of the platform, such as user authentication, recommendation algorithms, and video playback, are handled by independent, distributed services. This modularity allows for agile development and scaling, as each service can be updated or scaled independently without affecting others.

Netflix's reliance on cloud computing is another cornerstone of its distributed system. Leveraging the cloud enables Netflix to dynamically allocate resources based on demand, ensuring optimal performance during peak viewing times and cost-efficiency during lulls.

By mastering the art of distributed systems, Netflix has achieved unparalleled scalability, reliability, and performance, setting a benchmark for streaming services worldwide.

YouTube

YouTube, as a premier video-sharing platform, is another great example of distributed systems in action, catering to billions of users and hosting an immense library of content. Its infrastructure is designed to handle massive data volumes, ensuring videos are uploaded, stored, and streamed efficiently across the globe.

Central to YouTube's distributed architecture is its sophisticated content delivery network, which stores videos at multiple data centers worldwide. This distribution ensures that users can access content quickly, regardless of their location, by connecting to the nearest server, thereby reducing latency and improving streaming quality.

YouTube's backend is powered by a complex ecosystem of microservices, each responsible for different aspects of the platform, such as video encoding, metadata storage, recommendation algorithms, and user authentication. These services operate independently but communicate effectively, allowing YouTube to scale specific functions as needed without affecting the entire system.

Data is another critical aspect of YouTube's distributed system. The platform employs distributed databases to manage vast amounts of user data and video metadata, ensuring high availability and consistent performance even during peak usage times.

By leveraging distributed computing, YouTube can dynamically allocate resources, balance loads, and ensure high availability, providing a seamless viewing experience. This approach exemplifies how distributed systems can support scalable, resilient, and efficient service delivery on a global scale.

Conclusion

In this chapter, we looked at how evolution of hardware and ever-growing capabilities of computers led to the dawn of the internet age, pushing our civilization into a new world where we are seamlessly connected with one another at our fingertips. We purchase products on the internet and entertain ourselves using streaming services. Much of our day to day lives are governed by a plethora of software services. Underlying these services is a unique design and architecture which we collectively call distributed systems. We looked at an overview of how some of these challenges like scaling help. We looked at what scaling means and tried to understand different architectural patterns and techniques that help us scale system to hundreds and thousands of interconnected computing instances that serve our humanity in so many ways.

By now you may have realized that distributed systems are not a single technique but a collection of techniques that help us address the multitude of challenges.

In the next chapter, we will look at the microservices architecture and topics related to its design.

Join our book's Discord space

Join the book's Discord Workspace for Latest updates, Offers, Tech happenings around the world, New Release and Sessions with the Authors:

https://discord.bpbonline.com

CHAPTER 2

Monoliths and Microservices

Introduction

In this chapter we will learn on why microservices based architecture have become the design of choice for distributed systems. Software architectures have evolved to keep up with the growing demands of scalability, agility, and maintainability. Monolithic architectures, once the standard approach for building applications, have given way to microservices a modular, decentralized approach to system design.

In this chapter, we will try to understand the transition from monolithic to microservices architectures. We will explore the challenges and limitations of monoliths, such as tight coupling, scalability issues, and the difficulty of adopting new technologies. In contrast, we will discover how microservices offer a more flexible, resilient, and independently deployable approach to building complex systems.

We will use an example of a commonly used internet application like an ecommerce application for practical insights. We will dive into the benefits of microservices, including improved scalability, faster development cycles, and the ability to organize teams around specific business capabilities. However, we will also address the challenges that come with adopting microservices, such as increased complexity, data consistency concerns, and the need for robust inter-service communication.

By the end of this chapter, you will have a better understanding of the motivations behind the shift from monoliths to microservices, and the key considerations for successfully implementing a microservices architecture in an organization.

Structure

This chapter covers the following topics:

- Monoliths
- Microservices
- Benefits of microservices architecture
- Microservices and data persistence
- Orchestration
- Choreography
- Challenges with microservices

Objectives

By the end of this chapter, readers will have a comprehensive understanding of monolithic and microservices architectures. By the end of the chapter, readers will be able to understand the characteristics, benefits, and limitations of monolithic architectures, including their impact on scalability, maintenance, and development processes. They will be able to grasp the fundamental concepts and principles of microservices architectures, including their benefits such as scalability, flexibility, agility, and enabling independent deployments and team autonomy. We will also compare monolithic and microservices architectures, identifying scenarios where each is more suitable and assessing the trade-offs between simplicity and complexity. We will explore the challenges and considerations associated with adopting microservices, such as distributed systems, data consistency, service discovery, testing strategies, monitoring, and logging. We will additionally gain insights into the organizational and cultural shifts required for successful microservices adoption, including the importance of cross-functional teams, DevOps culture, collaboration, communication, governance, and continuous integration and deployment.

Monoliths

Consider an e-commerce platform like an online bookstore. In its early days, this bookstore operates as a single application. Everything from managing inventory, processing orders, handling customer reviews, and updating the website's front end is part of a single, cohesive codebase.

This setup allows the bookstore's developers to quickly implement changes, such as adding a new category of books or updating the checkout process, because they only need to work within one codebase. Deployment is a breeze too since there is just one application to push live.

As the bookstore expands, introducing new features or scaling to accommodate increased traffic becomes more challenging. The growing complexity of the codebase makes it difficult to modify one component, such as the payment processing system, without risking bugs in unrelated areas, like the recommendation engine. This is often due to the reuse of shared code, which gets adapted for use cases it was not originally designed for. Since developers in this growing application keep adding new changes across its vast code base and start sharing code which were not intended to be shared, things start breaking more often at build or integration test. Database interactions become more brittle; changes made to interact with one table or domain object causes updates at different places in this large code base. This interdependency slows down development and makes the application harder to maintain. Organization ends up creating quality specialists/testers thus adding more cost to maintain this monolith.

Inside of monolith

Diving into a monolith's architecture is like exploring a well-organized administrative building with three main sections. First, there is the database layer, the building's foundation, storing all the files (data). Then, we have the application layer, the bustling halls and rooms where work (business logic) happens. Finally, the client interface serves as the grand entrance, where guests (users) come in and interact. This setup fosters a cozy development environment, albeit one that might feel a bit cramped as the scope of what is done in this building (features) expands. *Figure 2.1* illustrates the architecture:

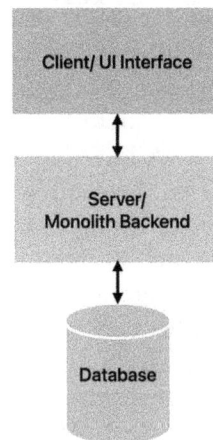

Figure 2.1: Illustration of a monolithic architecture

Advantage of monoliths

Now, monoliths are not without their charm; they offer a simplified development and deployment experience that is like having a direct expressway built from your idea to its execution, ideal for projects on the fast track. Testing is less of a headache when the application is not too large or complex since you're dealing with one big block rather than a jigsaw puzzle of services and when it comes to performance, monoliths can be predictably solid performers, provided they do not get too bloated.

Challenges with monoliths

As monoliths grow, they can become difficult to manage, making scalability feels like trying to fit a growing dragon into a room it is outgrown. The large codebase can turn into a maze, where making changes or adding new features feels like navigating through the maze without a map. Furthermore, trying to integrate new technologies can feel like retrofitting modern plumbing into an ancient building possible, but prone to break something unintended.

Usefulness of monoliths

Monoliths are well-suited for projects with a clearly defined scope, where scalability is a future concern rather than an immediate one. Think small to medium-sized enterprises with well-defined scope of systems or processes, e-commerce platforms with a manageable inventory, or startups in their sprint phase. These are the domains where the monolithic approach really shines, offering the simplicity and speed needed to get off the ground. In-fact monoliths do not start as monoliths, they end up as one due to explosive growth which is a great problem to have.

Building blocks of monoliths

Most commonly, the architecture is built using robust languages and frameworks like Java with Spring Boot, .NET, or PHP with Laravel each offering the tools and foundation necessary for constructing enterprise quality, well organized and well-structured applications. Supporting this structure, we have the infrastructure, which include servers, databases, and web services that act as the land on which these castles stand. If your application is running on WebSphere or WebLogic application servers, or you hear terms like EJBs you are in well entrenched monolith territory. It is not that these are bad, these are very good that can handle complex architectures and made develops rely on them too much to handle increasingly complex applications. However, server hardware has a limit to how much they can handle and scale for higher traffic. Managing such complex application servers need experienced engineers who know how to tune them well for their application's specific purpose.

In the grand scheme of software development, monolith applications are like the venerable castles of old majestic, sturdy, and sometimes, slightly cumbersome to expand. Yet, understanding when and how to use this architectural style can lead to successful projects, especially in scenarios where simplicity and speed are paramount.

Microservices

Imagine a bustling e-commerce platform. This application started with some basic services like *UserService* to enable users to register themselves with the platform. A

ProductCatalogService to enable users view various products available in the marketplace, A *ShippingService* to help the ecommerce company to handle shipping from seller to the user and an *OrderingService* to help visitors make payments, provide a delivery address and place orders. Ofcourse, even the most basic e-commerce platform would have lot many services but let us limit to these services for the purpose of this illustration. Now imagine developers making changes to some of these services while the system is live and having millions of active visitors at any minute. It will be quite a challenging exercise to ensure that a change to production does not break some flow when they are all running as a single application.

Figure 2.2 illustrates what a typical monolith looks like. So many important pieces all work together in the same application:

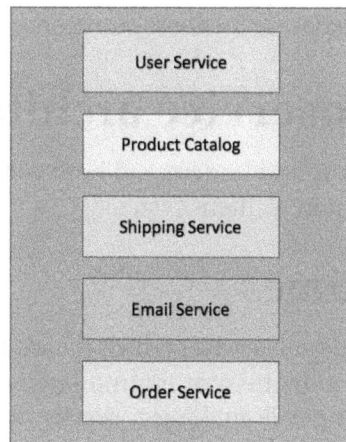

Figure 2.2: Ecommerce monolith starting up

Suppose a developer responsible for the Product Catalog component made a change to show product's customer ratings. While updating this component, they updated a common configuration property file that is shared with the other components in the monolith. One such component is the *Ordering* uses the same property file and the changes have now broken some functionality in the component. While this should have been avoided and the two services should not share such files if changes in one impacted another. However, the service has evolved and there may be many such interdependencies not just in this property file, but in shared libraries, shared data model and the database itself. As the changes get ready to be deployed, if the team is lucky and had added the right integration tests for those use cases, then this would get flagged early in the deployment and saved the day for all. If unlucky and found in production, this may cause some features to stop working to a direr situation of outage in one or all the services bringing the whole application down. These problems cannot always be solved by processes.

In this case even though the developers may have always avoided sharing across components, it might have been legacy code which was always there. A better approach would have been that developers of one component are never able to affect the stability of other components. At the core of the problem is that when too many components rely on each other, there is bound to be failures due to interdependencies. The solution to restrict this interdependencies via explicitly exposed interfaces instead of through shared files and sometimes even the database model where all components end up sharing the same data without any restrictions. We will discuss these in coming sections.

Splitting monolith into microservices

A microservice is a small, autonomous service that works together with other microservices to form a larger, application-wide system. Each microservice runs its own process and typically manages its own database. This approach to software architecture emphasizes dividing a traditionally monolithic application into a suite of independently deployable services, each scoped around a specific business function.

Benefits of microservice architecture

This section discusses the benefits and understand how various aspects of its architecture help towards building scalable and resilient systems.

Independent runtimes

Each microservice is an independent service, which means that it runs in its own process. This allows for each service to now be written in a language that suits its functionality better. For example, if a developer is making a service for multimedia processing like video transcoding, using an enterprise class managed runtime language like Java or C# will not provide the right performance/cost benefits. Using C, C++ or a language closer to machine code can be more efficient. At the same time if complex business logic and database interactions are concerned, it will be more efficient to use Java or C# where their strengths can be leveraged better. This ability of creating a polyglot application, that is, one with multiple technologies can bring efficiency in developments and maintenance. This independence is not possible in a monolith application.

Additionally, having independent smaller services help in isolating failures to that service, reducing the risk of a cascading failure that affects the entire application.

Not all parts of an application receive the same amount of traffic. In the e-commerce application, the *UserService* will handle user registration and other aspects of the customer signup flow, while the *ProductCatalogService* will serve displaying those customers the catalog of goods the website sells. The number of users registering themselves will often be less than the number of users browsing the catalog of goods. Discovering information like these in their own application, developers can choose to create the right combination of services to optimize their server resources effectively. In the above example, we will need fewer instances of *UserService* to run while reserving more server hardware for the *ProductCatalogService*e.

If the e-commerce application above is broke down into individual microservices, they could be arranged based on their traffic usage pattern as depicted in *Figure 2.3*:

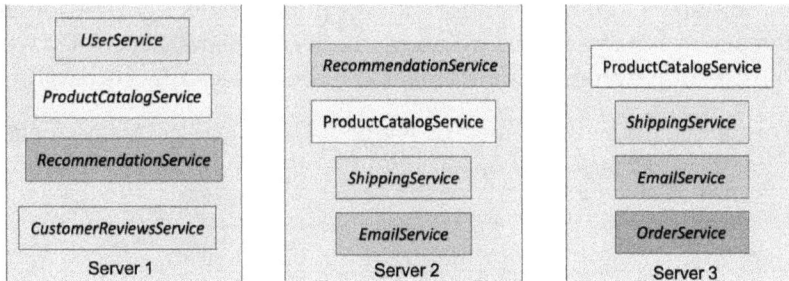

Figure 2.3: Distributing microservices among servers

Note that there is only one instance of the *UserService* running, while all three servers are running the *ProductCatalogService*. Number of instances of each service deployed on the server is dependent on their traffic, CPU, and memory requirements. Having this flexibility not just helps you focus on individual service needs and output you expect from them but also helps you optimize resource usage and costs.

Independent deployments

Microservices can be deployed independently of one another. This means updates, bug fixes, and feature releases for a specific service can occur without the need to redeploy the entire application. It boils down to the ability to maintain code in different repositories. Since microservices can be in different programming languages for the same application, it makes sense that each have their own independent repository. This in turn not only helps in simplifying the structure of the repository but setting up the environment and even understanding the purpose of the repository becomes easier. Moreover, understanding the code structure becomes simpler due to it being relatively more concise. If you have worked in a software organization, you are probably aware of how setting up a development environment can become a tedious and time taking job. When monoliths are involved, it is sometimes not even possible to setup the complete application due to its dependencies. These monolith deployment pipelines have an additional stage in the deployment pipeline where developers test their application in so called **dev stage** where developers test whether their changes actually work before, they move to a more elaborate testing stage. These complexities reduce speed of delivering a feature or fixing a bug.

Independent teams

In a monolithic architecture, an application is constructed as a single, indivisible unit often comprising the user interface, server-side application, and database. Teams working within this framework tend to be organized around layers of the application stack rather than distinct services, leading to a more centralized approach to development, deployment, and scaling.

With a monolith, a single team or multiple teams often work on the same codebase. They may divide responsibilities by application layer, such as front-end, back-end, or database or by features, but ultimately, all contributions merge into a single, tightly-coupled codebase. This necessitates a high degree of coordination between teams, especially when changes are made, to ensure that updates to one area do not adversely affect others.

This kind of organization as illustrated in *Figure 2.4* will lead to teams focused on their specific application stack they work on:

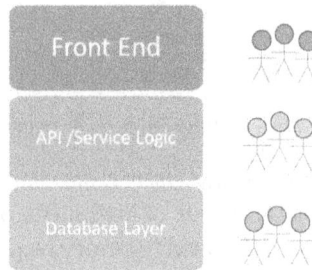

Figure 2.4: Illustrating teams organized based on the application layers they work on

Organizations, who design systems, are constrained to produce designs which are copies of the communication structures of these organizations.

– Conway's Law, Melvin Conway

Microservices are a perfect illustration of this law. When organizations adopt microservices, they often restructure their teams to mirror the services architecture. This reorganization minimizes communication overhead and aligns the software architecture with the business goals more naturally.

By structuring teams around services, organizations create clear lines of communication and decision-making. Each team's autonomy is reflected in the independent nature of their services, leading to a system architecture that directly represents the organizational structure. Refer to the following figure:

Figure 2.5: Teams arranged based on the services they support

The independent team structure inherent in microservices has facilitated a broader cultural shift within organizations. The small, focused teams foster a startup-like environment where agility, quick decision-making, and a sense of ownership are the norm. This shift has helped organizations become more responsive to market changes and better equipped to innovate.

Specialization and ownership

Each team in a microservices architecture typically takes responsibility for a single service. This ownership extends across the full application stack for that service, from the user interface to the data store. Teams become highly specialized around their service's business logic, which fosters a deep understanding of their domain and encourages a sense of pride and accountability in their work.

Cross-functional structure

These teams are usually cross-functional, comprising developers, testers, operations staff, and sometimes even a product owner. This mix of roles within a team encourages a holistic approach to service development, where every aspect, from coding to deployment, is everyone's responsibility. This structure eliminates silos and promotes a collaborative culture that aligns closely with DevOps principles.

DevOps and continuous delivery

The independent nature of microservices allows teams to adopt a DevOps culture, embracing practices such as **continuous integration and continuous delivery (CI/CD)**. Teams can independently deploy their services to production, leading to faster release cycles and a quick feedback loop with end-users. This autonomy also encourages innovation, as teams can experiment and iterate on their services without being hindered by the release cycles of other services or the application as a whole.

Testing at different layers

Testing becomes more focused and efficient in a microservices architecture. Teams are responsible for the testing of their individual services, which can range from unit testing of the code to integration testing with other services. By testing services in isolation, teams can ensure the robustness of their service without being affected by changes in other parts of the system. This leads to a more reliable overall application, as each microservice is thoroughly vetted before integration with the larger system.

Independent operations

The ability to independently operate each microservices helps the teams scale them according to demand. Rather than scaling an entire application, only the necessary microservice is scaled, optimizing resource utilization. Teams monitor their service's performance and respond to load changes dynamically.

Independent operations align closely with DevOps practices, blurring the lines between development and operations. Teams are equipped with the tools and permissions necessary to deploy and manage their services in production environments. CI and CD pipelines are managed at the microservice level, allowing for frequent and independent releases.

Full lifecycle ownership

Full lifecycle ownership incentivizes teams to create robust, self-sufficient services. Since the team is accountable for both the successes and failures of their service, there is a strong motivation to build resilient and maintainable systems. This responsibility includes not just writing code, but also choosing the right technology stack, setting up deployment pipelines, ensuring security standards. The team works on day-to-day operational challenges, for example ensuring that while a database version upgrade is happening, how can the team make sure that the application remains available.

Granular monitoring and fault isolation

In a traditional monolithic architecture, if the application experiences a slowdown, pinpointing the exact cause can be challenging since all components are tightly coupled. However, with a microservices architecture, each service is isolated. This means if there is an issue with the Order Service slowing down transactions, it can be quickly identified through service-specific monitoring tools without affecting the performance of the Product Catalog or Shipping Services. This isolation helps in rapidly addressing and rectifying the problem, ensuring minimal impact on the overall user experience.

Imagine a scenario where there is a sudden spike in traffic to the e-commerce application. The microservices architecture allows for real-time monitoring of each service. For instance, the *ProductCatalogService* might be handling the load efficiently, but the *OrderService* starts to lag due to the increased number of transactions. Real-time monitoring tools can immediately alert the operations team to this bottleneck, who can then scale up the resources allocated to the Order Service or optimize its performance on the fly, ensuring that the checkout process remains smooth for customers.

Enhanced fault tolerance

Microservices also enhance fault tolerance through better monitoring. If the *ShippingService* encounters a failure, monitoring tools can quickly detect the issue, and the service can be restarted or redirected without affecting the *ProductCatalogService* or *OrderServices*. This is because all these services are independently executing and interact with each other through a well-defined interface and without tight coupling with each other. So, while the shipping details which is service via the *ShippingService* might be temporarily unavailable, customers can still browse products using the *ProductCatalogService* and place orders via the *OrderService*, maintaining a level of operational functionality that would be difficult to achieve in a monolithic setup.

Customized health checks

Each microservice can have its own set of health checks based on its operational parameters. For instance, the *ProductCatalogService* might have health checks focused on response times to show items to users and database integrity, while the *OrderService* might monitor transaction completion rates and payment failure rates. This allows for more precise monitoring, ensuring that each service is performing optimally and that any issues are quickly identified and addressed.

Microservices and data persistence

When microservice share the same database, challenges arise. The database starts acting as the default integration point. This setup can lead to tight coupling, as changes in the database schema or business logic could impact multiple services, undermining the microservices principle of autonomy and independence. Shared databases constrain the ability of services to evolve independently, making deployments and scaling more complex and riskier.

An alternative approach is adopting the **polyglot persistence**, where each microservice uses a database technology that best fits its specific needs, whether it is a relational database, a NoSQL database, or even a graph database. This strategy aligns with the microservices ethos of decentralization and autonomy, enabling each service to optimize its persistence layer for its unique requirements.

When you take a deeper look at designing a data storage for *OrderService*, *ProductCatalogService* and the *PaymentService* in the ecommerce application, you will realize that expectations from these services are quite different. *ProductCatalogService* will be primarily a read heavy service because it supplies the catalog of items that the ecommerce application has. Writes will be limited to addition of new items. The ratio of **read versus write** may be a million read per write at a conservative level. Also, the consistency of data being updates immediately after a change in catalog is not needed. For such a service a NoSQL/ document-based database like MongoDB or AWS's DynamoDB may be a suitable fit. On the other hand, *PaymentService* would generally deal with large no of writes to DB and have minimal requirement for reading. Payment would also require updates to inventory, payment data, charging to the bank/card etc. to happen atomically, i.e. they should all happen or none of that happens. Any changes to payments should be immediately available. These requirements point to a transactional database, an RDBMS based database like Postgres or MySQL will be a suitable fit here.

The approach we discussed above is also called **Domain-Driven Design** (**DDD**). This approach significantly enhances the system's structure and clarity. DDD emphasizes the importance of aligning software designs closely with the business domain, promoting a deeper understanding of the business domain and its modelling. In a microservices architecture, DDD advocates for creating services around the domain model, encapsulating business logic, and fostering a modular structure.

Polyglot persistence introduces its own set of challenges. It demands diverse expertise from the development team, who must now manage and interact with multiple database systems. Moreover, it complicates data management and integration tasks, as data may need to be synchronized or aggregated across different storage systems.

In conclusion, while DDD provides a robust framework for designing microservices, the choice between a common database and polyglot persistence requires careful consideration of trade-offs between consistency, coupling, and complexity. Ultimately, the decision should be guided by the specific needs and context of the organization and the system it aims to build.

Orchestration

Orchestrated systems are systems having a centralized logic that calls multiple sub-systems one after the other or simultaneously, they may collect some data from those calls and then make another set of calls to other sub-systems and so on. The name refers to how a conductor in a musical orchestra conducts individual or set of instrument players to play tunes as per the conductor's directions. These systems rely on a central logic processor that may have the core business logic. For example, in our ecommerce application, suppose a user placed an order in the order service, it may make multiple calls to other systems, first it will verify that the inventory has the item being ordered by calling the *InventoryService*, then ask the *InventoryService* to reduce the inventory by the quantity being ordered. It would inform the *ProductCatalogService* that the items have been purchased so that it can adjust what the catalog should display based on this information. It may then make a call to the *ShippingService* to ensure that the item is delivered to the user. The *OrderService* would then notify the user via an email by triggering the *EmailService*.

Figure 2.6 illustrates some basic steps that can be involved, real ecommerce systems are vastly more complex but this illustration helps us to understand how the order service ensures the necessary steps are executed by **orchestrating** the whole business processing logic across multiple microservices:

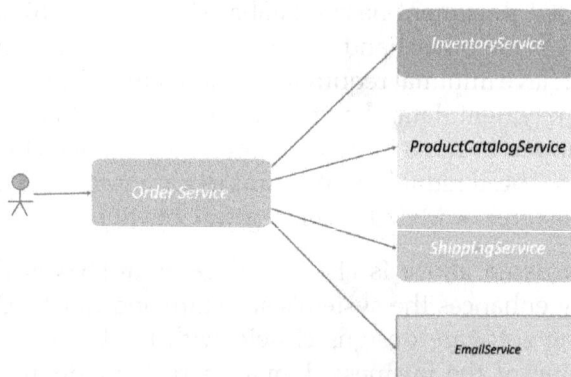

Figure 2.6: Illustration of orchestration

Benefits of orchestration

Orchestration based processing model is quite common. Let us look at some of the benefits to understand why they are so popular and useful.

Orchestration provides a bird's-eye view of business processes, allowing for easier control and management of service interactions. With a central orchestrator directing operations, developers can manage workflows in a straightforward way, understanding the entire process flow at a glance. This simplification is invaluable for maintaining complex systems, as it reduces the cognitive load required to comprehend the interactions between services.

Refer to the following:

- **Enhanced workflow efficiency**: By managing the sequence of service interactions centrally, orchestration ensures that workflows are executed efficiently. The orchestrator can optimize the order of operations, parallelize tasks where possible, and reduce unnecessary processing. For example, informing the *ProductCatalogService*, calling *ShippingService* and the *EmailService* can be parallelized while placing the order. This efficiency is crucial in high-load environments or when processing time-sensitive transactions, as it helps to minimize latency and resource consumption.

- **Improved error handling and recovery**: Orchestration facilitates centralized error handling, making it easier to implement uniform error recovery processes across different services. When a failure occurs in one part of the workflow, the orchestrator can decide on the appropriate action, whether it is retrying the operation, calling an alternative service, or aborting the process. This approach helps in maintaining the system's stability and ensures that errors are managed consistently and effectively.

- **Increased flexibility**: Orchestrator controls the interaction between services, updating or replacing a service involves minimal changes to the rest of the system, enhancing the architecture's flexibility. If the *OrderingService* has to now also make a call to the *PaymentsService* to verify that the payment has gone through, it can simply add that in the Ordering logic and orchestrate a call before calling the *ShippingService*.

- **Clearer audit trails and monitoring**: With all service interactions passing through a central point, orchestration inherently provides clearer audit trails and simplifies monitoring. It becomes easier to track the progress of specific transactions across multiple services, diagnose issues, and understand the system's behavior over time. This transparency is essential for compliance, troubleshooting, and performance optimization.

- **Streamlined implementation of business logic**: Orchestration allows for the centralized implementation of complex business logic that spans multiple services. Instead of embedding business decisions within individual services, the orchestrator can manage these decisions, making the system easier to update and maintain. This centralization of business logic helps in keeping the services themselves simple, focused, and loosely coupled.

- **Facilitates complex transactions and workflows**: Certain processes require transactions that span multiple services, where the success of the process depends on the successful completion of all constituent operations. Orchestration supports the implementation of such complex transactions, including compensating transactions for rollback in case of failures, ensuring data consistency and integrity across services. Consider for example that there is a sudden surge in traffic into the ecommerce application. The *OrderingService* start to get higher no of calls than usual. This service calls the *ShippingService* with the details of the delivery and also calls the *InventoryService* to keep its *Inventory* information up to date. Suppose the *InventoryService* is not able to keep up with this increased no of requests and starts to fail. The *OrderingService* will have to let the *ShippingService* to cancel the order and let the user know that it failed to place the order and try again after some time. Though this is not ideal and can be improved but the application is able to provide a consistent message to the user and keep its integrity when some systems were failing.

Challenges with orchestration

Centralization of logic, in an orchestration model, the orchestrator holds the majority of the business logic, directing the flow of operations and making decisions. This centralization can create a bottleneck, as the orchestrator becomes a critical point of failure. If the orchestrator service fails, the entire system's workflow can be disrupted. These systems evolve into an all-knowing single brain. Its dependencies sometimes get reduced to mere CRUD services that work to update the database. In the above example of the *OrderService*, suppose a new capability is needed to verify payments before shipping, it is easy for developers to load up the *OrderService* with the additional logic.

Refer to the following:

- **Scalability**: With the orchestrator managing the workflow, scaling the system can become challenging. As the number of services or the complexity of the processes increases, the orchestrator's workload intensifies, potentially leading to performance issues. In the *OrderService*, as more and more functionality are added, the service may become complex, error prone and slow.

- **Flexibility and agility**: One of the key benefits of microservices is the ability to develop, deploy, and scale services independently. However, with an orchestrator-heavy approach, changes in the workflow or business logic might require updates to the orchestrator, reducing the independence of individual services and potentially slowing down the development.

- **Service autonomy**: In a true microservices architecture, services are expected to be autonomous and loosely coupled. When an orchestrator controls skeletal CRUD services, these services may lose their autonomy, becoming overly reliant on the orchestrator for their operations, which contradicts the principles of microservices. Additionally, they create tight coupling between the Orchestrator and its dependencies. Not just that, when one service in the call chain is impacted, all other services see a spillover effect. In the *OrderService* example, if the service calls the other services sequentially and one of the service fails, the *OrderService* may simply start failing. No traffic will flow to the other services that follow this service in the call chain.

- **Complexity in maintenance**: Maintaining an orchestration-based architecture can become complex, particularly as the system evolves. The orchestrator's logic may grow increasingly intricate, making it harder to update or debug without affecting the entire system. The orchestrator code tends to move from merely being glue code to all powerful central brain. Making changes to this codebase becomes risky. This leads to additional cycles that developers need to review and test more thoroughly than other parts of the application.

- **Testing challenges**: Testing an orchestration-based system can be more complicated than testing a choreographed system. Since the orchestrator dictates the service interactions, end-to-end testing must account for various pathways and scenarios dictated by the orchestrator, which can be cumbersome and time-consuming.

Choreography

In the earlier section, we read how orchestration helps keep things simple. We also discussed their shortcomings when applications and services evolve with more and more features. distributed systems scale well when they have less tight coupling between components.

Choreography in microservices architecture represents a decentralized approach to service interaction, contrasting with the centralized nature of orchestration. In choreography, each service is designed to operate independently, reacting to events and communicating with other services through a shared event mechanism without relying on a central coordinator.

In a choreographed system, services publish events to a common event bus or use a message broker, allowing other services to subscribe to and react to these events. This model promotes loose coupling, as services do not need to be aware of each other's internal workings; they just need to understand the events they respond to. This enhances service autonomy, enabling teams to develop, deploy, and scale their services independently.

> **Note:** A message broker is an intermediary system that facilitates message exchange between different applications, ensuring that messages are appropriately routed and managed. It supports various messaging patterns and protocols, enabling asynchronous communication and decoupling of services. An event bus, on the other hand, is a type of message broker specifically designed for event-driven architecture, focusing on the publishing, and subscribing of events. While a message broker can handle a wide range of messaging patterns, an event bus typically focuses on broadcasting events to multiple subscribers, fostering a publish-subscribe model within a system. Examples of message brokers are AWS Simple Notification Service/Simple Queue Service, Kafka. Example of event bus: AWS Event Bridge

Before we move further on an example based on choreography, let us understand what a publish-subscribe model is. The model is not very different from say buying a magazine subscription. The magazine is delivered to your doorstep. The publisher knows your address and that you subscribed to the magazine. So, when the publisher has a new magazine edition, it sends you a copy.

Similarly, the publish-subscribe model in event-driven architecture is a messaging pattern where services (publishers) publish events and send them to a particular topic. Subscribers listen for specific events on a topic and when they receive an event in the topic, they read the event and react to it without knowing which service emitted the event. This decoupling allows for scalable, flexible systems where components can be added or removed without affecting others. It is particularly effective in distributed systems for enhancing communication efficiency, enabling independent service scaling, and improving system resilience by minimizing dependencies.

Now, let us take the example of the *OrderService* and try to redesign it based on choreography. Let us imagine that instead of the *OrderService* making specific calls to other services as illustrated in *Figure 2.6*, it makes a call to the inventory service to ensure that there are enough items to fulfill an order. After verifications, it updates its own storage with relevant information to process the order. It then emits a message to a topic called *OrderPlaced*. Following is an illustration of this process:

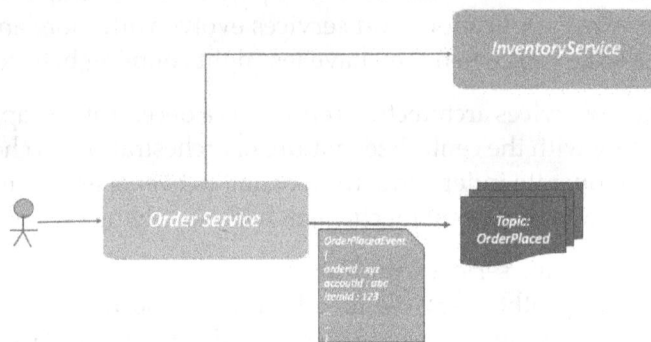

Figure 2.7: OrderService emitting a message to topic OrderPlaced

Individual services like *ProductCatalogService*, *ShippingService* and *EmailService* that were being called directly by *OrderService*, now subscribe to the *OrderPlaced* topic. When a new order is placed, each receive a copy of the message that the *OrderService* put into the topic. Each service starts processing as soon as they receive a copy of the message, parallelization of processing is implicit in event-driven systems. *Figure 2.8* illustrates the new event-driven model of processing an order:

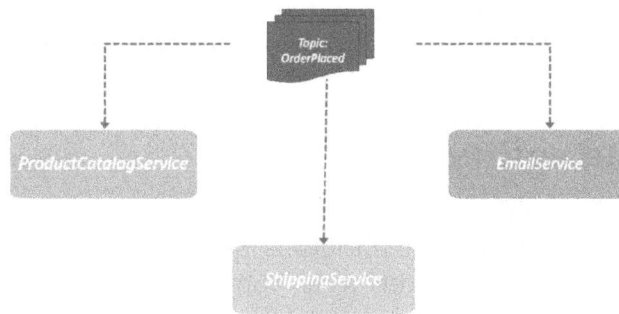

Figure 2.8: Event-driven processing of order

This process makes the *OrderService* light. The developers who maintained the *OrderService* now have more flexibility as the service is not a single point of failure for myriad of cases. Earlier, a change in its code base would need to be vetted across all its downstream services to make sure each respond within an agreed upon time/permitted limits on latency. One downstream service failing would not fail the complete order itself, or multiple if-then-else maze of code do not have to be written for various failure modes. As long as all services that depend on the *OrderService's* message, have all agreed upon the message content and its format, *OrderService* is doing its job well.

> **Note: In the context of software and systems, upstream and downstream dependencies refer to the relationships between services or components in a workflow or data flow. An upstream dependency is a service or component that provides data or functionality needed by another service, which is considered downstream. For instance, if Service A must process data before Service B can operate on it, Service A is an upstream dependency for Service B, and Service B is a downstream dependency for Service A. Understanding these dependencies is crucial for managing data flow, troubleshooting, and ensuring system reliability.**

The choreography approach offers several advantages, let us look at them from the lens of the *OrderService* example.

Decentralization

Without a central orchestrator dictating interactions, services can evolve independently, reducing the risk of a single point of failure that could cripple the entire system. The *OrderService* logic now does not have to depend on all failure modes of each service it interacts with.

Scalability

Services can be scaled independently based on demand, improving the system's ability to handle varying loads efficiently. If there is a high demand and a sudden surge in orders, the *OrderService* does not have to wait for each service to respond. At the same time, individual services consume events from the topic on their own pace, this ensures that the services are never overwhelmed. However, this comes with certain caveats that we will look at later.

Flexibility and agility

Changes to one service require minimal to no changes in other services, as long as the event contracts are maintained. This facilitates quicker adaptations to new business requirements or technological advancements. Suppose there is a need to notify users with text messages when the order has been shipped, all that is required will be simply adding the *TextNotificationService* to start listening to the *OrderPlaced* topic and its ability to understand the messages coming from that topic.

Figure 2.9 illustrates this where multiple services are dependent on messages from this topic:

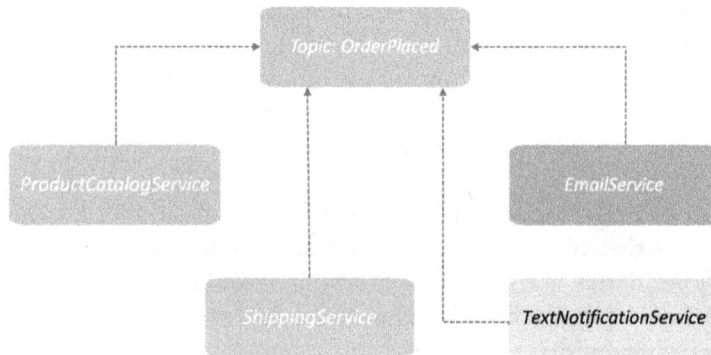

Figure 2.9: *Introducing new capabilities like TextNotificationService in an event-based model*

Resilience

The system is more resilient to failures, as the breakdown of one service does not directly impede the operations of others. Services can be designed to handle the absence or delay of expected events, enhancing overall system robustness.

However, choreography is not without challenges. It can lead to complex event chains that are hard to track and debug, potentially creating a scenario where tracing the flow of operations across services becomes cumbersome. Ensuring data consistency and managing distributed transactions can also be more complex in a choreographed environment.

In the context of microservices, choreography is well-suited for systems where services need to maintain high autonomy and the business processes are naturally event-driven. When developing your application, think about whether the dependencies of your service need to be tightly coupled due to the business use case or not. If not, then they should not be held to such constraints. Your design or the system adds tangible costs on your business that may surface in different manifestations like operational cost of maintaining the system, dependencies on thorough integration tests and deployment agility of your application to name a few of such real manifestations.

It is particularly effective in environments where agility and resilience are prioritized, loosely coupled systems are easy to ship with new features and bug fixes without worrying about its impact on other services.

The system's complexity is manageable with well-defined events and responses, do no try to retrofit a design style where they may not be appropriate. If you have too many different event types from the same service that is always directed to specific services, then there is an implicit coupling. The design needs a larger overhaul than moving to a choreographed system and you may be making your application more complicated than necessary.

We looked at the benefits of moving to microservices, we also talked about different architectural models. Let us also understand some challenges and practical problems that teams deal with when implementing and maintaining systems that work on top of microservices.

Challenges with microservices

Adopting a microservices architecture offers numerous benefits, such as improved scalability and agility, but it also introduces several challenges. These challenges require careful consideration and planning to ensure a successful implementation.

Complexity

Microservices increase system complexity. Developers must manage numerous independent services, each with its own lifecycle, dependencies, and configurations. This complexity can make understanding the system as a whole more difficult and increase the overhead for maintenance and monitoring. Imagine the ecommerce application example. A real-world application may easily have hundreds of microservices across catalog, ordering, notifications, fulfillment, payments and seller services etc. Though microservices make such an internet scale application even possible to exists, each of those services will need its own deployment cycle, operations and monitoring.

Data management

Data consistency and management become more complex in a microservices architecture. Each service may have its own database, leading to challenges in ensuring data consistency and integrity across the system. Services may need to exist in more than one geographic region, they may need to communicate with each other and ensure that their data integrity is maintained. Implementing distributed transactions can be complex and may require patterns like *Saga* (we will discuss about them in another chapter) to maintain consistency without tight coupling. Distributed systems encourage making tradeoffs between strong consistency and availability. Due to these factors, a balancing tradeoff is achieved by supporting eventual consistency which is quite among such systems.

Network latency

Communication between microservices over a network introduces latency. This can impact the overall performance of the system, especially if services require synchronous communication or if there are a large number of inter-service calls. Latency becomes particularly challenging when services are distributed across different geographical regions or when they rely on complex network topologies. The physical distance between services, network congestion, and the number of hops required for data to reach its destination all contribute to increased latency. Developers must carefully design their services to minimize the impact of network latency, considering factors such as the choice of communication protocols, the use of caching mechanisms and collocating services that frequently communicate with each other.

Inter-service communication

Designing effective communication strategies between services is crucial. Developers must choose appropriate communication protocols and patterns (for example, synchronous RESTful APIs, asynchronous messaging) and handle partial failures gracefully to ensure system resilience.

In addition to choosing the right communication patterns, developers must also consider how to handle partial failures and ensure system resilience. Services should be designed to gracefully handle scenarios where other services are unavailable or responding slowly. Techniques like circuit breakers, retries with exponential backoff, and bulkheads can help isolate failures and prevent cascading effects across the system. Developers must also consider security aspects when designing inter-service communication. Securing communication channels, implementing authentication and authorization mechanisms, and encrypting sensitive data are critical to prevent unauthorized access and protect the integrity of the system.

Service discovery and load balancing

As services scale and instances change dynamically, services need mechanisms for service discovery and load balancing to route requests to the correct instances efficiently. Service discovery allows services to locate and communicate with each other without hard-coding network addresses, using approaches like centralized service registries or distributed key-value stores.

Load balancing distributes incoming requests across multiple service instances to optimize resource utilization and improve performance. It can be implemented at the application level, for example, API gateway or infrastructure level, for example, dedicated load balancers and is often managed by container orchestration platforms like Kubernetes.

Robust service discovery and load balancing are essential for managing the complexity and dynamicity of microservices, enabling seamless communication and efficient resource utilization.

Security

Ensuring security in a microservices architecture is more complex compared to monolithic systems. With numerous services communicating over a network, each service becomes a potential attack surface. Developers must implement secure communication channels, such as using HTTPS and SSL/TLS encryption, to protect data in transit. Authenticating and authorizing requests between services is crucial to prevent unauthorized access. Implementing consistent security policies across all services can be challenging, requiring the use of centralized authentication and authorization mechanisms like *OAuth* or *JWT*. Managing and distributing secrets, such as database credentials or API keys, securely across services adds another layer of complexity. Developers must follow security best practices, regularly update dependencies, and conduct thorough security testing to identify and mitigate vulnerabilities in the microservices ecosystem.

Testing

Testing microservices is more complex than testing monolithic applications. With numerous interdependent services, testing requires a comprehensive approach that covers individual services, their integrations, and the overall system behavior. Developers must create and maintain a suite of automated tests, including unit tests, integration tests, contract tests, and end-to-end tests. Testing the interactions between services is crucial to ensure they work together as expected and handle failure scenarios gracefully. Setting up test environments that mimic production can be challenging, requiring the use of containers, mocks, and stubs. Automated testing pipelines are essential to catch regressions and ensure the system remains stable as services evolve independently. Debugging and troubleshooting issues across multiple services can be time-consuming, requiring robust logging and tracing mechanisms. Effective testing strategies, combined with continuous integration and delivery practices, are critical to maintaining the quality and reliability of microservices-based systems.

Continuous integration/continuous delivery

Implementing effective CI/CD processes is crucial for successfully managing microservices. With multiple services developed and deployed independently, automating the build, test, and deployment processes becomes essential. Each service should have its own CI/CD pipeline, enabling frequent updates and faster time-to-market. However, coordinating the deployment of multiple services can be challenging, requiring careful planning and orchestration. Automating the integration and testing of services is necessary to ensure compatibility and catch any issues early in the development cycle. Containerization technologies like Docker and orchestration platforms like Kubernetes play a vital role in simplifying the deployment and scaling of microservices. Implementing blue-green deployments, canary releases, and rolling updates helps minimize downtime and reduce the risk of faulty deployments. Monitoring and logging throughout the CI/CD process are essential for identifying and resolving issues quickly. Embracing a DevOps culture and collaboration between development and operations teams is key to streamlining the CI/CD process in a microservices environment.

Monitoring and logging

Monitoring and logging are critical for maintaining the health and reliability of microservices. With a distributed system, it becomes challenging to gain a holistic view of the system's behavior. Each service generates its own logs and metrics, making it difficult to correlate and analyze data across multiple services. Centralized logging and monitoring solutions are necessary to aggregate and visualize data from various sources. Implementing distributed tracing helps track requests as they flow through different services, enabling developers to identify performance bottlenecks and diagnose issues. Setting up alerts and notifications based on predefined thresholds is crucial for proactively identifying and resolving problems. Ensuring consistent logging formats and propagating correlation IDs across services is important for effective troubleshooting. Monitoring and logging in microservices require careful planning, tooling, and collaboration between teams to maintain system observability and quickly resolve issues.

Cultural and organizational changes

Adopting microservices often requires significant cultural and organizational changes. Teams need to adopt a DevOps culture, embrace new tools and processes, and often reorganize around cross-functional teams responsible for individual services. Generally, teams align based on the microservices they own, depending on the size and complexity of the service themselves, a team may manage one or more of these services on their own. While independence brings flexibility, it also introduces challenges. Each team must have members with a diverse skill set to cover the various operational aspects of their service. There can be a learning curve as teams adapt to managing operations traditionally handled by dedicated ops teams. Overcoming these challenges requires a combination of technological solutions, skilled personnel, and a culture that promotes collaboration, continuous learning, and adaptation. While microservices can offer significant advantages, organizations must approach this architectural style with a clear understanding of the associated challenges and a solid strategy for addressing them.

Standardization and governance

While teams operate independently, there is still a need for some level of standardization and governance across services. Organizations often establish a set of best practices and common tools to ensure consistency and facilitate inter-service compatibility for logging, monitoring and request processing across services. Standardization and governance in microservices implementation could involve defining a standard set of APIs. For example, an organization might mandate that all microservices must be accessed through RESTful APIs adhering to OpenAPI specifications. This ensures that different teams develop APIs that are consistent, well-documented, and easy to integrate across the organization. Governance might include policies on service deployment, ensuring that all microservices are containerized and managed through a platform like Kubernetes, providing a unified approach to deployment, scaling, and management. This standardization aids in maintaining consistency, efficiency, and compatibility across various microservices within the organization.

Conclusion

This chapter discussed the transition from monolithic to microservices architectures. We went through an example of an e-commerce platform can split its service into independent microservices. We looked at the inherent complexities and challenges of monoliths, such as scalability and integration difficulties. We also looked at how that contrasts with the segmented, agile nature of microservices. We further explored benefits of microservices like independent runtimes, deployments, and team structures, while also acknowledging the challenges such as increased system complexity and data management. The chapter emphasized the importance of adopting a microservices architecture to enhance scalability, flexibility, and maintainability in modern software development. We also looked at how microservices impact overall organizational and technical landscape.

In the next chapter, we will be introduced to various aspects of distributed system architecture. We will look at how systems receive request traffic, compute responses and technologies involved within those components. We will also look at security and modern trends in designing such systems.

Join our book's Discord space

Join the book's Discord Workspace for Latest updates, Offers, Tech happenings around the world, New Release and Sessions with the Authors:

https://discord.bpbonline.com

CHAPTER 3
Architecture of Distributed Systems

Introduction

Distributed systems deal with innumerous scaling and availability bottlenecks which is directly proportional to how complex a problem those systems are trying to solve. Most of these problems though can be divided into three wide aspects, managing incoming traffic and redirecting them to the right location, serving the traffic and common concerns around managing the traffic like authentication. Some of these problems require various aspects of the software stack right from OS to the application code to be considered. In this chapter, we will dive deeper to introduce ourselves to some of these problems and ways to deal with them.

Structure

This chapter covers the following topics:

- Microservices architecture
- API Gateways
- Serving requests
- Request processing
- Designing effective API interfaces
- Fault tolerance and resilience
- Server infrastructure considerations

Objectives

By the end of this chapter, readers will dive into API Gateways and Load balancers to understand why they are instrumental tools for request processing in distributed systems. We will also look at how the infrastructure stack architecture covering **virtual machines (VMs)** and the container technology. Going deeper with a request flow, we look at **identity and access management (IAM)** to understand how authentication and authorizations work in distributed systems. Finally, we look at some recent technologies around serverless computing services and how they are changing the distributed systems landscape where developers are shielded by some aspects of scaling applications.

At the heart of distributed systems architecture lie three key architectural patterns: microservices, event-driven architecture, and service mesh. Each of these patterns addresses specific challenges and contributes to the overall robustness and flexibility of the system. Let us look at each of them.

Microservices architecture

The microservices architectural style is a fundamental building block of distributed systems. It advocates for breaking down a monolithic application into a collection of small, independent services, each focused on a specific business capability or domain. These services are loosely coupled, independently deployable, and communicate with each other through well-defined interfaces, typically using lightweight protocols like HTTP or message queues.

By embracing microservices, organizations can scale individual services independently, foster agility through continuous delivery and deployment, and promote autonomy among cross-functional teams. Additionally, microservices enable organizations to adopt different technologies and programming languages for each service, allowing them to leverage the most appropriate tools for the job. Microservices have enabled distributed systems but they have also made managing systems more complex. Managing multiple technologies and programming languages need engineers and architect to know their nuances, it needs a talented group of engineers to master multiple programming languages and help deploy them seamlessly in a medium to large system.

Event-driven architecture

In a distributed system, where components are decoupled and operate independently, event-driven architecture plays a crucial role in facilitating communication and coordination. This architectural pattern revolves around the production, detection, consumption, and reaction to events, which represent significant occurrences within the system.

Events can be generated by various sources, such as user interactions, system activities, or external triggers. These events are then propagated through an event stream or message queue, where interested services can subscribe to receive and react to specific events. This decoupled approach promotes loose coupling, scalability, and resilience, as services can independently consume and process events without being tightly coupled to the event producers.

Service mesh

As distributed systems grow in complexity, with an increasing number of microservices and interdependencies, managing and securing communication between services becomes a daunting task. This is where the service mesh pattern comes into play, providing a dedicated infrastructure layer for service-to-service communication.

A service mesh comprises a network of lightweight proxies deployed alongside each microservice, handling tasks such as load balancing, service discovery, encryption, observability, and traffic control. By offloading these cross-cutting concerns from the application code, service meshes simplify the development and operation of microservices, enabling teams to focus on business logic while ensuring consistent and secure communication across the distributed system.

Let us understand this with some examples, as follows:

- **Traffic management**: During a major product launch, an online ecommerce platform could use Istio's traffic splitting to perform canary deployments, gradually shifting user requests to a new service version while monitoring error rates. This prevents outages caused by abrupt rollouts.

- **Security**: A financial institution can leverage Linkerd's automatic **mutual TLS (mTLS)** to encrypt service-to-service communication without modifying application code, ensuring compliance with strict regulatory standards.

- **Resilience**: A bank could use Linkerd's circuit-breaking features to halt requests to failing payment services, preventing cascading failures during high-traffic events like *Black Friday*.

The combination of microservices, event-driven architecture, and service mesh provides a powerful foundation for building robust, scalable, and resilient distributed systems. Microservices enable modular and independent development; event-driven architecture facilitates decoupled communication and asynchronous processing, while service meshes ensure secure and reliable service-to-service communication.

As organizations continue to embrace digital transformation and strive to deliver innovative solutions rapidly, distributed systems architecture offers a compelling approach to address the challenges of modern software development. By embracing these architectural patterns, organizations can unlock the true potential of distributed computing, enabling them to build highly available, scalable, and adaptable applications that can withstand the ever-increasing demands of today's dynamic business landscape.

API Gateways

Every component of distributed systems solves a specific aspect of the problem space that distributed systems present. They can be related to accepting requests at different scale of requirements from a hundred to a million requests per second, or could be related to processing of those request. In the world of distributed systems, where applications are composed of numerous independent and decoupled services, the need for a unified entry point and a centralized controller becomes quite useful. This is where API Gateways play a crucial role, acting as a strategic orchestration layer that streamlines communication, enhances security, and simplifies the overall management of distributed architectures.

Simplification of client interaction

API Gateways present a single-entry point for all client requests, simplifying the interaction with various microservices in a distributed system. Clients no longer need to manage multiple endpoints or understand the internal architecture of the backend services. API Gateways help provide a façade to separate the backend system complexities from external consumers. Internally a backend system may be composed of hundreds of microservices, some of them accepting external requests while other microservices supporting other microservices accepting external requests. As a developer or architect responsible for exposing these external facing endpoints, API Gateways come in handy in creating sophisticated traffic routing patterns based on various request attributes. For example, an order processing request need to be sent to only *OrderProcessingService* while a request to view the next page of the product catalog need to be only sent to the *ProductCatalogService*.

Modern API Gateways offer fine-grained routing control through multiple mechanisms. Path-based routing allows directing traffic based on URL patterns requests to **/api/ orders/** might route to the *OrderProcessingService*, while **/api/products/** routes to *ProductCatalogService*. Header-based routing enables even more sophisticated patterns, such as routing requests with specific API versions (via custom-version header) to different service implementations, or directing traffic based on user demographics stored in authorization headers. This granular control becomes especially valuable in large organizations where different teams might maintain separate microservices for distinct consumer segments or geographic regions.

Service abstraction and encapsulation

By hiding the internal structure of microservices, an API Gateway provides an abstraction layer that decouples the client-side of an application from its backend. This abstraction allows backend services to evolve independently without affecting the client. This is done by making API contracts as first-class citizens of distributed systems land. Microservices that service those requests lie behind the gateway and are configurable from the gateway itself. In a sense the API Gateway is where the system wide knowledge resides of which microservices serve what kind of requests. In the e-commerce example, if we add a new service for customers to add product review and ratings, it is the API Gateway where we configure the microservice where the requests should be directed to.

Cross-cutting concerns

The API Gateway can abstract away the primary authentication and authorization of every request from the backend services, serving as the first line of defense. While the API Gateway maintains the primary knowledge of who is authorized to call a particular service, it is considered a security best practice for the backend microservices to also implement their own lightweight authentication checks. This defense-in-depth approach ensures that even if the gateway's configuration is compromised or misconfigured, the individual services maintain a basic security posture and are not left completely exposed. For example, in our ecommerce application, adding new product categories to the application may need a separate service, but this functionality is only available to a specific team within the organization and is out of bounds to public users of the application. The category management service will verify not only the requests that arrive through the gateway but also that they contain valid internal authorization tokens. API Gateway also has the ability to throttle requests for services that have specific rate limits and are prone to cyclical spikes of requests. For example, a 10x increase in requests on a specific promotion or event that the ecommerce application marketed could cost the system to go down due to heavy load. By associate specific rate limits for various APIs of the application, the API Gateway can safeguard the application.

Functionality of API Gateway

Let us look deeper into the functionality of API Gateways. API Gateways primarily provide a single point of access to all internal services with a coherent API contract thus providing a unified entry point. API Gateways also help the underlying service by taking care of traffic managements and load balancing of requests. They also help in handling multiple protocols, authentication and authorization, monitoring and logging.

Let us look at each of them in more detail.

Unified entry point

API Gateways serve as a single-entry point for clients, abstracting the complexity of the underlying services and providing a consistent interface for accessing the distributed system. This centralized access point simplifies client integration, reduces the need for clients to understand the intricate details of service locations and protocols, and enables easier management of cross-cutting concerns like authentication, rate limiting, and caching.

Following our analogy of an ecommerce application, the user places an order via the website or the app. The app does not need to know where is the OrderService running, instead of calling the OrderService directly, they would send the request to the API Gateway.

The gateway can then perform various operations before forwarding the request to the OrderService. For instance, it can authenticate the client, validate the request payload, and even enrich the request with additional context or metadata.

Figure 3.1 shows the various components that an API Gateway can interact with while serving a request. Notice that backend services are totally abstracted away from the various management aspects of handling the traffic. External requests simply interact with a single endpoint and a URI that indicates which service the requests may be meant for, although it is the API Gateway which decides which service the request should be sent to for servicing.

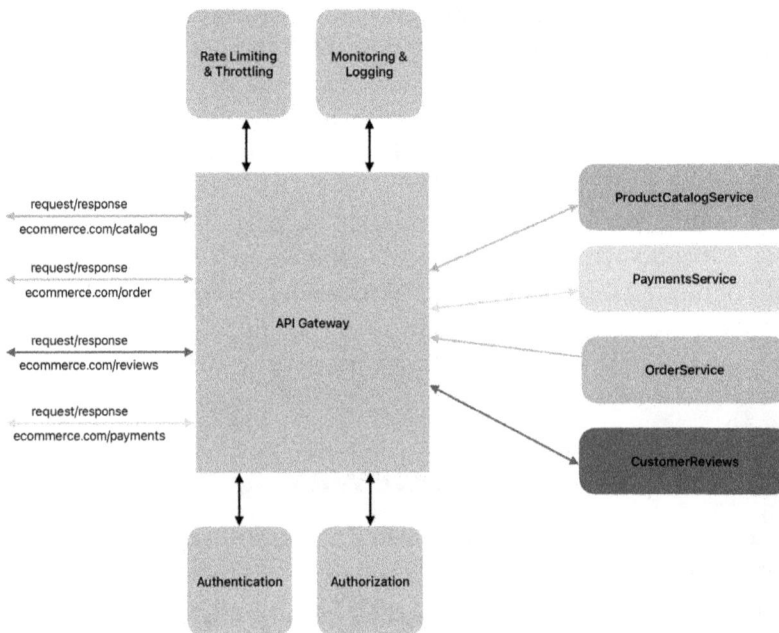

Figure 3.1: *API Gateway illustration of components while serving a request*

Traffic management and load balancing

API Gateways act as a traffic control and load balancing layer, distributing incoming requests across multiple instances of backend services based on predefined rules and algorithms. This ensures optimal resource utilization, improves overall system performance, and provides a seamless failover mechanism in case of service outages or failures.

So, while several thousand users may be placing an order in our ecommerce application, the API Gateway can handle the traffic and load balance it across multiple instances of the OrderService. It is like having a team of valets who ensure that incoming cars are distributed evenly across the available parking spots, preventing any one spot from getting overcrowded.

Protocol translation

Distributed systems employ various protocols and data formats, such as REST, WebSockets or gRPC. API Gateways can handle protocol translation, allowing clients to communicate using their preferred protocol while transparently translating requests and responses to the appropriate formats required by the backend services.

What if our e-commerce platform supports different protocols, like REST and WebSockets? The API Gateway can act as a protocol translator, allowing clients to communicate using their preferred protocol while seamlessly translating requests and responses to the formats expected by the backend services. Having a multilingual receptionist who can converse with guests in their language of preference.

Authentication and authorization

API Gateways play a critical role in enforcing security policies and safeguarding the distributed system from unauthorized access and potential threats. They can implement authentication and authorization mechanisms, apply rate limiting and quotas, perform input validation, and provide protection against common web vulnerabilities like SQL injection, cross-site scripting, and distributed denial-of-service attacks.

Monitoring and observability

By acting as a central point of control, API Gateways enable comprehensive monitoring and observability of the distributed system. They can collect and aggregate metrics, logs, and traces from various services, providing a consolidated view of the system's health, performance, and usage patterns. This valuable insight aids in detecting and resolving issues, optimizing resource allocation, and making informed decisions about system improvements.

Transformation and enrichment

API Gateways can perform data transformations and enrichment on incoming and outgoing requests, enabling them to adapt to different client requirements or backend service expectations. This capability includes tasks like payload marshaling, content filtering, request/response caching, and injecting additional context or metadata into requests.

Service composition and orchestration

In complex distributed systems, API Gateways can facilitate service composition and orchestration by combining and coordinating multiple service invocations into a single, cohesive response. This functionality simplifies the client experience and abstracts the intricate details of inter-service communication, enabling the creation of more sophisticated and comprehensive APIs.

Suppose when the user places an order, we want the user to get a consolidated view of order acknowledgement along with the date of shipment arrival via a single. The API Gateway can coordinate the invocation of the OrderService and the ShippingService, combine their responses, and present a cohesive result to the client.

So, in a nutshell, API Gateways are the unifying layer that brings order and control to your distributed system, acting as a strategic orchestration point for communication, security, observability, and service composition. They provide a simple interface externally while handling the internal complexities of managing hundreds of services, managing request and responses making life easier for clients and developers alike, while promoting scalability, resilience, and agility within your distributed architecture.

Popular API Gateway implementations

There are various popular API Gateway solutions and tools available in the market, each with its own strengths and features. Let us look at some of the more popular products which you may encounter. Please note, that they may not be popular later, it is always a good idea to look at specific requirements and how each of these tool weigh on those requirements, their cost structure, are they deployed on the cloud on premise, maintenance requirements like patching for bugs and security and complexity of configuration before selecting one.

Refer to the following:

- **NGINX**: NGINX is a high-performance web server and reverse proxy that can act as a lightweight API Gateway. It provides features like load balancing, caching, access control, and protocol translation. NGINX's lightweight nature and ease of configuration make it a popular choice for API Gateway implementations.

  > **Note: Reverse proxy operates in the opposite direction of request processing. Instead of being client-facing, it sits in front of one or more backend servers and acts as an intermediary for incoming client requests.**

- **Kong**: Kong is an open-source, cloud-native API Gateway built on top of NGINX. It offers a rich set of features, including load balancing, caching, authentication, rate limiting, transformations, and analytics. Kong supports a wide range of plugins and integrates well with various service discovery tools and distributed tracing solutions.

- **Amazon API Gateway**: Part of the AWS suite of services, Amazon API Gateway is a fully managed API Gateway solution. It handles tasks like traffic management, authentication, monitoring, and API versioning. Amazon API Gateway integrates seamlessly with other AWS services, making it a popular choice for AWS-based architectures.

- **Google Cloud Endpoints**: Google Cloud Endpoints is a fully managed API Gateway service offered by **Google Cloud Platform (GCP)**. It provides features like API monitoring, caching, logging, and integration with other GCP services like Cloud Functions and Cloud Run for serverless deployments.

- **Azure API management**: Azure API Management is a turnkey API Gateway solution from Microsoft Azure. It offers a wide range of features, including API publishing, access control, rate limiting, caching, and integration with Azure's monitoring and logging services.

- **Tyk**: Tyk is an open-source API Gateway and management platform that supports various deployment options, including cloud, on-premises, and hybrid environments. It offers features like API versioning, rate limiting, analytics, and a plugin architecture for extending its functionality.

- **Gloo**: Gloo is an open-source, Kubernetes-native API Gateway and ingress controller. It integrates seamlessly with Kubernetes and service mesh solutions like *Istio* and *Linkerd*. Gloo provides features like rate limiting, authentication, and advanced routing capabilities.

- **Envoy Proxy**: Envoy Proxy is a high-performance, open-source edge and service proxy that can act as an API Gateway. It was originally developed by Lyft and is now part of the **Cloud Native Computing Foundation** (**CNCF**). Envoy provides features like load balancing, circuit breaking, and advanced routing capabilities.

- **Ambassador Edge Stack**: Ambassador Edge Stack is a Kubernetes-native API Gateway and ingress controller. It offers features like authentication, rate limiting, caching, and support for various protocols like gRPC, WebSockets, and HTTP/2. Ambassador Edge Stack is designed to work seamlessly within Kubernetes environments.

- **Ocelot**: Ocelot is an open-source API Gateway specifically designed for .NET and ASP.NET Core applications. It provides features like request aggregation, caching, rate limiting, and authentication. Ocelot integrates well with the .NET ecosystem and is a popular choice for .NET-based distributed systems.

These API Gateway solutions and tools offer varying levels of functionality, performance, and integration capabilities. The choice of an API Gateway depends on factors such as the technology stack, deployment environment (cloud, on-premises, or hybrid), scalability requirements, and the specific needs of the distributed system architecture.

Serving requests

One of the key responsibilities of a distributed system is to handle and serve incoming requests from clients. In a typical distributed architecture, requests are received by one or more server nodes and then processed to generate a response that is returned to the client. Let us explore some important aspects and best practices for effectively serving requests.

Load balancing

In a distributed system with multiple server nodes, incoming requests need to be efficiently distributed across the nodes to balance the load and maximize throughput. This is often accomplished using a load balancer, which acts as the entry point for client requests. The load balancer employs algorithms like round-robin, least connections, or hash-based distribution to determine which server node should handle each request. It ensures that requests are evenly distributed, preventing any single node from becoming overloaded. Let us take a deeper look at load balancers.

Let us explore the importance of load balancing in distributed systems and how it contributes to building scalable, resilient, and high-performing applications.

Load balancing is the process of distributing incoming network traffic across multiple servers or resources to optimize resource utilization, maximize throughput, minimize response time, and avoid overloading any single resource. In a distributed system, where multiple servers or nodes work together to handle client requests, load balancing plays a vital role in ensuring that the workload is evenly distributed among the available resources.

The primary goal of load balancing is to prevent any single server or resource from becoming a bottleneck or a single point of failure. By distributing the traffic intelligently across multiple servers, load balancing helps to improve the overall performance, scalability, and availability of the system.

Load balancing in distributed systems is essential in distributed systems for several reasons, as follows:

- **Scalability**: As the number of users and the volume of traffic increase, a single server may not be able to handle the load efficiently. Load balancing allows the system to scale horizontally by adding more servers to the pool and distributing the traffic among them. This enables the system to handle a higher number of concurrent requests and accommodate growth without compromising performance. In our sample ecommerce application, as our application becomes popular, the number of users and requests will increase. Load balancing will allow us to scale our services.

- **High availability:** We do not want our customers to face downtime or errors when they are trying to browse products or place orders. Distributed systems aim to provide high availability by minimizing downtime and ensuring that the system remains operational even in the face of failures. Load balancing helps achieve high availability by directing traffic away from failed or unresponsive servers and routing it to healthy servers. If one server goes down, the load balancer can automatically redirect the traffic to other available servers, ensuring that the system continues to serve requests without interruption.

- **Improved performance**: By distributing the workload evenly across multiple instances, load balancing helps us optimize resource utilization and improve overall performance. For example, if a particular instance of the Shipping Service is experiencing high CPU usage, the load balancer can redirect some of the requests to other instances with more available resources. This way, we can maintain fast response times and by distributing the workload evenly across multiple servers. Load balancing prevents any single server from becoming overwhelmed and ensures that each server operates at an optimal capacity. This leads to reduced latency and a better user experience overall.

- **Fault tolerance**: Distributed systems are designed to be fault-tolerant, meaning they can continue functioning correctly even in the presence of failures. Load balancing contributes to fault tolerance by detecting and isolating failed servers and redirecting traffic to healthy servers. This ensures that the system remains available and responsive even if some components fail. If an instance of the product catalog service encounters an error, the load balancer can detect the failure and route the requests to the remaining healthy instances.

- **Observability and monitoring**: Load balancers serve as strategic monitoring points in distributed systems, offering valuable insights into the overall health and performance of your application ecosystem. Since all traffic flows through the load balancer layer, it becomes a natural aggregation point for collecting vital system metrics. Load balancers can track request rates across different services, helping teams understand traffic patterns and identify potential bottlenecks. They measure response latencies at a granular level, enabling operators to quickly spot performance degradation before it impacts end users.

  The error tracking capabilities of load balancers are particularly valuable for maintaining system reliability. By monitoring HTTP status codes and connection failures, operators can detect when specific service instances are struggling or failing entirely. For example, if a particular service instance starts returning an unusually high number of 5xx errors, the load balancer can not only route traffic away from that instance but also provide detailed metrics about when and how the problems began.

  These observability features transform load balancers from simple traffic directors into essential monitoring tools that provide real-time visibility into system health. When integrated with modern monitoring and alerting systems, load balancer metrics become a fundamental part of a comprehensive observability strategy, enabling teams to maintain reliable and performant distributed systems at scale.

- **Maintenance and upgrades**: Load balancing facilitates maintenance and upgrades in a distributed system. When performing maintenance tasks or deploying updates, individual servers can be taken offline without disrupting the entire system. The load balancer can route traffic to the remaining servers, allowing for seamless maintenance and reducing the impact on end-users.

Types of load balancing

Load balancing can be implemented at different layers of the network stack and can be categorized into several types, as follows:

- **Server-side load balancing**: Server-side load balancing involves distributing incoming requests across a group of servers. Common algorithms used for server-side load balancing include round-robin, least connections, weighted round-robin, and IP hash.

- **Client-side load balancing**: Client-side load balancing involves the client application or device making decisions about which server to send requests to. This can be achieved through techniques like DNS load balancing or client-side software load balancing.

- **Layer 4 load balancing**: Layer 4 load balancing operates at the transport layer (TCP/UDP) and distributes traffic based on IP address and port information. It is efficient and fast but does not consider the content of the requests.

- **Layer 7 load balancing**: layer 7 load balancing operates at the application layer (HTTP/HTTPS) and distributes traffic based on the content of the requests, such as URLs, headers, or cookies. It allows for more advanced request routing and content-based load balancing.

Popular load balancing software

Some popular load balancing solutions are as follows:

- **Hardware load balancers**: some of the dedicated hardware appliances designed for high-performance load balancing are F5 BIG-IP and Citrix ADC.

- **Software load balancers**: Examples of server applications or open-source solutions that provide load balancing capabilities are NGINX, HAProxy, and Apache mod_proxy.

- **Cloud load balancers**: managed load balancing services are offered by cloud platforms, such as Amazon **Elastic Load Balancer** (**ELB**), Google Cloud Load Balancer, and Azure Load Balancer.

Request processing

Serving requests in distributed systems efficiently is a fundamental aspect of building robust and scalable applications. Understanding how to handle requests effectively is crucial for delivering a seamless user experience. Let us explore the two primary approaches to request handling: synchronous and asynchronous processing, and dive into the various considerations and techniques involved.

Synchronous request processing

Synchronous request processing is the traditional approach where a service handles each request from start to finish before moving on to the next one. When a client sends a request, the service processes it immediately and returns a response. This model is straightforward and easy to understand, making it a good choice for simple use cases or when real-time responses are required.

Refer to the following:

- **Blocking and latency**: One potential drawback of synchronous processing is that it can lead to blocking and increased latency if the request involves time-consuming tasks. While the service is processing a request, it cannot handle any other incoming requests, which can result in a bottleneck and slow down the overall system performance. This is especially problematic when dealing with long-running operations or high-latency dependencies.

  For example, consider the Order Service in an e-commerce application. When a customer places an order, the Order Service needs to perform several tasks, such as validating the order details, calculating the total price, and updating the inventory. If these tasks are performed synchronously, the service will be blocked until all the operations are completed, potentially leading to increased response times and reduced throughput.

- **Threading and concurrency**: To mitigate the limitations of synchronous processing, services often employ multi-threading or concurrency techniques. By creating multiple threads or processes, a service can handle multiple requests simultaneously. Each thread takes care of processing a single request, allowing the service to achieve parallel execution and improve throughput. However, managing concurrency introduces additional complexity, such as thread synchronization and resource sharing, which must be carefully handled to avoid issues like race conditions and deadlocks.

  Let us take our *ProductCatalogService* as an example. When multiple customers are browsing the product catalog simultaneously, the service needs to handle concurrent requests efficiently. By leveraging multi-threading, the service can spawn multiple threads, each responsible for processing a specific customer request. This enables the service to serve multiple customers in parallel, improving response times and overall performance.

Synchronous request processing frameworks

There are several popular frameworks and technologies that support synchronous request processing.

Following are a few examples:

- **Express.js**: Express.js is a lightweight and flexible web application framework for Node.js. It provides a simple and intuitive way to handle HTTP requests and responses synchronously. With Express.js, you can define routes, middleware, and handlers to process incoming requests and send back responses.

- **Spring Boot**: Spring Boot is a powerful and opinionated framework for building Java applications. It provides a wide range of features and abstractions for handling synchronous request processing. With Spring Boot, you can create RESTful APIs, define controllers and services, and leverage the rich ecosystem of Spring libraries for various aspects of request handling.

- **Flask**: Flask is a popular Python web framework known for its simplicity and ease of use. It allows you to build synchronous request processing applications by defining routes and view functions. Flask provides a straightforward way to map URLs to Python functions and handle incoming requests synchronously.

These frameworks simplify the process of building synchronous request processing applications by providing abstractions and utilities for handling HTTP requests, parsing request data, and generating responses.

Asynchronous request processing

Asynchronous request processing is an alternative approach that addresses the limitations of synchronous processing. In this model, a service accepts a request, acknowledges its receipt, and then processes it independently, allowing the client to continue without waiting for the completion of the request. Asynchronous processing enables services to handle a large number of requests concurrently and improve overall system responsiveness. Synchronous processing requires the client to wait or be blocked until a response is received from the server. On the other hand, an asynchronous execution does not block the client and hence considered non-blocking.

Non-blocking design

With asynchronous processing, services can quickly respond to clients with an acknowledgment, indicating that the request has been accepted for processing. This non-blocking behavior allows the service to remain responsive and handle other incoming requests, even if the actual processing of the request takes some time. Clients can continue their work or perform other tasks without being blocked, leading to a more fluid and responsive user experience.

Consider the *OrderService,* when customers place an order, order service should be able to provide a success as soon as possible. This is the most critical part of the application and brings business to the organization. A good design will ensure that any processing that is critical to respond to the user with a success or failure is only processed in this blocking path. In the case of order processing, the system has to absolutely check that the item customer is purchasing is available in the inventory, every other aspect of placing an order does not need to block a success or failure response. *Figure 3.2* visually illustrates this. The *OrderService* publishes a message to a topic which is listened by all other services that need to react to an order request. This event-driven approach also enables loose coupling between services and allows for scalable and resilient request processing.

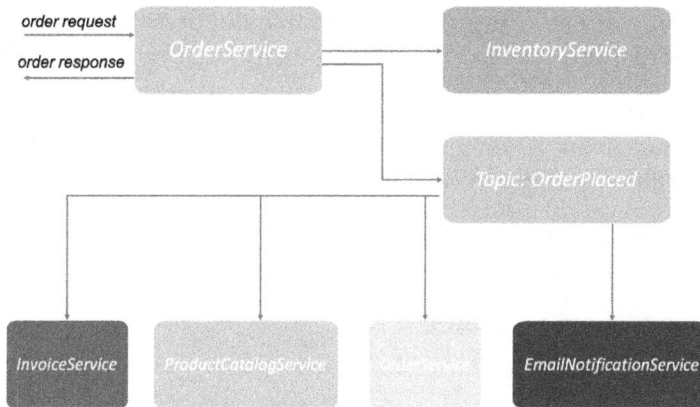

Figure 3.2: *Unblocking requests with event-driven design*

Reactive request processing

Reactive request processing is a programming paradigm and architectural style that addresses the challenges of handling high volumes of concurrent requests and dealing with latency-sensitive operations in distributed systems. In traditional request processing, each request is handled synchronously, blocking the processing thread until the request is complete. This approach can lead to poor resource utilization, limited scalability, and reduced responsiveness, especially when dealing with long-running or I/O-bound operations.

Reactive request processing solves these problems by adopting non-blocking I/O, asynchronous processing, and event-driven architectures. It allows systems to handle a large number of concurrent requests efficiently by avoiding thread blocking and enabling better resource utilization. Asynchronous processing enables the system to initiate long-running tasks without blocking the main execution thread, improving concurrency and responsiveness.

Moreover, reactive systems incorporate *backpressure* and flow control mechanisms to regulate the rate of incoming requests based on the system's capacity. This prevents overload and ensures stability under high load. Reactive systems are also designed to be resilient and fault-tolerant, employing techniques like circuit breakers and retries to handle failures gracefully.

Note: Backpressure is a mechanism in reactive systems that allows a component to signal its upstream components to slow down or pause the flow of data when it reaches its processing capacity. It is a way to regulate the rate of incoming requests to prevent overload and maintain system stability. When a component is unable to keep up with the incoming flow, it can apply backpressure to its upstream components, requesting them to send data at a slower rate. This helps to avoid buffer overflows, memory exhaustion and issues caused by resource not being available. Backpressure handling ensures that the system remains responsive and resilient under high load.

By embracing reactive request processing, distributed systems can achieve better scalability, resilience, and responsiveness, making them well-suited for handling high-concurrency scenarios and real-time data processing.

Several programming languages and frameworks have emerged to support reactive request processing.

Some popular examples are as follows:

- **Java**: RxJava, Project Reactor, Vert.x
- **JavaScript**: Node.js, RxJS
- **Scala**: Akka, Play Framework
- **C#**: Reactive Extensions (Rx.NET)
- **Python**: AsyncIO, Twisted

Designing effective API interfaces

When serving requests in a distributed system, designing effective **application programming interface** (**API**) is crucial for ease of use, maintainability, and scalability. API interfaces define the contract that the service exposes to the outside world. Consider a RESTful API, it defines whether an HTTP request is more commonly GET, POST, PUT or DELETE. Additionally, an API interface can define headers which are used as additional information to the service. The OpenAPI initiative has defined a specification for standardizing descriptions of API interfaces (learn more about them at **https://spec. openapis.org**). There are multiple considerations when defining an API. This section discusses some key considerations.

Protocol selection

Choosing the right protocol for your API is important. ReSTful APIs using HTTP are widely adopted due to their simplicity and compatibility with web technologies. They leverage HTTP methods (GET, POST, PUT, DELETE) to perform operations on resources. GraphQL is another popular choice that allows clients to query for specific data fields, reducing over-fetching and under-fetching. gRPC is a high-performance RPC framework that uses protocol buffers for efficient binary serialization and supports streaming.

For example, in our e-commerce application, the *ProductCatalogService* can expose a RESTful API that allows clients to retrieve product information using GET requests, update product details using PUT requests, and create new products using POST requests. The *OrderService* can use a GraphQL API to enable clients to query for specific order details, such as the order status, shipping address, and associated products, in a single request.

API versioning

As your system evolves, it is essential to version your API to maintain backward compatibility. API versioning allows you to introduce changes and new features without breaking existing clients. Common approaches include using version numbers in the URL path or headers, or employing content negotiation to specify the desired version.

Let us say the Shipping Service in our e-commerce application needs to introduce a new feature that requires changes to the API contract. By versioning the API, the Shipping Service can support both the old version (v1) and the new version (v2), simultaneously. Clients can specify the desired version in the URL path, such as **/v1/shipping** or **/v2/shipping**, ensuring a smooth transition for existing integrations.

Authentication and authorization

Securing your API is critical to protect sensitive data and ensure that only authorized clients can access the system. Authentication mechanisms like **JSON Web Tokens (JWT)** or OAuth 2.0 can be used to verify the identity of clients. **Role-based access control (RBAC)** or **attribute-based access control (ABAC)** can be implemented to define and enforce authorization rules based on user roles or attributes.

In our e-commerce application, the *OrderService* may require authentication to ensure that only registered users can place orders. JWTs can be used to authenticate requests, with the client including the token in the request headers. The Order Service can verify the token's validity and extract user information to authorize access to specific order-related operations based on the user's role or permissions.

Documentation and developer experience

Providing clear and comprehensive documentation is essential for developers who will be consuming your API. Use tools like Swagger or OpenAPI to generate interactive API documentation that describes endpoints, request/response formats, and authentication requirements. Include code samples and tutorials to help developers get started quickly. Consider providing client libraries or SDKs in popular programming languages to simplify integration.

For instance, the *ProductCatalogService* can provide API documentation using Swagger, which allows developers in internal teams of the organization to explore the available endpoints, view request and response examples, and even try out the API directly from the documentation. Additionally, the service can offer client libraries in languages like JavaScript, Python, and Java to facilitate easy integration with the API.

Fault tolerance and resilience

Distributed systems are inherently prone to failures, and serving requests reliably requires building fault-tolerant and resilient services. This is because when you are dealing with multiple services spread across hundreds of hardware hosts, sometimes running into hundreds or thousands of instances, the chances of failures linearly increase with the number of provisioned hosts.

Circuit breakers

Implement circuit breakers to prevent cascading failures and protect services from being overwhelmed by excessive requests. Circuit breakers monitor the health of downstream services and can automatically trip open when a certain failure threshold is reached, redirecting requests to fallback mechanisms or returning error responses.

In our e-commerce application, the *OrderService* may depend on the *InventoryService* to check the availability of products before placing an order. If the *InventoryService* becomes unresponsive or experiences a high error rate, the *OrderService* can use a circuit breaker to avoid repeatedly calling the failing service. The circuit breaker can trip open and either invoke a fallback mechanism, such as using cached inventory data, or return an appropriate error response to the client.

Figure 3.3 illustrates different states that a circuit breaker could be in:

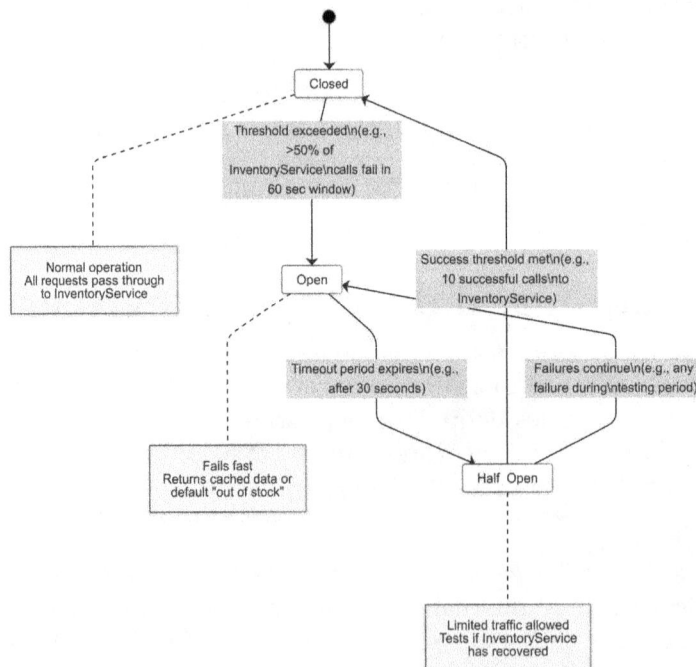

Figure 3.3: Illustration of circuit breaker states

Retry mechanisms

Incorporate retry mechanisms to handle transient failures, such as network hiccups or temporary service unavailability. Retry policies can be configured to specify the number of retries, delay between retries, and backoff strategies. Be cautious not to overload the system with excessive retries and consider rate limiting and exponential backoff.

Let us consider a scenario where the *EmailNotificationService* experiences a temporary network issue while sending order confirmation emails. Instead of immediately failing, the service can implement a retry mechanism. It can attempt to resend the email after a specified delay, gradually increasing the delay between retries using exponential backoff. This helps handle transient failures gracefully and ensures that emails are eventually delivered successfully.

Timeouts and deadlines

Set appropriate timeouts and deadlines for requests to prevent them from hanging indefinitely. Timeouts ensure that services do not wait too long for a response and can move on to serving other requests. Deadlines specify the maximum time allowed for a request to complete, including all retries and fallbacks.

In the context of our e-commerce application, the *ShippingService* may integrate with external shipping providers to obtain shipping rates and labels. If an external provider becomes unresponsive or slow to respond, setting a timeout ensures that the *ShippingService* does not block indefinitely. It can either retry the request with a different provider or return an error response to the client, indicating that the shipping information is currently unavailable.

To summarize, serving requests efficiently and reliably in distributed systems requires careful design, implementation, and operation. By understanding the trade-offs between synchronous and asynchronous processing, designing effective API interfaces, building fault-tolerant services, and implementing robust monitoring and observability practices, you can create a scalable and resilient request serving infrastructure.

Remember, the key to success lies in continuously iterating and improving your system based on real-world usage patterns and feedback. Embrace best practices, leverage modern technologies, and foster a culture of collaboration and learning within your team.

As you embark on your journey of building distributed systems, keep these principles in mind, and you will be well-equipped to tackle the challenges and deliver exceptional user experiences. Stay curious, experiment with different approaches, and always strive for excellence in serving requests and building reliable distributed systems.

Server infrastructure considerations

In the world of distributed systems, architects and developers have a wide array of tools and technologies at their disposal to design and implement scalable and resilient applications. Here we explore the cross-cutting infrastructure which is common across all distributed systems irrespective of their purpose. By understanding these concepts and their applications, you can make informed decisions when architecting distributed systems at scale.

Virtual machines

VMs have been a cornerstone of distributed system architecture for decades. A VM is an emulation of a physical computer system, running on top of a hypervisor that manages the allocation of hardware resources. VMs provide a high level of isolation and encapsulation, allowing multiple operating systems to run concurrently on a single physical machine.

One of the primary benefits of using VMs in distributed systems is the ability to achieve strong isolation between applications and services. Each VM runs its own operating system and has its own allocated resources, such as CPU, memory, and storage. This isolation ensures that applications running in separate VMs do not interfere with each other, providing a secure and stable environment for each workload.

VMs also offer flexibility in terms of operating system choice and configuration. Different VMs can run different operating systems and versions, enabling the coexistence of legacy systems alongside modern applications. This flexibility is particularly valuable in distributed systems where various components may have specific operating system requirements.

However, VMs come with some overhead in terms of resource consumption and startup time. Each VM requires its own operating system, which consumes additional memory and storage. Starting up a new VM can take several minutes, as the entire operating system needs to be booted. This overhead can impact the agility and scalability of distributed systems, especially when rapid provisioning and scaling are required.

Despite these limitations, VMs still play a significant role in distributed system architecture. They provide a robust and secure foundation for running applications and services, particularly in scenarios where strong isolation and compatibility with legacy systems are crucial.

Figure 3.4 illustrates the infrastructure stack for an application running on a VM:

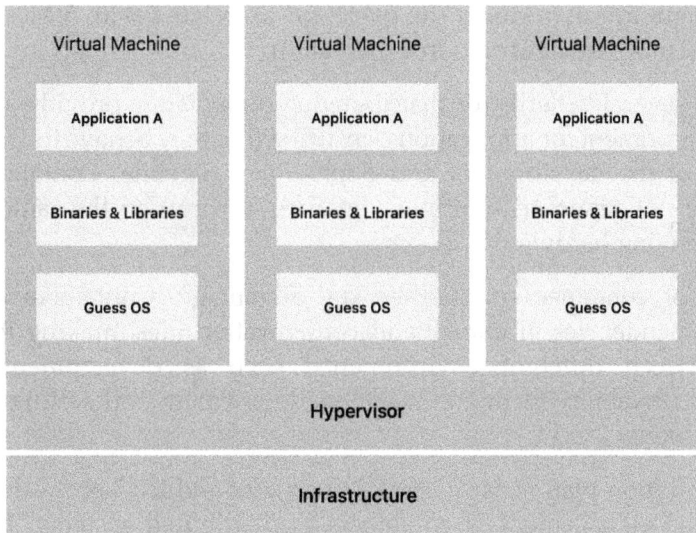

Figure 3.4: *Virtual machine-based application's server architecture*

Containers

Containers have emerged as a lightweight and efficient alternative to VMs in distributed system architecture. Containers provide a way to package an application along with its dependencies into a single, portable unit that can be easily deployed and run consistently across different environments. However, it's important to understand that containers are particularly well-suited for stateless applications services that do not need to maintain data between requests, like web servers, API endpoints, or application logic layers. These workloads can be easily scaled, restarted, or replaced without worrying about data persistence.

For stateful workloads that need to maintain data across container lifecycles such as databases, message queues, or long-running data processing jobs containers require additional consideration and infrastructure. These applications need specialized container runtimes or orchestration systems that can manage persistent storage volumes, handle data replication, and ensure proper backup and recovery procedures. For instance, while you might run your e-commerce application's product catalog service in a standard container, running its PostgreSQL database would require careful planning around storage management, backup strategies, and coordination during container restarts or migrations. Modern container orchestration platforms like Kubernetes provide solutions for managing stateful workloads, but these implementations are more complex than their stateless counterparts and require deeper operational expertise.

Unlike VMs, containers do not require a separate operating system for each instance. Instead, containers share the host operating system kernel and leverage kernel-level isolation mechanisms, such as cgroups and namespaces, to provide process-level isolation.

This approach significantly reduces the overhead associated with VMs, enabling faster startup times and more efficient resource utilization.

Containers offer several benefits for distributed systems. They provide a consistent and reproducible environment for applications, ensuring that they behave the same way across different stages of the development and deployment pipeline. Containers also enable efficient resource utilization, as multiple containers can run on the same host machine, sharing the underlying hardware resources.

The portability of containers is another key advantage. Containers encapsulate all the necessary dependencies, libraries, and configuration files, making it easy to move applications between different environments, such as development, testing, and production. This portability facilitates seamless deployment and scaling of applications in distributed systems.

Container orchestration platforms, such as Kubernetes and Docker Swarm, have further revolutionized the management of containers in distributed systems. These platforms provide powerful abstractions and automation capabilities for deploying, scaling, and managing containerized applications across clusters of machines. They handle tasks such as container scheduling, load balancing, service discovery, and self-healing, simplifying the operational complexity of distributed systems.

Containers have become a fundamental building block for modern distributed system architecture, enabling agility, efficiency, and scalability. They provide a lightweight and portable way to package and deploy applications, making it easier to build and manage large-scale distributed systems. *Figure 3.5* illustrates the infrastructure stack for an application running on containers:

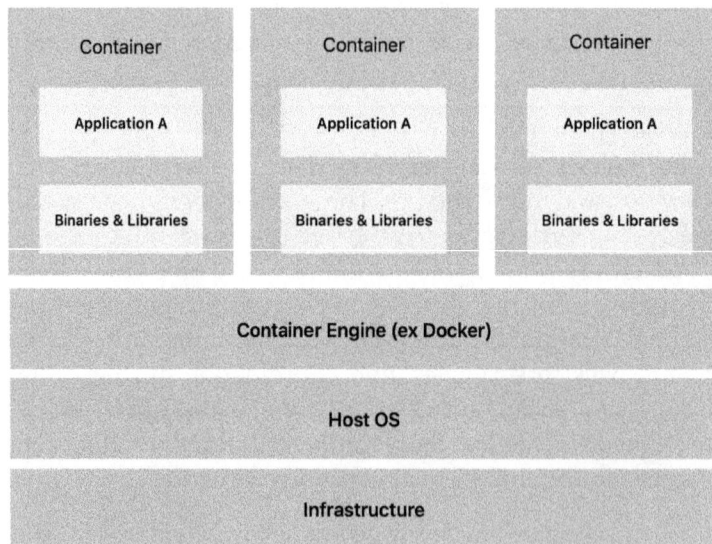

Figure 3.5: Container based application's server architecture

Serverless compute services

Serverless compute services, such as Google Cloud Functions, AWS Lambda, and Azure Functions, have emerged as a compelling alternative to traditional VM and container-based infrastructure. These services provide a platform where developers can focus on writing code and implementing business logic without the burden of managing the underlying infrastructure. Let us explore the advantages of serverless compute services and when they are more advantageous compared to container-based services.

Serverless compute services abstract away the complexities of infrastructure management, allowing developers to concentrate on writing code and solving business problems. With serverless, developers no longer need to provision, configure, or scale servers. The cloud provider takes care of these tasks, enabling faster development and deployment cycles. This simplified infrastructure management reduces operational overhead and allows teams to focus on delivering value to their customers.

Benefits of serverless computer services

One of the key benefits of serverless compute services is automatic scaling. As the incoming workload increases, the platform seamlessly provisions more instances to handle the load. Conversely, when the workload decreases, the platform scales down the resources, ensuring optimal utilization. This automatic scaling capability eliminates the need for manual capacity planning and enables applications to handle variable traffic patterns effortlessly. In contrast, with container-based services, scaling often requires manual intervention or complex orchestration mechanisms.

Cost efficiency is another significant advantage of serverless compute services. With the pay-per-use pricing model, you only pay for the actual execution time and resources consumed by your code. There is no need to pay for idle server time or overprovisioned capacity. This model can result in significant cost savings, especially for applications with sporadic or unpredictable workloads. In comparison, container-based services typically require a certain level of resource allocation, even when the application is not actively processing requests, leading to potential cost inefficiencies.

Serverless compute services promote a modular and event-driven architecture, enabling rapid development and deployment. Developers can focus on writing small, self-contained functions that perform specific tasks. These functions can be easily developed, tested, and deployed independently, allowing for faster iteration and shorter time-to-market. Serverless platforms often provide a wide range of triggers and integrations, making it simple to compose and orchestrate complex workflows. While containers also support modular architectures, serverless functions offer a finer-grained level of granularity and simplify the development process.

Scalability and high availability are inherent characteristics of serverless compute services. The platform automatically distributes the workload across multiple instances and ensures that the application can handle a large number of concurrent requests. Serverless providers typically offer built-in redundancy and fault tolerance, minimizing the risk of downtime. Achieving the same level of scalability and availability with container-based services requires additional effort in terms of cluster management, load balancing, and failover mechanisms.

Serverless compute services are particularly advantageous in certain scenarios. They excel in handling event-driven workloads, such as processing data streams, responding to changes in storage, or reacting to user actions. Serverless is also well-suited for building microservices architectures, where each service can be implemented as a set of functions. Additionally, serverless is ideal for applications with unpredictable or highly variable traffic patterns, as it automatically scales based on the incoming workload.

Challenges of serverless compute services

However, it is important to note that serverless compute services have some limitations and may not be suitable for all scenarios. Serverless functions have limited execution duration, typically up to a few minutes, making them less suitable for long-running tasks or complex computations. Container-based services offer more flexibility in terms of execution duration and can handle long-running processes more effectively. They may also not be suitable for long running memory and CPU intensive jobs due to relatively higher cost. However, cost should always take into consideration engineering effort saved in managing infrastructure which is close to negligible in case of serverless cloud services.

Container-based services are more appropriate when you require more control over the underlying infrastructure, or have specific performance requirements. Containers provide a consistent and portable runtime environment, making them suitable for applications that need to be deployed across different platforms or on-premises. They also offer more flexibility in terms of resource allocation and can be optimized for specific workloads.

In summary, serverless compute services provided by cloud providers like GCP, AWS, and Azure offer an alternative to traditional VM and container-based infrastructure. They provide simplified infrastructure management, automatic scaling, cost efficiency, rapid development, and inherent scalability and availability. However, they may not be suitable for all scenarios, particularly those involving long-running tasks or requiring fine-grained control over the infrastructure. When deciding between serverless and container-based services, it is essential to evaluate the specific requirements, performance needs, and architectural goals of your application.

Identity and access management

In distributed systems, where multiple services and components interact with each other and with external users, ensuring secure and controlled access is crucial. IAM plays a vital role in managing authentication, authorization, and access control within these systems. IAM is a critical aspect of information security that involves controlling and managing who has access to various IT systems and resources within an organization. IAM helps ensure that the right individuals have the appropriate level of access to the resources they need to perform their job functions, while also protecting sensitive data and systems from unauthorized access.

IAM is not limited to managing user-level access. In modern distributed architectures, particularly in microservices environments, IAM also encompasses service-to-service permissions. This involves controlling which services can communicate with each other and access specific APIs.

For example, consider a microservices-based application where numerous services interact to provide functionality. Ensuring that only authorized services can invoke specific APIs is crucial to maintaining security and preventing unauthorized access or data leakage. To achieve this, organizations often implement mechanisms like OAuth2 or mTLS. OAuth2 can be used to issue tokens that services must present when calling APIs, ensuring that only services with valid tokens can gain access. Similarly, mTLS establishes trust by requiring both the client and server to authenticate each other through certificates before communication is allowed.

These measures play a vital role in enforcing granular access controls within an internal service mesh, enabling secure and efficient communication between microservices while safeguarding sensitive data and preventing unauthorized access at the service level. As a result, IAM in distributed systems is not just about managing access for users but also about ensuring robust permissions and authentication mechanisms for the services that underpin modern applications.

Authentication mechanisms

Authentication is the process of verifying a user's identity to ensure they are who they claim to be before granting access.

Common authentication mechanisms include the following:

- **Passwords**: Users enter a secret password that is matched against a stored hash. Passwords should enforce complexity requirements and be rotated periodically.

- **Multi-factor authentication (MFA)**: Requires users to present multiple credentials, such as a password plus a one-time code from a hardware token or mobile app. MFA significantly enhances security over passwords alone.

- **Biometrics**: Uses physical characteristics like fingerprints, facial recognition, or iris scans to authenticate users. Biometrics are highly secure but require specialized hardware.

- **PKI certificates**: Users are issued a digital certificate that is validated against a trusted certificate authority to prove their identity. Certificates are frequently used for servers, devices, and API authentication.

- **Identity federation and single sign-on (SSO)**: With the proliferation of cloud services, identity federation has become a key aspect of IAM. Federation enables a user's identity to be shared across different systems and organizations in a secure manner. This allows for **single sign-on (SSO)**, where a user can authenticate once and gain access to multiple applications and services without needing to re-enter their credentials.

- **Security Assertion Markup Language (SAML)** is an open standard for exchanging authentication and authorization data between parties, in particular between an identity provider and a service provider. SAML uses XML-based assertions and protocols to communicate identities between systems. It is widely used for enabling SSO for enterprise applications.

Authorization and access control

Once a user is authenticated, the next step is authorization to determine what actions they are permitted to take and what resources they are allowed to access. Access control models define the rules and policies governing authorization.

Common models include the following:

- **RBAC**: Access is granted based on a user's role or job function. Roles are assigned permissions to different resources. Users acquire access through their assigned roles.

- **ABAC**: Access is determined dynamically based on attributes about the user, resource, action and environment. Policies define what combinations of attributes are required for access. ABAC allows for more granular access decisions.

- **Principle of least privilege (PoLP)**: Users should only be granted the minimum level of access needed to perform their duties. Excess privileges should be avoided.

Secure communication between services is also a critical aspect of IAM in distributed systems. **Transport Layer Security (TLS)** is commonly used to encrypt communication channels and establish secure connections between services. mTLS extends this by requiring both the client and server to present their own certificates, providing strong authentication and encryption for service-to-service communication.

Auditing and monitoring

Auditing and monitoring of IAM systems is essential for security and compliance. Detailed logs should be maintained of all authentication attempts, authorization decisions, administrative changes, etc. These logs need to be continuously monitored for signs of malicious activity or policy violations. Anomaly detection and security analytics tools can be leveraged to identify potential issues.

Best practices for access management

To ensure effective access management, organizations should have the following:

- Implement strong authentication, preferably MFA, for all critical systems
- Use SSO and federation to simplify access across applications
- Apply granular authorization policies based on least privilege
- Regularly review and adjust user roles and permissions
- Promptly deprovision access for terminated users
- Enable comprehensive auditing and monitoring of all IAM activities

By implementing a comprehensive IAM strategy encompassing secure authentication, granular authorization, federated identity, and robust auditing, organizations can effectively manage and control access to their critical systems and data. A well-designed IAM system is essential for preventing data breaches, ensuring compliance with regulations, and enabling the business to operate efficiently and securely.

Conclusion

In this chapter, we explored the key architectural patterns and components that form the foundation of distributed systems. We understood the importance of microservices, event-driven architecture, and service mesh in building scalable, resilient, and flexible distributed applications.

We discussed the role of API Gateways in simplifying client interactions, abstracting service complexities, and handling cross-cutting concerns. We also examined the significance of effective request processing, including synchronous and asynchronous approaches, and the benefits of reactive programming paradigms.

We highlighted the criticality of fault tolerance and resilience in distributed systems, emphasizing techniques such as circuit breakers, retry mechanisms, and timeouts to ensure reliable request serving.

We also explored server infrastructure considerations, comparing VMs, containers, and serverless compute services. Each approach offers unique benefits and trade-offs, and the choice depends on factors such as isolation requirements, resource utilization, scalability needs, and operational complexity.

Finally, we emphasized the importance of IAM in securing distributed systems. IAM covers authentication, authorization, and access control mechanisms, ensuring that only authorized entities can access system resources and perform permitted actions.

As we continue our journey into the world of distributed systems, it is crucial to understand and apply these architectural patterns and best practices. By leveraging the power of microservices, event-driven design, and service mesh, along with effective request processing, fault tolerance, and IAM, we can build distributed systems that are scalable, resilient, and secure.

In the next chapter, we will understand about ensuring consistency and availability in distributed systems and discuss tradeoffs that is needed to provide these capabilities in our systems.

Join our book's Discord space

Join the book's Discord Workspace for Latest updates, Offers, Tech happenings around the world, New Release and Sessions with the Authors:

https://discord.bpbonline.com

CHAPTER 4
Consistency and Availability

Introduction

In the world of distributed systems, ensuring consistency and availability is crucial for providing reliable services and maintaining data integrity. Consistency ensures that all nodes in a distributed system have a shared, identical view of data at any given point in time while availability ensures that the system remains operational and responsive to user requests, even in the face of failures.

Consistency is about ensuring that various parts of the system see the same data without variation. Let us consider our e-commerce application as an example. In such a system, consistency is important to ensure that product inventory, order information, and user data remain accurate and coherent across all nodes. Imagine a customer ordering the last pair of limited-edition sneakers in their size. The order succeeds because the shopping cart service sees one unit in stock, but the inventory management service due to delayed synchronization in a distributed system had already marked the item as sold out. The customer receives a confirmation email, only to be notified hours later that their order is canceled. This inconsistency not only frustrates the user but may cost the company future business as the customer loses trust. Such glitches epitomize why distributed systems demand rigorous consistency guarantees, especially in high-stakes domains like e-commerce.

On the other hand, availability is critical for an e-commerce application to ensure that customers can access the system, browse products, and place orders at any time, even if some nodes in the system are experiencing issues. If the system becomes unavailable during peak shopping periods, such as during a flash sale or holiday season, it can lead to lost revenue and customer dissatisfaction.

Structure

This chapter covers the following topics:

- CAP theorem
- Consistency models
- Locking strategies
- Availability
- Protocols for consistency
- Availability techniques
- Real-world systems
- Emerging trends and future directions

Objectives

By the end of this chapter, readers will have a solid foundation in the concepts, challenges, and techniques related to consistency and availability in distributed systems, enabling them to make informed decisions when designing and building robust, scalable, and reliable systems. Readers will learn about different consistency models and their trade-offs, factors that affect availability and how to measure them. Readers will look at techniques to maintain consistency, learn from real world examples with practical insights coming from them.

CAP theorem

The CAP theorem, proposed by *Eric Brewer*, is a fundamental principle that highlights the trade-offs between consistency and availability in distributed systems. It states that in the presence of network **partitions (P)**, a distributed system can only guarantee either strong **consistency (C)** or **availability (A)**, but not both simultaneously. This theorem has become a guiding light for system architects and developers when making design decisions and understanding the limitations of distributed systems.

Continuing with our ecommerce application analogy, imagine the online store is distributed across multiple data centers to ensure high availability and low latency for customers in different regions. In this scenario, consistency and availability are closely tied together.

Let us say a customer in New York adds a product to their cart, and the inventory count is updated in the US data center. At the same time, another customer in London tries to add the same product to their cart. If the system prioritizes strong consistency, it will ensure that the London customer sees the updated inventory count from the US data center before allowing them to add the product to their cart. This ensures that the inventory count remains consistent across all data centers. However, if there is a network partition or a communication delay between the data centers, the London customer may experience higher latency or even be unable to add the product to their cart until the partition is resolved, impacting availability.

On the other hand, if the system prioritizes availability, it may allow the London customer to add the product to their cart based on the local inventory count in the UK data center, even if it has not received the updated count from the US data center. This ensures that both customers can continue to shop without interruption, maintaining high availability. However, this approach may lead to inconsistencies, such as overselling the product if the inventory count is not updated fast enough across all data centers.

In this example, the CAP theorem comes into play. The system can either prioritize consistency by ensuring that all data centers have the same inventory count before allowing purchases, or it can prioritize availability by allowing purchases based on local inventory counts. In a distributed system, network partitions are inevitable, and according to the CAP theorem, the system must choose between consistency and availability during a partition.

Distributed systems may prioritize consistency or availability, a public-facing service like an ecommerce store will often prioritize availability over strong consistency because they do not want to lose sales or provide a poor user experience due to network issues. They may use eventual consistency models, where the system allows temporary inconsistencies but ensures that all data centers eventually converge to the same state. This approach provides a balance between availability and consistency, allowing the system to continue functioning during network partitions while gradually resolving inconsistencies.

The CAP theorem forces system designers to make a choice between strong consistency and high availability based on the specific requirements of their application. In some cases, strong consistency may be prioritized, such as in financial transactions where data accuracy is paramount. In other cases, availability may be more important, such as in a recommendation system where providing continuous access to product suggestions is crucial for user engagement.

Throughout this chapter, we will explore different consistency models, ranging from strong consistency to eventual consistency, and discuss their implications. We will also examine factors that affect availability and strategies to improve it, such as replication techniques and distributed consensus algorithms.

By understanding the CAP theorem and the trade-offs between consistency and availability, system architects and developers can make informed decisions when designing and building distributed systems. They can choose the appropriate consistency model based on the application's requirements, employ techniques to enhance availability, and use distributed consensus algorithms to achieve agreement among nodes.

Consistency, availability, and partition tolerance

In this chapter, we examined in detail the definitions of consistency and availability.

Following is a summarization:

- **Consistency**: It ensures that all nodes in a distributed system have the same view of the data at any given time. Strong consistency models, such as linearizability or serializability guarantee that all nodes always see the most up-to-date data. Weaker consistency models, such as eventual consistency allow for temporary inconsistencies but ensure that all nodes eventually converge to the same state.

- **Availability**: It ensures that every request received by a non-failing node in the system must result in a response. In other words, the system remains operational and responsive even in the presence of failures. High availability is critical for many applications, particularly those serving end-users or supporting mission-critical functions.

- **Partition tolerance**: It is a communication break between two or more nodes in a distributed system. Partition tolerance ensures that the system continues to function even if there are network partitions. In large-scale distributed systems, network partitions are considered inevitable and the system must be designed to handle them gracefully.

Note: Real-world scenarios are rarely so black-and-white. Network partitions can also manifest as latent partial failures. For instance, a slow or unreliable link between nodes might mimic the behavior of a partition by significantly delaying communication. These subtle issues can cause inconsistencies or timeouts without an obvious meltdown, making them harder to detect and resolve. Such latent failures are common in production systems, especially in geographically distributed environments where network conditions can vary unpredictably. Recognizing that partitions are not always catastrophic disruptions helps system architects design for resilience against these more frequent, subtle failures. By accounting for both obvious and latent partitions, teams can better understand the trade-offs imposed by the CAP theorem and make informed decisions about which guarantees to prioritize based on their application's needs.

Trade-offs between consistency and availability

In the presence of a network partition, a distributed system must choose between consistency and availability. This trade-off is often referred to as the *CAP trade-off* or the *consistency-availability trade-off*.

If a system prioritizes consistency, it may choose to sacrifice availability during a network partition. In this case, the system will reject some requests to ensure that all nodes always see the same, consistent data. This approach is suitable for applications that require strong consistency, such as financial systems or databases supporting strict transactional semantics.

On the other hand, if a system prioritizes availability, it may choose to sacrifice consistency during a network partition. In this case, the system will continue to accept requests and provide responses, even if some nodes have outdated or inconsistent data. This approach is suitable for applications that can tolerate temporary inconsistencies, such as social media platforms or content delivery networks.

Implications of CAP theorem in design

The CAP theorem has significant implications for the design and operation of distributed systems, as follows:

- System designers must carefully consider the specific requirements of their application and choose the appropriate trade-off between consistency and availability.

- Distributed systems should be designed with partition tolerance in mind as network partitions are considered inevitable in large-scale deployments.

- The choice of consistency model (for example, strong consistency, eventual consistency) should be based on the application's needs and the acceptable level of data inconsistency.

- Monitoring and alerting mechanisms should be put in place to detect and handle network partitions, as well as to ensure that the system behaves as expected during such events.

By understanding the CAP theorem and its implications, system designers can make informed decisions about the architecture and trade-offs of their distributed systems, ensuring that they meet the specific requirements of their applications and users.

Figure 4.1 illustrates the various tradeoffs that help you map multiple permutations in order to understand the CAP theorem:

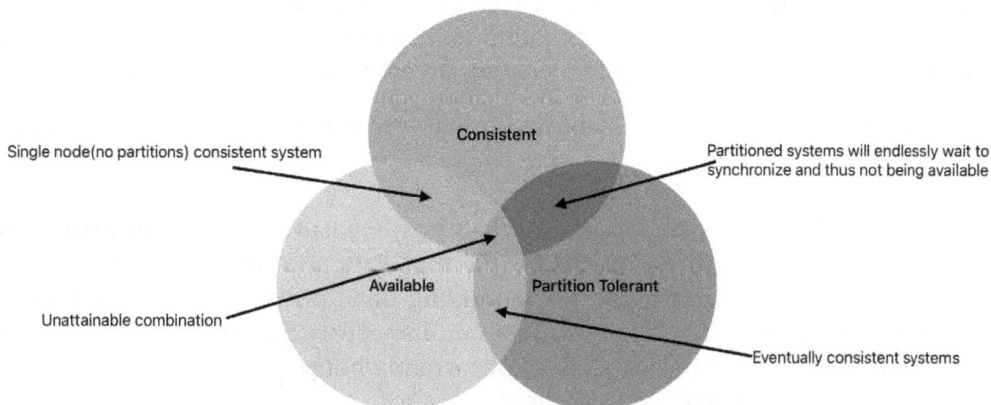

Figure 4.1: *Illustration of CAP theorem and implications of various permutations*

Consistency models

Consistency models define the rules and guarantees that a distributed system provides regarding the visibility and ordering of data updates across multiple nodes. They specify how the system behaves when multiple clients concurrently access and modify shared data. Different consistency models offer varying levels of strictness and have different implications for system performance and availability. Let us explore some common consistency models and their characteristics.

Strong consistency

Strong consistency, also known as **strict consistency** or **linearizability**, is the most stringent consistency model. In a strongly consistent system, all nodes always see the same data at the same time. Any data updates are immediately visible to all nodes and the system behaves as if there is a single, up-to-date copy of the data. Strong consistency provides a simple and intuitive behavior as it guarantees that read operations always return the most recent write.

Strong consistency is ideal for systems where data accuracy and real-time consistency are critical, though it comes with notable performance implications. In financial systems, such as banking applications, transactions must be processed in a strictly consistent manner, which often means waiting for confirmation across multiple geographic regions. For instance, when processing an international wire transfer, the system might need to wait for acknowledgments from data centers in both Asia and Europe before confirming the transaction, introducing latency in the range of hundreds of milliseconds.

In an e-commerce application, strong consistency can be applied to critical data, such as order processing and inventory management, to ensure that multiple customers cannot purchase the same item simultaneously if there is only one item left in stock. However, this level of consistency requires all nodes in the distributed system to synchronize before completing each transaction. For a global e-commerce platform, this synchronization overhead might mean that order confirmation takes longer, especially during high-traffic periods like holiday sales, as the system ensures inventory accuracy across all regions.

Strong consistency is enforced in databases through various mechanisms and techniques.

Following are a few common approaches:

- **Locking**: Databases use locking mechanisms to ensure that only one transaction can access and modify a particular piece of data at a time. Exclusive locks are acquired by a transaction before modifying data, preventing other transactions from reading or writing the same data simultaneously. Shared locks allow multiple transactions to read the same data concurrently but prevent any transaction from modifying it until the lock is released.

- **Two-Phase Locking (2PL)**: 2PL is a concurrency control protocol used to maintain serializability and ensure strong consistency. In the first phase (growing phase), transactions acquire locks on the data items they need to access or modify. In the second phase (shrinking phase), transactions release all the locks they have acquired. Strict 2PL, a variant of 2PL, holds exclusive locks until the transaction commits or aborts, preventing other transactions from accessing the modified data until the transaction is complete.

- **Multi-Version Concurrency Control (MVCC)**: MVCC maintains multiple versions of data items to provide concurrent access while ensuring strong consistency. Each transaction sees a consistent snapshot of the database at a particular point in time. Reads and writes are isolated from each other, allowing transactions to operate on different versions of the data without conflicts. MVCC is commonly used in databases like PostgreSQL and Oracle.

- **Consensus protocols**: In distributed database systems, consensus protocols like Paxos or Raft are used to ensure strong consistency across multiple nodes. These protocols ensure that all nodes in the system agree on the order and state of transactions, even in the presence of failures or network partitions. Transactions are committed only when a majority of nodes reach consensus, guaranteeing that all nodes have the same consistent view of the data.

- **Synchronous replication**: Synchronous replication involves replicating data to multiple nodes or replicas before confirming the success of a transaction. When a transaction is executed, it is applied to all replicas, and the transaction is considered successful only when all replicas have confirmed the write operation.

  This ensures that all replicas have a consistent view of the data, but it can impact performance and availability if replicas are slow or unavailable.

- **Strong consistency models**: Some databases offer strong consistency models, such as serializable isolation or linearizability. Serializable isolation ensures that transactions appear to execute in a serial order, providing a strong consistency guarantee. Linearizability provides real-time ordering of operations, ensuring that each operation appears to take effect instantaneously at a point between its invocation and completion.

It is important to note that enforcing strong consistency often comes with trade-offs in terms of performance and availability. Databases may offer different isolation levels and consistency models to balance consistency, performance, and concurrency requirements based on the specific needs of the application.

Weak consistency

Weak consistency, also known as **eventual consistency**, is a more relaxed consistency model. In a weakly consistent system, nodes may have different views of the data at a given point in time. Updates made by one node may not be immediately visible to other nodes, and there can be a delay in propagating the changes. However, the system guarantees that all nodes will eventually converge to the same state, given enough time and no further updates.

Weak consistency is suitable for systems where eventual consistency is acceptable and immediate data consistency is not critical. Social media platforms, such as *Facebook* or *Twitter*, often employ weak consistency for features like news feeds or timelines. In an e-commerce application, product reviews or ratings can be managed using weak consistency, allowing users to see the most recent reviews eventually but not necessarily in real-time.

Eventual consistency

Eventual consistency is a specific form of **weak consistency**. In an eventually consistent system, all nodes will converge to the same state over time but there may be temporary inconsistencies. Reads may return stale data for some time, but eventually, all nodes will agree on the same data. Eventual consistency sacrifices immediate consistency for increased availability and scalability.

Eventual consistency is commonly used in distributed databases and storage systems, such as *Amazon's DynamoDB* and *Apache Cassandra*. In an e-commerce application, eventual consistency can be applied to non-critical data, such as product catalog updates or user preferences. While users may temporarily see inconsistent information, the system ensures that the data will eventually become consistent across all nodes.

Causal consistency

Causal consistency is a consistency model that preserves the causal relationships between operations. In a causally consistent system, if one operation happens before another, all nodes will observe the operations in the same order. Causal consistency ensures that causally related operations are seen in the correct order but it allows concurrent operations to be reordered.

Causal consistency is useful in scenarios where the order of related operations is important but the absolute order of all operations is not critical. In an e-commerce application, causal consistency can be applied to order processing. For example, if a customer updates their shipping address and then places an order, causal consistency ensures that the order is shipped to the updated address, even if other unrelated orders are processed concurrently.

Choosing the appropriate consistency model depends on the specific requirements of the application. Strong consistency provides the highest level of data accuracy but may impact availability and performance. Weak consistency, including eventual consistency, sacrifices immediate consistency for better availability and scalability. Causal consistency strikes a balance by preserving the causal relationships between operations while allowing some flexibility in the ordering of concurrent operations.

In practice, distributed systems often employ a combination of consistency models, applying stronger consistency for critical data and operations while leveraging weaker consistency for less sensitive or frequently accessed data. By understanding the characteristics and trade-offs of different consistency models, system architects can make informed decisions based on the needs of their specific application.

Locking strategies

In the realm of consistency in distributed systems, locking plays a crucial role in ensuring data integrity and preventing conflicts when multiple transactions or processes access shared resources concurrently. Locking strategies can be broadly categorized into two main approaches: pessimistic locking and optimistic locking.

Pessimistic locking

Pessimistic locking follows a conservative approach, assuming that conflicts are likely to occur and proactively taking measures to prevent them. Before accessing or modifying a shared resource, a transaction must acquire a lock on that resource. The lock can be either an exclusive lock (write lock) or a shared lock (read lock), depending on the nature of the operation. Exclusive locks are used for write operations and prevent other transactions from accessing the resource simultaneously, while shared locks are used for read operations and allow multiple transactions to read the resource concurrently.

If a transaction attempts to acquire a lock on a resource that is already locked by another transaction, it is blocked and must wait until the lock becomes available. This blocking behavior can lead to reduced concurrency and potential performance issues if locks are held for long durations or if there is high contention for resources. Pessimistic locking systems often include mechanisms to prevent or detect deadlocks, such as timeout mechanisms or deadlock detection algorithms.

Pessimistic locking is suitable for scenarios where data consistency is critical, and conflicts are expected to be frequent. It provides a high level of data integrity and prevents inconsistencies caused by concurrent modifications. However, it can impact performance and scalability, especially in systems with high contention for resources.

Optimistic locking

Optimistic locking, on the other hand, assumes that conflicts are rare and allows transactions to proceed without locking. It relies on version control to detect conflicts. Each resource is assigned a version number or a timestamp, and when a transaction reads a resource, it retrieves the current version number along with the data.

When a transaction wants to modify a resource, it first checks if the version number of the resource matches the version number it initially read. If the version numbers match, it means no other transaction has modified the resource since it was read, and the transaction can proceed with the modification. If the version numbers do not match, it indicates that another transaction has modified the resource, and a conflict has occurred.

In case of a conflict, the transaction that attempts to modify the resource is typically aborted and rolled back. The transaction can then retry the operation by re-reading the resource, getting the updated version number, and attempting the modification again. Alternatively, the transaction can employ conflict resolution strategies, such as merging the changes or presenting the conflict to the user for manual resolution.

Optimistic locking is suitable for systems where conflicts are expected to be rare and where the cost of occasional rollbacks and retries is acceptable. It can provide better scalability and performance compared to pessimistic locking, especially in systems with low contention for resources. However, in scenarios with high contention and frequent conflicts, optimistic locking may lead to increased rollbacks and retries, impacting performance.

Availability

Availability refers to the ability of a system to be operational and accessible to users at any given time. It is often measured as a percentage of uptime which represents the proportion of time that the system is functioning correctly and available for use. For example, if a system has an availability of 99.9% (often referred to as **three nines** availability), it means that the system is operational and accessible for 99.9% of the time, with only 0.1% downtime.

Importance of availability

In distributed systems, availability is crucial because these systems are designed to serve multiple users simultaneously often across different geographical regions. High availability ensures that users can access the system and its services whenever they need to, without experiencing significant downtime or interruptions. This is particularly important for mission-critical applications, such as financial systems, healthcare systems, and emergency response systems where downtime can have severe consequences.

Several factors can impact the availability of a distributed system, as follows:

- **Hardware failures**: The failure of physical components, such as servers, storage devices, and network equipment can cause system downtime.

- **Software bugs**: Errors in software code can lead to system crashes or unexpected behavior, reducing availability.

- **Network issues**: Problems with network connectivity, such as network partitions can prevent users from accessing the system or cause communication failures between system components.

- **Human errors**: Mistakes made by system administrators or operators, such as misconfiguration or accidental deletion of data can result in system downtime.

- **Environmental factors**: Natural disasters, power outages, and other external events can disrupt the operation of a distributed system.

Challenges in achieving high availability

Achieving high availability in distributed systems is challenging due to several factors, as follows:

- **Complexity**: Distributed systems are inherently complex with many interconnected components and interactions between them. This complexity makes it difficult to design, implement, and maintain highly available systems.

- **Scalability**: As distributed systems grow in size and complexity, ensuring high availability becomes more challenging. Scaling the system while maintaining availability requires careful design and management of system resources. Components designed assuming a certain scale start breaking beyond a certain throughput, which can pose challenges towards availability.

- **Consistency**: Ensuring data consistency across multiple nodes in a distributed system can be challenging, especially in the presence of network partitions or node failures. Balancing consistency and availability is the key challenge in distributed systems design.

- **Fault tolerance**: Building fault-tolerant systems that can withstand hardware failures, software bugs, and network issues requires sophisticated techniques, such as replication, failover, and recovery mechanisms.

- **Monitoring and management**: Monitoring the health and performance of a distributed system, detecting issues, and taking corrective actions are essential for maintaining high availability. However, these tasks can be complex and time-consuming, requiring specialized tools and expertise.

By understanding the challenges and factors affecting availability, system designers and developers can make informed decisions and implement appropriate techniques to achieve high availability in distributed systems.

Measuring availability

Measuring availability is essential to monitoring and maintaining high availability in distributed systems. This section will discuss common metrics and techniques used to measure availability along with their definitions and significance.

Uptime and downtime

Uptime and downtime are the most basic metrics used to measure availability. Uptime refers to the amount of time that a system is operational and accessible to users while downtime is the amount of time that the system is not available or not functioning correctly. Availability is typically expressed as a percentage of uptime over a given period and can be calculated as follows:

$$Availability = (Uptime) / (Uptime + Downtime) \times 100\%$$

For example, if a system has an uptime of 99 hours and a downtime of one hour over 100 hours, its availability would be as follows:

$$Availability = \frac{99}{99+1} \times 100$$

Nines of availability

Availability is often expressed in terms of *nines* which represent the percentage of uptime. The higher the number of nines, the greater the availability.

Following are some common availability levels:

- **Two nines (99%)**: 3.65 days of downtime per year
- **Three nines (99.9%)**: 8.76 hours of downtime per year
- **Four nines (99.99%)**: 52.56 minutes of downtime per year
- **Five nines (99.999%)**: 5.26 minutes of downtime per year

Achieving higher levels of availability becomes increasingly challenging and expensive as it requires more sophisticated fault-tolerance mechanisms, redundancy, and monitoring.

Mean Time Between Failures

Mean Time Between Failures (MTBF) is a metric that measures the average time between system failures. It represents the expected time a system will operate before experiencing a failure.

Let us calculate the MTBF, as follows:

$$MTBF = (Total\ operational\ time) / (Number\ of\ failures)$$

A higher MTBF indicates a more reliable system as it experiences fewer failures over a given period.

Mean time to repair

Mean time to repair (MTTR) is a metric that measures the average time it takes to repair a system after a failure occurs. It includes the time required to detect the failure, diagnose the problem, and restore the system to its operational state.

To calculate MTTR, refer to the following equation:

$$MTTR = (Total\ downtime) / (Number\ of\ failures)$$

A lower MTTR indicates that the system can be repaired quickly, minimizing the impact of failures on availability.

Service level agreements

Service level agreements (**SLAs**) are contracts between service providers and customers that define the expected level of service, including availability. SLAs specify the minimum availability levels that the service provider commits to maintaining along with the consequences of failing to meet those levels (for example, financial penalties or service credits). Measuring and reporting on availability metrics help service providers ensure compliance with SLAs and maintain customer satisfaction.

Monitoring and alerting

In order to effectively measure availability; distributed systems must be continuously monitored. Monitoring tools can track system metrics, such as uptime, response times, and error rates, and provide real-time visibility into the system's health. Alerting mechanisms should be in place to notify system administrators or support teams when availability falls below pre-defined thresholds or when critical failures occur. This allows for prompt intervention and minimizes the impact of availability issues on end-users.

By understanding and applying these availability measurement techniques, system designers and operators can assess the reliability of their distributed systems, identify areas for improvement, and ensure that they meet the availability requirements of their users and stakeholders.

Protocols for consistency

Protocols help maintain consistency in distributed systems. They define the rules that help guarantee consistency when data is accessed, updated, and synchronized among the nodes in the system. In this section, we will explore several common consistency models and protocols used in distributed systems.

Consensus protocols

Consensus protocols are a class of algorithms that allow a group of nodes in a distributed system to agree on a single value or state, even in the presence of failures or network partitions. Two of the most well-known consensus protocols are *Paxos* and *Raft*.

Paxos

Paxos is a family of protocols for solving consensus in a network of unreliable processors. In the context of distributed systems, consensus refers to the process of getting all nodes to agree on a single value or state, despite the presence of failures or network partitions. Paxos is particularly useful in scenarios where strong consistency is required, such as in e-commerce systems that need to maintain accurate inventory counts and process financial transactions reliably.

Imagine our online inventory data replicated across multiple data centers. When a customer places an order, the system must ensure that the inventory count is updated consistently across all data centers, even if some data centers are unavailable or network partitions occur.

In a Paxos-based system, the nodes are classified into three roles, as follows:

- **Proposers**: These are the nodes that propose a value, for example, an updated inventory count to be agreed upon.

- **Acceptors**: These are the nodes that accept or reject the proposed value based on certain criteria.

- **Learners**: These are the nodes that learn the final agreed-upon value.

The Paxos protocol consists of two main phases, that is, the prepare phase and the accept phase.

In the **prepare phase**, a proposer node sends a prepare request to a majority of acceptor nodes with a unique proposal number. Each acceptor node compares the received proposal number with the highest proposal number it has seen so far. If the received proposal number is higher, the acceptor node promises not to accept any proposals with lower proposal numbers and sends back the last accepted value (if any) to the proposer.

In the **accept phase**, if the proposer receives promises from a majority of acceptor nodes, it sends an accept request to those acceptors with the value to be agreed upon. The value is either the one received from the acceptors (if any) or the proposer's own proposed value. Acceptor nodes then accept the value if the proposal number is equal to or greater than the highest proposal number they have promised.

Once a majority of acceptor nodes have accepted a value, consensus is reached, and the learner nodes can safely learn the agreed-upon value. In our e-commerce example, this means that the updated inventory count is consistently replicated across all data centers, ensuring that customers see accurate product availability and the system can process orders reliably.

In practice, a single node may run as a proposer, acceptor, and learner. Indeed, Paxos usually coexists with the service that requires consensus, with each node taking on all three roles. For the sake of understanding the protocol, however, it is useful to consider them to be independent entities.

Paxos ensures safety and liveness properties in distributed systems. Safety means that the protocol will never allow two different values to be agreed upon, while liveness means that the protocol will eventually reach consensus as long as enough nodes are available and communicating properly.

However, implementing Paxos can be complex as it involves multiple rounds of communication and requires careful handling of node failures and network partitions. To simplify the implementation, some systems use variants of Paxos, such as *Multi-Paxos* which allows for multiple instances of the protocol to run concurrently, or *Cheap Paxos* which reduces the number of messages exchanged between nodes.

In summary, Paxos is a powerful consensus protocol that enables distributed systems, such as e-commerce platforms to maintain strong consistency and reliability in the face of failures and network partitions. By ensuring that all nodes agree on a single value, Paxos helps prevent data inconsistencies and ensures that critical operations, like inventory updates and financial transactions, are processed correctly. While implementing Paxos can be challenging, its benefits make it a crucial tool for building robust and reliable distributed systems.

Figure 4.2 illustrates the protocol and its interaction visually:

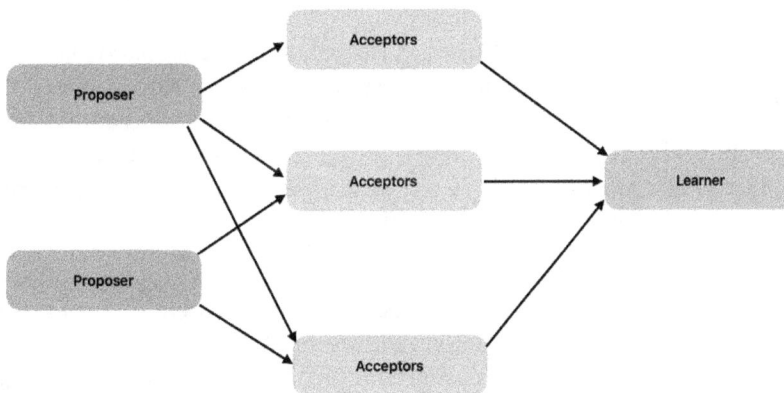

Figure 4.2: Paxos consensus protocol

Raft

Raft is a consensus algorithm designed to be more understandable and easier to implement than Paxos. It provides strong consistency and is based on a leader-follower model where a leader node is elected and is responsible for managing the replication of data to the follower nodes. Like *Paxos*, Raft ensures that a distributed system can reach consensus on a single value, even in the presence of node failures or network partitions.

In order to illustrate how Raft works, let us continue with our e-commerce example. Suppose the online store uses a distributed database to store customer information, orders, and inventory data. To ensure that all nodes in the database cluster have a consistent view of the data, the system uses Raft to achieve consensus.

In a Raft-based system, the nodes are organized into a leader-follower model. At any given time, one node is elected as the leader, while the others serve as followers. The leader is responsible for accepting client requests, replicating data to the followers, and managing the overall state of the system.

The Raft algorithm consists of the following three main phases:

- **Leader election**: When the system starts or the current leader fails, the nodes initiate a leader election process. Each node begins as a follower and can transition to a candidate if they do not receive a heartbeat from the leader within a specified timeout period. Candidates request votes from the other nodes, and if a candidate receives votes from a majority of nodes, they become the new leader.

- **Log replication**: Once a leader is elected, it starts accepting client requests and appending them to its log. The leader then replicates the log entries to the follower nodes. Each follower appends the entries to its own log and sends an acknowledgment back to the leader. Once a majority of followers have acknowledged an entry, it is considered committed, and the leader can apply it to its state machine and respond to the client.

- **Safety and consistency**: Raft ensures the safety and consistency of the replicated log through a few key mechanisms. First, it enforces a strict ordering of log entries, with each entry assigned a unique index. Second, it uses a term number to identify each round of leader election, ensuring that stale leaders cannot overwrite newer log entries. Finally, Raft employs a quorum-based approach, requiring a majority of nodes to agree on the log entries before they are considered committed.

In our e-commerce example, when a customer updates their shipping address, the client request is sent to the leader node in the database cluster. The leader appends the address update to its log and replicates it to the follower nodes. Once a majority of followers have acknowledged the update, the leader commits it and applies the change to its local state. The updated address is now consistently replicated across all nodes in the cluster.

One of the key advantages of Raft is its strong leadership model which simplifies the replication process and makes it easier to reason about the system's behavior. Raft also provides a clear separation of concerns between leader election, log replication, and safety, making it more modular and easier to implement compared to Paxos.

However, like any consensus algorithm, Raft has its trade-offs. It prioritizes consistency over availability, meaning that in the event of a network partition or a majority of node failures, the system may become unavailable until the issues are resolved. Additionally, Raft's strong leadership model can limit its scalability in certain scenarios as the leader node may become a bottleneck under high write loads.

Despite these limitations, Raft has gained significant popularity in the distributed systems community due to its simplicity and ease of understanding. It has been implemented in various distributed systems, including etcd, HashiCorp Consul, and MongoDB, among others.

In order to summarize, Raft is a powerful and easy-to-understand consensus algorithm that enables distributed systems, such as e-commerce platforms, they are used to maintain a consistent and reliable state across multiple nodes. By providing a clear leader-follower model and a modular approach to consensus, Raft offers a simpler and more pragmatic alternative to Paxos, making it an attractive choice for many distributed systems in practice.

Figure 4.3 illustrates this protocol:

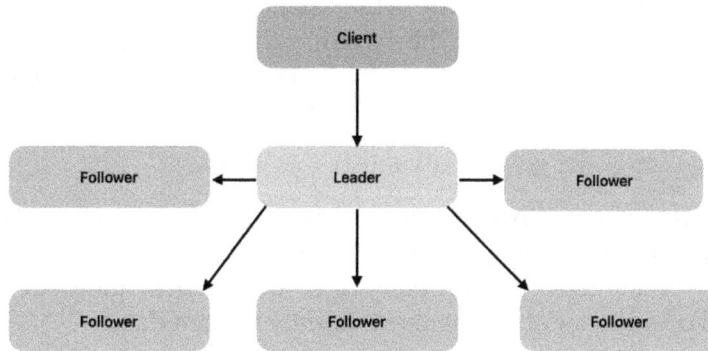

Figure 4.3: *Raft consensus protocol*

Quorum-based systems

Quorum-based systems are a class of distributed systems that employ quorums to ensure data consistency and availability in the presence of failures or network partitions. A quorum is a subset of nodes in the system that is sufficient to perform a particular operation, such as reading or writing data while guaranteeing consistency.

In order to illustrate how quorum-based systems work, let us revisit our e-commerce example. Suppose the online store uses a distributed storage system to manage product information and inventory data. To ensure that the data remains consistent and available, even in the face of node failures or network issues, the system employs a quorum-based approach.

In a quorum-based system, data is typically replicated across multiple nodes. Each read or write operation requires a quorum of nodes to participate to be considered successful. The quorum size is determined based on the desired level of consistency and fault tolerance.

The two main types of quorums are as follows:

- **Read quorums**: A read quorum is the minimum number of nodes that must be contacted to perform a read operation. The read quorum ensures that the system returns the most up-to-date data by contacting enough nodes to guarantee that at least one node has the latest version of the data.

- **Write quorums**: A write quorum is the minimum number of nodes that must be contacted to perform a write operation. It ensures that the system maintains data consistency by updating enough nodes to guarantee that any subsequent read operation will see the updated data.

The quorum sizes are typically chosen such that the read quorum and the write quorum intersect. This intersection property guarantees that any read operation will always see the most recently written data.

In our e-commerce application, when a customer requests product information, the system contacts a read quorum of nodes to retrieve the data. If the quorum is satisfied (i.e., enough nodes respond with the same data), the system returns the product information to the customer. Similarly, when an inventory update is performed, the system contacts a write quorum of nodes to ensure that the update is consistently applied across the replicas.

Quorum-based systems offer several advantages, as follows:

- **Consistency**: Quorum-based systems ensure that data remains consistent across the replicas by requiring a quorum of nodes to participate in each read or write operation. The intersection property of read and write quorums guarantees that any read operation will see the most recently written data.

- **Availability**: Quorum-based systems can tolerate node failures or network partitions as long as the remaining available nodes form a quorum. This means that the system can continue to serve read and write requests even if some nodes are unavailable.

- **Tunable consistency**: Quorum-based systems allow for tunable consistency levels by adjusting the quorum sizes. Smaller read quorums favor availability as fewer nodes need to be contacted while larger write quorums favor consistency., as more nodes must be updated before a write is considered successful.

However, quorum-based systems also have limitations, as follows:

- **Overhead**: Contacting a quorum of nodes for each read or write operation can introduce overhead, especially in large-scale systems. This overhead can impact the system's performance and latency.

- **Consistency-availability trade-off**: The choice of quorum sizes involves a trade-off between consistency and availability. Larger quorums favor consistency but may reduce availability while smaller quorums favor availability but may compromise consistency.

- **Network partitions**: In the presence of network partitions, quorum-based systems may struggle to maintain both consistency and availability. If a partition causes the system to split into two or more subsets, each unable to form a quorum, the system may become unavailable or risk violating consistency guarantees.

Despite these limitations, quorum-based systems have been widely adopted in various distributed storage systems, such as *Amazon's Dynamo, Cassandra*, and *Riak*. These systems leverage quorums to provide high availability and eventual consistency while tolerating node failures and network partitions.

Quorum-based systems offer a powerful approach to ensuring data consistency and availability in distributed environments. By leveraging the concept of quorums and carefully choosing the quorum sizes, these systems can provide tunable consistency guarantees and remain available even in the face of failures. While quorum-based systems have their trade-offs, they have proven to be a valuable tool in building resilient and scalable distributed systems, such as those powering modern e-commerce platforms.

Operating a distributed system based on Paxos or Raft requires meticulous handling of cluster management operations. For instance, when upgrading the software version of a five-node cluster, administrators must carefully orchestrate the process to maintain quorum. They typically need to upgrade nodes one at a time, ensuring that at least three nodes (a majority) remain operational throughout the process. If this quorum is lost during an upgrade, the cluster can become unavailable or, worse, split into multiple partitions.

Scaling operations present similar challenges. Adding new nodes to a Raft cluster requires a careful bootstrapping process where the new node must first catch up with the cluster's state before it can participate in voting. During this time, the cluster is more vulnerable to failures since losing existing nodes could break quorum. Similarly, removing nodes requires reconfiguring the cluster while ensuring the remaining nodes can still form a majority to make progress.

These operational considerations extend to routine maintenance as well. Even simple tasks like replacing a failed disk or applying security patches require careful planning to maintain the cluster's availability and consistency guarantees. System architects must design their deployment and maintenance procedures with these constraints in mind, often implementing sophisticated automation to manage these operations safely.

Gossip protocols

Gossip protocols, also known as **epidemic protocols**, are a class of decentralized communication protocols that enable efficient and robust information dissemination in large-scale distributed systems. These protocols are inspired by the way rumors or gossip spread in social networks where each shares information with a subset of their peers, eventually leading to the rapid propagation of the message throughout the entire network.

In the context of our e-commerce example, let us consider a scenario where the online store needs to propagate information about a promotional event to all nodes in its distributed system. Instead of relying on a centralized approach which might be inefficient and prone to single points of failure, the system can employ a gossip protocol to disseminate the information efficiently.

The basic idea behind gossip protocols is simple: each node in the system periodically selects a random subset of its peers and shares the information it has with them. The recipient nodes then update their state based on the received information and continue the process by gossiping with their own randomly selected peers. Over time, the information spreads throughout the entire network, even in the presence of node failures or network partitions.

Following are the two main types of gossip protocols:

- **Push-based gossip**: In this variant, a node actively pushes the information it has to its selected peers. The recipient nodes update their state and continue the gossiping process. Push-based gossip is particularly effective for rapidly disseminating new information across the network.

- **Pull-based gossip**: In this variant, a node periodically selects a random subset of peers and requests the latest information from them. The node then updates its own state based on the received information. Pull-based gossip is useful for repairing inconsistencies and ensuring that all nodes eventually converge to the same state.

Many gossip protocols employ a combination of push and pull mechanisms to achieve efficient and robust information dissemination.

In our promotional event example, the node that initiates the event can start by pushing the information to a random subset of nodes in the system. These nodes then update their state and continue gossiping with their own randomly selected peers. As the gossip process continues, the information about the promotional event rapidly spreads throughout the entire network, ensuring that all nodes are aware of the event.

Gossip protocols offer several key benefits in distributed systems, as follows:

- **Scalability**: Gossip protocols are highly scalable as they do not rely on centralized coordination and can efficiently handle large numbers of nodes. The communication overhead is typically logarithmic with respect to the number of nodes, making gossip protocols suitable for large-scale systems.

- **Fault-tolerance**: Gossip protocols are inherently fault-tolerant as they do not depend on any single node for information dissemination. Even if some nodes fail or become unreachable, the gossip process continues, and the information eventually reaches all available nodes.

- **Decentralization**: Gossip protocols are decentralized by nature as each node independently decides which peers to communicate with and what information to share. This decentralization eliminates single points of failure and makes the system more resilient to failures and attacks.

- **Eventual consistency**: Gossip protocols ensure that all nodes eventually converge to the same state, even in the presence of temporary inconsistencies or network partitions. This eventual consistency model is well-suited for many distributed applications that can tolerate short periods of inconsistency.

However, gossip protocols also have some limitations. They are not suitable for applications that require strong consistency or real-time information dissemination as the gossip process takes time to propagate information throughout the network. Additionally, gossip protocols can generate significant network traffic, especially in large-scale systems which may impact overall performance.

Despite these limitations, gossip protocols have found wide adoption in various distributed systems, such as peer-to-peer networks, distributed databases, and large-scale monitoring and management systems. They provide a simple, efficient, and robust way to disseminate information and maintain consistency in decentralized environments.

In summary, gossip protocols offer a scalable, fault-tolerant, and decentralized approach to information dissemination in distributed systems. By leveraging the power of peer-to-peer communication and eventual consistency, gossip protocols enable large-scale systems, such as e-commerce platforms, in order to efficiently propagate information and maintain a consistent state across all nodes, even in the face of failures and network partitions.

Conflict-free replicated data types

Conflict-free replicated data types (**CRDTs**) are a class of data structures designed to simplify the development of distributed systems by allowing for seamless and conflict-free replication of data across multiple nodes. CRDTs ensure that the replicated data remains consistent, even in the presence of concurrent updates and network partitions, without requiring complex coordination or consensus protocols.

In the context of our e-commerce example, let us consider a scenario where the online store needs to maintain a distributed product catalog. The product catalog contains information about various products, such as their names, descriptions, prices, and available inventory. Multiple nodes in the system may need to concurrently update the product catalog, for example, when the inventory of a product changes or when a new product is added. CRDTs can be employed to achieve this goal without the need for a centralized coordination mechanism.

The two main types of CRDTs are as follows:

- **Operation-based CRDTs (op-based CRDTs)**: In this type of CRDT, each node maintains a local copy of the data and applies updates in the form of operations. When a node performs an update, it generates an operation that is then propagated to the other nodes in the system. The receiving nodes apply the operation to their local copy of the data, ensuring that all nodes eventually converge to the same state.

- **State-based CRDTs (state-based CRDTs)**: In this type of CRDT, each node maintains a full copy of the data and periodically shares its entire state with the other nodes. When a node receives the state from another node, it merges the received state with its own local state using a merge function that ensures conflict-free convergence.

In our product catalog example, we can use a state-based CRDT called an **LWW-Element-Set** (**Last-Write-Wins-Element-Set**) to manage the products and their details. An LWW-Element-Set allows for adding and removing elements, and it automatically resolves conflicts by favoring the most recent update based on a timestamp or a logical clock.

When a node needs to update the details of a product, such as its price or inventory, it updates its local copy of the LWW-Element-Set with the new information. Periodically, each node shares its entire product catalog state with the other nodes in the system. When a node receives the state from another node, it merges the received state with its local state using the LWW-Element-Set's merge function. This merge function ensures that the product catalog remains consistent across all nodes, even if multiple nodes concurrently update the same product.

The key advantage of CRDTs in this scenario is that they allow for efficient and conflict-free replication of the product catalog without the need for complex coordination protocols. By designing the data structure (LWW-Element-Set) to handle concurrent updates in a conflict-free manner, CRDTs enable the distributed system to achieve eventual consistency while maintaining high availability and fault tolerance.

Other benefits of CRDTs in the context of the product catalog include the following factors:

- **Scalability**: CRDTs can scale horizontally by allowing for the seamless addition of new nodes to the system. Each node can operate independently and share its state with the others, enabling the system to handle increased loads and a growing product catalog.

- **Offline support**: CRDTs can support offline operations as each node can continue to accept updates to the product catalog even when disconnected from the network. When the node reconnects, it can share its updated state with the other nodes, ensuring that all changes are eventually propagated.

- **Simplified programming model**: CRDTs provide a simpler programming model compared to traditional distributed data structures as developers do not need to worry about complex coordination and conflict resolution mechanisms. CRDTs handle these aspects automatically, allowing developers to focus on the application logic.

However, CRDTs also have limitations, some are as follows:

- **Increased storage overhead**: Since each node maintains a full copy of the product catalog, CRDTs can have higher storage requirements compared to systems that partition data across nodes.

- **Limited data types**: CRDTs are designed for specific data types and operations that can be merged in a conflict-free manner. Not all data types and operations are suitable for CRDTs which may limit their applicability in certain scenarios.

- **Eventual consistency**: CRDTs provide eventual consistency which means that there may be temporary inconsistencies between nodes until all updates are propagated and merged. This may not be suitable for applications that require strong consistency guarantees.

Despite these limitations, CRDTs have gained popularity in recent years and have been adopted by various distributed systems, such as *Riak, SoundCloud's Roshi*, and *Akka Distributed Data*. They provide a powerful tool for building scalable and resilient distributed systems that can handle concurrent updates and network partitions.

In summary, CRDTs offer a novel approach to achieving consistent and conflict-free replication of data in distributed systems. By designing data structures that can be merged in a conflict-free manner, CRDTs enable systems, such as e-commerce platforms in order to maintain a consistent and highly available product catalog, even in the presence of concurrent updates and network issues. While CRDTs have their limitations, they provide a valuable tool for simplifying the development of scalable and resilient distributed systems.

Availability techniques

Achieving high availability is a critical goal for most distributed systems. In this section, we will explore various techniques and strategies used to ensure that a distributed system remains available and responsive, even in the face of failures or high loads.

Replication

Replication involves maintaining multiple copies of data or services across different nodes in a distributed system. The system can continue to function by replicating data and services even if some nodes fail. There are two main replication strategies.

Primary-secondary replication

Primary-secondary replication is a data replication strategy used in distributed systems to enhance data availability, reliability, and read scalability. In this replication model, one node is designated as the Primary while one or more nodes are designated as secondary.

Following is how primary-secondary replication works:

- **Data writes**: All write operations, such as data inserts, updates, and deletes are performed on the primary node. The primary is responsible for handling these write requests and updating its own data.

- **Replication**: After the primary node processes a write operation, it propagates the changes to the secondary nodes. This process is called replication. The primary sends the updated data or the replication log to the secondary nodes, which then apply the changes to their own data, keeping it in sync with the primary.

- **Data reads**: Read operations can be performed on both the primary and secondary nodes. Clients can read data from any of the secondary nodes, which helps distribute the read load and improve read performance. However, reads from the secondary might return slightly stale data compared to the primary as there can be a short replication lag.

- **Failover**: If the primary node fails, one of the secondary nodes can be promoted to become the new primary. This failover process ensures high availability and minimizes downtime. The promoted secondary takes over the role of the primary and the other secondary starts replicating from the new primary.

The benefits of primary-secondary replication are as follows:

- **High availability**: If the Primary node fails, a secondary node can be promoted to take over as the new Primary, ensuring that the system remains available and operational.

- **Read scalability**: Primary-secondary replication can distribute the read load across multiple nodes, improving read performance and scalability by allowing read operations on secondary nodes.

- **Data durability**: It replicates data to multiple secondary nodes provides data redundancy and protects against data loss in case of hardware or node failures.

- **Backup and disaster recovery**: Secondary nodes can be used for backup purposes and to enable disaster recovery in case of catastrophic failures.

Some considerations and challenges are as follows:

- **Replication lag**: There can be a short delay between the time a write is performed on the Primary and when it is replicated to the secondary. This replication lag can lead to temporary data inconsistencies between the primary and secondary.

- **Consistency**: Ensuring strong consistency in a primary-secondary setup can be challenging as reads from secondary might return slightly stale data. Consistency requirements should be carefully considered based on the specific needs of the application.

- **Scalability limitations**: While primary-secondary replication improves read scalability, write scalability is still limited by the capacity of the Primary node. As the write load increases, the Primary can become a bottleneck.

- **Failover complexity**: Promoting a secondary to become the new primary during a failover can be complex and may require manual intervention or additional tools to ensure a smooth transition.

Primary-secondary replication is commonly used in various systems, such as databases (e.g., MySQL, PostgreSQL), messaging systems (e.g., Apache Kafka), and distributed file systems (e.g., HDFS). It provides a simple and effective way to achieve data availability, reliability, and read scalability in distributed environments.

When implementing primary-secondary replication, it is important to consider factors such as consistency requirements, replication lag, failover mechanisms, and scalability limitations based on the specific needs of the application. Proper monitoring, fault detection, and automated failover processes can help ensure the reliability and robustness of the replication setup.

Peer-to-peer replication

In the peer-to-peer replication model, all nodes in the distributed system are equal peers and each node can handle both read and write operations. When a write operation is performed on one node, the changes are propagated to the other nodes in the system. This ensures that all nodes eventually have a consistent view of the data.

Peer-to-peer replication can be applied to the e-commerce application's product catalog and user information. Each node in the system can handle read and write operations for the product catalog and user data. When a new product is added or user information is updated, the changes are replicated across all the nodes. This allows for better fault tolerance and scalability as the system can continue functioning even if some nodes fail, and the workload can be distributed among the available nodes.

The advantages of peer-to-peer replication are as follows:

- **Improved fault tolerance**: If one node fails, the other nodes can continue to serve read and write requests.

- **Better scalability**: The workload can be distributed evenly among the nodes, allowing the system to handle higher loads.

- **No single point of failure**: Since all nodes are equal, there is no single point of failure, unlike in the primary-secondary model.

However, peer-to-peer replication also has challenges, as follows:

- **Consistency**: Ensuring data consistency across all nodes can be more complex as there may be conflicts when multiple nodes perform write operations simultaneously.

- **Increased network overhead**: Propagating changes to all nodes can result in higher network overhead compared to the primary-secondary model.

When choosing a replication strategy, it is essential to consider factors, such as data consistency requirements, scalability needs, fault tolerance goals, and the specific characteristics of the application. The e-commerce application can benefit from a combination of primary-secondary replication for critical data like inventory and peer-to-peer replication for less critical data like product catalogs and user information. This hybrid approach allows for a balance between consistency, availability, and scalability.

Partitioning and sharding

Database partitioning and sharding are different but related techniques of dividing data across nodes so that it is manageable to handle them.

Partitioning

Partitioning a database involves dividing a large table or index into smaller, more manageable parts called **partitions** within a single database. Each partition contains a subset of the data based on a specified partitioning scheme.

Let us consider the *orders* table in our hypothetical e-commerce order processing database that stores information about customer orders. As the table grows large, we can partition it based on the order date.

We might create partitions as follows:

- **Partition 1**: Orders from January 2024 to March 2024
- **Partition 2**: Orders from April 2024 to June 2024
- **Partition 3**: Orders from July 2024 to September 2024
- **Partition 4**: Orders from October 2024 to December 2024

By partitioning the *orders* table, we improve query performance by accessing only the relevant partitions for a given query. If we want to retrieve orders from August 2022, the database can quickly locate and scan only partition three instead of scanning the entire *orders* table.

Thus, partition can be done at a logical level keeping into consideration the data and querying pattern.

There are several strategies for partitioning data, as follows:

- **Range partitioning**: Data is partitioned based on a specific range of values, such as alphabetical ranges or numerical ranges.

- **Hash partitioning**: Data is partitioned based on a hash function applied to a key, ensuring an even distribution of data across the partitions.

- **Directory-based partitioning**: A separate directory service is used to map data to the appropriate partitions based on specific criteria.

Sharding

Sharding a database involves distributing the data across multiple independent databases, called shards, running on separate servers or instances. Each shard contains a subset of the overall data, and the shards collectively make up the entire database.

In our e-commerce application, we can shard the database based on the customer's geographic regions. You will have the following shards:

- **Shard 1**: Customers from North America
- **Shard 2**: Customers from Europe
- **Shard 3**: Customers from Asia-Pacific

Each shard would contain the complete set of tables required for the e-commerce application, but only for customers within its assigned geographic region. When a customer from North America places an order, the application would direct the write operation to *Shard 1*. Similarly, when retrieving data for a customer from Europe, the application would query *Shard 2.*

Sharding allows you to distribute the data and the load across multiple servers, enabling horizontal scalability. Each shard can be hosted on a separate server, and additional shards can be added as the data and traffic grow. This approach helps to handle high volumes of data and concurrent users in the e-commerce application.

The benefits of partitioning are as follows:

- Partitioning improves query performance by reducing the amount of data scanned for a given query.
- Sharding enables horizontal scalability by distributing the data and load across multiple servers.
- Sharding can help to alleviate storage constraints by allowing data to be spread across multiple machines.

The considerations for partitioning are as follows:

- Partitioning requires careful design and management to ensure optimal performance and data integrity.
- Sharding introduces complexity in data management, such as data consistency, cross-shard queries, and data rebalancing.
- Sharding may require changes to the application architecture to handle distributed data access and routing.

When implementing sharding, one of the most crucial yet often overlooked decisions is the selection of the shard key, as this choice has long-lasting implications for your system's scalability and maintenance.

Consider a social media application that initially shards user data based on user ID. As the user base grows from millions to hundreds of millions, the system might require re-sharding to maintain balanced data distribution and optimal performance. This re-sharding process involves moving massive amounts of data between shards while the system remains operational, imagine carefully relocating books between libraries while people are still trying to check them out and return them.

The complexity of re-sharding operations becomes apparent when we examine the process in detail. During re-sharding, the system must maintain data consistency, handle incoming requests, and manage the migration of terabytes of data. For instance, if you are moving User A's data from Shard 1 to Shard 2, you need to ensure that any updates to User A's profile during the migration are not lost, and that other users can still interact with User A's content without interruption. This often requires implementing a two-phase migration approach where data is first copied to the new shard while keeping the old shard as the source of truth, then carefully switching over once synchronization is complete.

To minimize the need for re-sharding, careful upfront planning of your sharding strategy is essential.

When choosing a shard key, consider the following factors:
- The expected growth patterns of your data
- The natural access patterns of your application
- The potential for uneven data distribution
- The feasibility of future redistribution

For example, in an e-commerce system, sharding by customer region might seem logical initially, but could lead to significant imbalances if certain regions grow faster than others. A composite shard key combining region and customer ID might provide better long-term distribution characteristics, even though it adds some complexity to the initial implementation.

Some modern distributed databases offer auto-sharding capabilities that can help manage these challenges, but they often come with their own operational considerations and limitations. Understanding these trade-offs early in the design phase can save substantial operational effort and potential system downtime later in your application's lifecycle.

To summarize, partitioning is done at the logical level within a single database. It focuses on dividing a large table or index into smaller, more manageable parts based on a specific partitioning scheme. The partitioning scheme is typically based on the values of one or more columns in the table, such as date ranges, discrete values, or hash functions. Partitioning is primarily aimed at improving query performance and manageability of large tables within a single database. On the other hand, sharding is done with the functional aspects of the business domain in mind. Sharding involves distributing the entire database across multiple independent databases, called shards, based on a sharding key or strategy. The sharding key is chosen based on the functional requirements and characteristics of the application.

Both partitioning and sharding are powerful techniques for optimizing database performance and scalability in large-scale applications like e-commerce systems. The choice between them depends on the specific requirements, data characteristics, and scalability needs of the application.

Load balancing

Load balancing is the process of distributing workload evenly across multiple nodes in a distributed system. By ensuring that no single node is overwhelmed with requests, load balancing helps maintain high availability and responsiveness.

Load balancing can be achieved through various techniques, as follows:

- **Round-robin**: Requests are distributed sequentially across the available nodes in a circular manner.

- **Least connections**: Requests are sent to the node with the least number of active connections, ensuring an even distribution of workload.

- **IP hash**: The client's IP address is hashed to determine which node should handle the request, providing a form of sticky sessions.

- **Consistent hashing**: A hashing algorithm is used to map requests to nodes in a way that minimizes the redistribution of workload when nodes are added or removed from the system.

Failover and recovery mechanisms

Failover and recovery mechanisms are essential for ensuring high availability in distributed systems. Failover refers to the process of automatically switching to a redundant or standby component when a primary component fails. Recovery involves the steps taken to restore a failed component to its operational state.

Some common failover and recovery techniques are as follows:

- **Active-Passive failover**: One node is designated as the active node while another is designated as the passive node. If the active node fails, the passive node takes over.

- **Active-Active failover**: Multiple nodes are active simultaneously, and if one node fails, the others continue to handle the workload.

- **Checkpointing**: The state of a node is periodically saved to persistent storage, allowing for faster recovery in case of a failure.

- **Logging and replay**: All actions performed by a node are logged, and in case of a failure, the logs are replayed to bring the node back to its pre-failure state.

By employing a combination of these availability techniques, distributed systems can achieve high levels of availability and fault tolerance, ensuring that the system remains operational and responsive even in the presence of failures or high load.

Real-world systems

Let us explore how consistency and availability are handled in real-world distributed systems. We will look at well-known systems and discuss the lessons learned from their implementations.

Amazon DynamoDB

Amazon Dynamo is a highly available key-value store that prioritizes availability over strong consistency. Dynamo uses a combination of techniques, including partitioning, replication, and eventual consistency to achieve high availability and scalability.

In Dynamo, data is partitioned across multiple nodes using consistent hashing. Each data item is replicated across multiple nodes to ensure fault tolerance. When a write operation occurs, it is applied to a single node and then propagated to the other replicas asynchronously. This allows for high write availability as the system can continue to accept writes even if some nodes are unavailable.

Dynamo employs an eventual consistency model, which means that reads may return stale data until all replicas have been updated. To resolve conflicts between replicas, Dynamo uses a vector clock mechanism and a set of conflict resolution strategies, such as Last-Write-Wins or application-specific resolvers.

Google Spanner

Google Spanner is a globally distributed database system that provides strong consistency and high availability. Spanner achieves this by using a combination of techniques, including a novel time synchronization mechanism called **TrueTime** and a two-phase commit protocol for distributed transactions.

Spanner partitions data across multiple nodes and replicates each partition across multiple data centers. It uses a Paxos-based consensus algorithm to ensure that all replicas agree on the order of transactions. Spanner's TrueTime mechanism provides a highly accurate and synchronized clock across all nodes, allowing for globally consistent timestamps and enabling linearizability for reads and writes.

By leveraging TrueTime and two-phase commit, Spanner can provide strong consistency guarantees for distributed transactions, ensuring that all nodes always see a consistent view of the data. However, this strong consistency comes at the cost of higher latency compared to eventually consistent systems.

Cassandra

Apache Cassandra is a highly scalable and available distributed database that prioritizes availability and partition tolerance over strong consistency. Cassandra is designed to handle large amounts of structured data across multiple commodity servers providing high write throughput and low latency.

Cassandra uses a peer-to-peer architecture where each node in the cluster is equal and can serve both read and write requests. Data is partitioned across nodes using a consistent hashing mechanism and each partition is replicated across multiple nodes for fault tolerance.

Cassandra provides tunable consistency levels allowing developers to choose the desired level of consistency for each operation. It supports eventual consistency by default but also offers strong consistency options, such as quorum-based reads and writes. Cassandra uses a gossip protocol to propagate data updates and maintain consistency across replicas.

Emerging trends and future directions

Distributed systems are hard. They are difficult to build and required a team of experienced engineers, they also require significant maintenance. Small changes can lead to unexpected impact on latency, availability of the system. They require meticulous monitoring to ensure each part of the system works as expected. Small degradation in a critical component can have a domino effect causing catastrophic impact somewhere else. Cloud providers and hyper scalers like GCP, AWS and Azure are working on providing solutions for their customers that solve these problems, bringing them a ready solution that can be customized by their customers. One such solution is serverless computing.

Serverless computing

Serverless computing is an emerging trend in cloud computing that allows developers to build and run applications without the need to manage the underlying infrastructure. In a serverless architecture, the cloud provider dynamically manages the allocation of resources, scaling the application up or down based on the workload. This model offers several benefits, such as reduced operational complexity, cost efficiency, and automatic scalability.

However, ensuring data consistency in a serverless environment can be challenging. Serverless functions are typically short-lived and stateless, meaning they do not maintain a persistent state between invocations. This can make it difficult to enforce strong consistency, as the state needs to be externalized and managed separately.

In order to address this challenge, serverless platforms are exploring various approaches, as follows:

- **Stateful serverless**: Some platforms, such as AWS Step Functions and Azure Durable Functions, provide mechanisms for maintaining state across function invocations. These approaches allow for stateful workflows and can help enforce consistency by managing the state transitions.

- **Eventual consistency**: Many serverless applications rely on eventual consistency models where the state is updated asynchronously and may be temporarily inconsistent. This approach can be suitable for applications that can tolerate some level of inconsistency and prioritize availability and scalability.

- **External state management**: Serverless applications can use external storage services, such as databases or key-value stores, to manage and persist the state. By leveraging the consistency guarantees provided by these services, serverless functions can ensure data consistency.

As serverless computing continues to evolve, we can expect to see more research and development in the area of consistency management for serverless applications. This may include new programming models, frameworks, and best practices that help developers build consistent and reliable serverless systems.

Consistency in edge computing and IoT systems

Edge computing and the **Internet of Things** (**IoT**) are rapidly growing fields that involve processing data and making decisions closer to the source of the data, rather than relying on centralized cloud infrastructure. Edge computing brings computation and storage closer to edge devices, such as sensors, mobile devices, and industrial equipment, reducing latency and enabling real-time processing.

Ensuring data consistency in edge computing and IoT systems presents unique challenges, as follows:

- **Limited resources**: Edge devices often have limited computational power, storage capacity, and battery life, making it difficult to implement complex consistency protocols.

- **Intermittent connectivity**: Edge devices may have intermittent or unreliable network connectivity, leading to temporary disconnections and partitions. This can impact the ability to maintain strong consistency across the system.

- **Heterogeneity**: IoT systems often involve a diverse range of devices, protocols, and data formats, making it challenging to ensure consistent data representation and exchange.

In order to address these challenges, researchers and practitioners are exploring various approaches, as follows:

- **Eventual consistency**: Many edge computing and IoT systems rely on eventual consistency models where data updates are propagated asynchronously and may result in temporary inconsistencies. This approach can be suitable for applications that can tolerate some level of inconsistency and prioritize availability and scalability.

- **Hybrid consistency models**: Some systems employ hybrid consistency models where different consistency levels are used for different parts of the system or different types of data. For example, strong consistency can be used for critical data or control operations while eventual consistency can be used for less critical data or sensor readings.

- **Edge-cloud collaboration**: Edge devices can collaborate with cloud services to achieve consistency. For example, edge devices can perform local processing and caching while periodically synchronizing with the cloud to ensure global consistency.

- **Conflict resolution strategies**: IoT systems need to have well-defined conflict resolution strategies to handle concurrent updates and reconcile inconsistencies. This may involve techniques such as Last-Write-Wins, merging, or application-specific conflict resolution logic.

As edge computing and IoT systems continue to grow and evolve, ensuring data consistency will remain a critical challenge. Future research and development in this area will focus on developing scalable, efficient, and robust consistency mechanisms that can operate in resource-constrained and dynamically changing environments.

Research challenges and opportunities

Consistency and availability in distributed systems present several ongoing research challenges and opportunities, as follows:

- **Formal verification and analysis**: Developing formal methods and tools for verifying and analyzing the consistency and availability properties of distributed systems is an active area of research. This includes techniques for modeling, specifying, and reasoning about consistency models, as well as tools for automated verification and testing.

- **ML and consistency**: Applying ML techniques to consistency management is an emerging research direction. This includes using ML for predicting and optimizing consistency levels, detecting and resolving inconsistencies, and adapting consistency strategies based on workload patterns and system dynamics.

- **Consistency in multi-cloud and federated environments**: As applications increasingly span multiple cloud providers and federated environments, ensuring consistency across these heterogeneous systems becomes a significant challenge. Research in this area focuses on developing consistency protocols and mechanisms that can operate across different cloud platforms and administrative domains.

- **Consistency for new application domains**: As new application domains emerge, such as blockchain systems, virtual and augmented reality, and collaborative editing, novel consistency challenges arise. Researchers are exploring new consistency models, algorithms, and architectures that can meet the specific requirements of these domains.

- **Human factors and usability**: Consistency and availability trade-offs have a direct impact on the user experience. Researching the human factors aspects of consistency, such as how users perceive and interact with eventually consistent systems can provide valuable insights for designing more usable and user-centric distributed systems.

As distributed systems continue to evolve and become more complex, research in consistency and availability will play a crucial role in enabling the development of reliable, scalable, and user-friendly applications. By addressing these research challenges and exploring new opportunities, the distributed systems community can advance the state of the art and provide better tools and techniques for building consistent and available systems in the face of ever-increasing demands and expectations.

Conclusion

In this chapter, we have explored the critical concepts of consistency and availability in distributed systems, and the trade-offs between them as described by the CAP theorem. We have examined various consistency models, such as strong consistency and eventual consistency, and discussed their implications for system design and operation.

We have also investigated the factors that affect availability and explored techniques for achieving high availability, such as replication, partitioning, and load balancing. The role of consensus protocols, like *Paxos* and *Raft*, in ensuring consistency and availability has been discussed along with real-world examples of distributed systems and their design choices.

Furthermore, we have delved into emerging trends and future directions, such as serverless computing, edge computing, and IoT systems, and the unique challenges they present in terms of consistency and availability. Finally, we have provided practical insights and best practices for designing and operating distributed systems that meet the specific requirements of different applications and use cases.

As distributed systems continue to evolve and become more complex, understanding the principles of consistency and availability remains crucial for building reliable, scalable, and user-friendly applications. By carefully considering the trade-offs between consistency and availability, and leveraging the appropriate techniques and protocols, system designers and developers can create robust distributed systems that meet the ever-growing demands of modern applications.

Ongoing research in areas such as formal verification, ML, multi-cloud environments, and new application domains will continue to advance the state of the art in consistency and availability providing better tools and techniques for tackling the challenges of building reliable distributed systems in the face of increasing complexity and scale.

In the next chapter, we will look at how to designs systems to be highly performant, efficient and maintainable. We will look at best practices related to codebases, designing and coding best practices.

CHAPTER 5

Design for Speed and Efficiency

Introduction

The chapter delves into the art of designing distributed systems optimized for speed and efficiency, which is crucial in today's fast-paced digital world. It introduces the twelve-factor app principles as a set of industry-adopted best practices that provide a solid foundation for building resilient, scalable, and maintainable applications.

The passage explores various essential topics, including the significance of having a single codebase tracked in version control, the power of **continuous integration and continuous delivery (CI/CD)** in automating deployments, the benefits of stateless application processes, the philosophy of simplicity in execution, the role of concurrency and horizontal scaling, the concept of ephemeral processes, the advantages of serverless architectures, the importance of environment parity, the significance of logging and monitoring, the application of SOLID design principles, and various performance optimization techniques.

By applying these principles and practices, developers can create high-performance distributed systems that are fast, efficient, and responsive to the demands of the modern digital landscape. The chapter aims to equip readers with a comprehensive understanding of the key considerations and best practices for designing distributed systems that are optimized for speed and efficiency, enabling them to tackle the challenges of building high-performance distributed applications in today's demanding digital world.

Structure

The chapter covers the following topics:

- Codebase, dependencies, and configuration
- Continuous integration and continuous delivery
- Stateless application processes
- Concurrency and horizontal scaling
- Ephemeral processes and disposability
- Leveraging serverless architectures
- Environment parity
- Applying SOLID design principles

Objectives

By the end of this chapter, readers will be familiar with and understand the importance of designing distributed systems for speed and efficiency, as well as the twelve-factor app principles and their application in designing high-performance distributed systems. You will learn about the benefits of maintaining a single codebase in version control, implementing explicit dependency management and isolation, and the role of CI/CD in automating and streamlining the deployment process. Additionally, you will explore the significance of stateless application processes and their advantages in terms of scalability and fault tolerance, the philosophy of simplicity in execution, techniques for simplifying deployment and maximizing robustness, concurrency and horizontal scaling techniques for handling increased loads and achieving better performance, the concept of ephemeral processes and the benefits of designing processes to be disposable and quickly restartable, the advantages of leveraging serverless architectures for increased efficiency in distributed systems, the importance of environment parity and techniques for maintaining consistency across development, staging, and production environments, and the application of SOLID design principles in the context of distributed systems to promote maintainability, extensibility, and loose coupling.

Codebase, dependencies and configuration

Consider a scenario where development teams maintain environment-specific code forks a separate branch for production containing TLS certificate handling, while staging uses hardcoded API endpoints from an older branch. When a developer updates a core dependency (e.g., database client v4.2 in dev) but neglects to synchronize this across environments, staging deployments might silently inherit v3.9 from its branch. This mismatch could surface as catastrophic runtime errors perhaps a changed connection pooling syntax but only during production load testing. Teams then waste hours chasing

works on my machine phantom bugs, unaware their fragmented version control created hidden dependency timebombs. Such configuration drift directly undermines the speed, and reliability gains distributed systems aim to achieve, highlighting why environment parity must be codified through a single source of truth rather than tribal knowledge.

One of the fundamental principles of designing distributed systems for speed and efficiency is maintaining a single codebase that is tracked in version control. This principle emphasizes the importance of having a unified and consistent source of truth for the application code, regardless of the number of deployments or environments.

In a distributed system, multiple instances of the application may be running simultaneously across different servers or even different geographical regions. By keeping the codebase in a centralized version control system, such as *Git*, developers can ensure that all instances of the application are built from the same codebase.

This approach provides several benefits, as follows:

- **Consistency**: With a single codebase, all deployments of the application are based on the same code, ensuring consistency across environments. This reduces the risk of discrepancies and makes it easier to identify and troubleshoot issues.

- **Collaboration**: Version control systems facilitate collaboration among team members. Developers can work on different features or bug fixes concurrently, merging their changes back into the main codebase. This enables efficient teamwork and helps maintain a cohesive and up-to-date codebase.

- **Versioning and rollbacks**: Version control allow for tracking changes over time and creates a history of the codebase. This makes it possible to revert to previous versions if needed, providing a safety net in case of unexpected issues or bugs introduced in new releases.

- **Automated deployments**: With a single codebase, automated deployment processes can be set up to build, test, and deploy the application consistently across multiple environments. This ensures that the same codebase is used for all deployments, reducing the risk of manual errors and improving efficiency.

In order to implement this principle effectively, it is recommended to follow best practices, as follows:

- Using a distributed version control system like Git to manage the codebase.

- Establishing clear branching and merging strategies to maintain a stable and predictable codebase.

  For instance, teams often adopt frameworks like GitFlow or trunk-based development for systematic collaboration. GitFlow formalizes long-lived branches (e.g., develop for integration and main for production) with strict rules for merging feature branches and hotfixes. This prevents merge day chaos in distributed systems where multiple teams work concurrently, imagine a payment service team merging a feature branch prematurely, destabilizing the shared develop branch relied upon by inventory and shipping services. Conversely, trunk-based development prioritizes small, frequent commits directly to the main branch, enforced by automated testing and feature flags. A streaming platform using this approach could deploy 50+ microservices daily without version skew, as all components evolve atomically from the same trunk. Both strategies codify workflow guardrails, ensuring distributed teams do not inadvertently compromise system stability through uncoordinated changes.

- Implementing code review processes to ensure code quality and catch potential issues early.

- Automating the build and deployment processes to minimize manual intervention and reduce the risk of errors.

By adhering to the principle of a single codebase tracked in version control, developers can streamline the development and deployment workflows, ensure consistency across environments, and promote collaboration within the team. This lays the foundation for building efficient and maintainable distributed systems. You can leverage GitHub, GitLab, or one of the cloud service provider's code management services to start with.

Dependency management and isolation

In a distributed system, managing dependencies is crucial for ensuring the stability, reliability, and efficiency of the application. The principle of explicit dependency management and isolation emphasizes the need to declare and isolate the external dependencies of an application explicitly.

External dependencies, such as libraries, frameworks, or third-party services, can introduce complexities and potential points of failure in a distributed system. Even with careful planning, distributed systems often grapple with version conflicts, scenarios where incompatible library versions create cascading failures. Consider a Node.js microservice requiring library-auth@2.5 that itself depends on utils-common@^1.4, while another service uses data-processor@3.1 needing utils-common@1.9. These overlapping but mismatched sub-dependencies can silently corrupt data flows. Such version conflicts are magnified in distributed architectures, where inconsistent dependency trees across services lead to unreproducible bugs (works in QA, breaks in production) and operational paralysis. Explicit dependency management, containerized builds, and strict semantic versioning policies becomes essential to prevent these invisible fault lines.

Explicit dependency management involves the following practices:

- **Dependency declaration**: All dependencies required by the application should be explicitly declared, typically in a configuration file or manifest. This includes specifying the exact versions of the dependencies to ensure consistency across different environments.

In a Node.js application, dependencies are declared in the **package.json** file. Each dependency is listed with its name and version, as follows:

```json
  "dependencies": {
    "express": "^4.17.1",
    "mongoose": "^5.12.5",
    "lodash": "^4.17.21"
  }
```

- **Dependency isolation**: Each application should have its own isolated set of dependencies, independent of other applications or the underlying system. This isolation prevents conflicts between different versions of dependencies and ensures that the application has a consistent and reproducible runtime environment.

  For example, in a microservices architecture, each microservice is deployed as a separate container using technologies like *Docker*. Each container has its isolated filesystem and includes only the dependencies required by that specific microservice. This isolation ensures that different microservices can use different versions of the same dependency without conflicts.

- **Dependency resolution**: Automated tools and package managers, such as *npm* for *Node.js* or *Maven* for *Java*, can be used to resolve and install the declared dependencies. These tools handle the retrieval and installation of the required packages, making the dependency management process more efficient and reliable.

  For example, when running **npm install** in a Node.js project, **npm** reads the **package.json** file, resolves the dependencies, and installs them in the **node_modules** directory. It automatically downloads the required packages from the **npm** registry and ensures that the correct versions are installed based on the declared dependencies.

- **Dependency tracking**: Version control systems should be used to track changes to the dependency configuration files. This allows for auditing and reproducing the exact set of dependencies used in a specific version of the application.

  For example, in a Git repository, the **package.json** file (for Node.js) or **pom.xml** file (for Java Maven projects) should be committed along with the application code. This enables tracking changes to the dependencies over time and makes it possible to reproduce the exact environment used for a specific version of the application.

Note: While dependency managers resolve version compatibility, they do not inherently address security risks. For example, running npm install might inadvertently pull a package with known vulnerabilities. Tools like npm audit (built into npm) or third-party scanners like Snyk automatically flag such risks by cross-referencing dependencies against vulnerability databases. Integrating these tools into CI/CD pipelines ensures vulnerabilities in distributed components—like a compromised Redis client or a logging library with injection flaws—are detected during builds, not in production. This complements version management by adding a critical layer of proactive security validation.

Implementing explicit dependency management and isolation offers several benefits, as follows:

- **Reproducibility**: By explicitly declaring and isolating dependencies, the application can be easily reproduced in different environments, ensuring consistency and reducing the risk of runtime issues caused by conflicting dependencies.

- **Portability**: The application becomes more portable, as it carries its dependencies and is not tightly coupled to the underlying system. This makes it easier to deploy the application across different platforms or cloud providers.

- **Scalability**: Isolating dependencies allows for independent scaling of different components of the application. Each component can have its own set of dependencies, enabling teams to develop, test, and deploy them independently.

- **Maintainability**: Explicit dependency management makes it easier to update and manage dependencies over time. It provides clarity about the dependencies used by the application and helps in identifying and resolving any potential issues or vulnerabilities.

In order to implement explicit dependency management effectively, consider the following best practices:

- Use versioned dependency configuration files to specify the exact versions of the required dependencies.

- Utilize dependency-locking mechanisms to ensure deterministic builds and prevent unintended updates to dependencies.

- Regularly review and update dependencies to address security vulnerabilities and take advantage of new features and bug fixes.

- Automate the dependency resolution and installation process to ensure consistency and efficiency across different environments.

By embracing explicit dependency management and isolation, developers can create more stable, portable, and maintainable distributed systems. It reduces the complexity of managing dependencies, improves the reliability of the application, and facilitates independent development and deployment of different components.

Storing configuration in the environment

In addition to explicit dependency management and isolation, another key principle of designing distributed systems for speed and efficiency is storing configuration in the environment. This principle advocates for separating the configuration settings from the application code and storing them in the environment where the application is deployed.

Configuration settings, such as database connection strings, API keys, server endpoints, or feature flags, can vary across different environments (e.g., development, staging, production). By externalizing these settings and storing them in the environment, the application becomes more flexible, portable, and easier to manage.

Hardcoding credentials like API keys or database passwords in configuration files creates catastrophic exposure risks, imagine a developer accidentally committing a .env file with production credentials to a public GitHub repository. Even externalized settings stored in plaintext, for example, **appsettings.json**) remain vulnerable. Tools like **HashiCorp Vault** or **AWS Secrets Manager** solve this by injecting secrets at runtime via secure APIs. For instance, a Kubernetes-based system might retrieve database credentials from Vault dynamically during pod initialization, avoiding persistent storage of sensitive data. These tools also enforce encryption, access auditing, and automatic secret rotation, mitigating risks like credential leakage or stale keys lingering in deployment scripts. In distributed architectures, where secrets may span hundreds of microservices, centralized management becomes non-negotiable for both security and operational sanity.

Advantages of storing configuration in the environment as follows:

- **Separation of concerns**: Decoupling the configuration from the application code promotes a clear separation of concerns. It allows the application to focus on its core functionality while the configuration is managed independently.

  In a Java application deployed on a Kubernetes cluster, the database connection string can be stored as an environment variable in the Kubernetes deployment configuration file, for example, **deployment.yaml**. This way, the application code remains independent of the specific database connection details, and the configuration can be easily modified without changing the code.

- **Environment-specific settings**: Storing configuration in the environment enables the use of different settings for different environments. This is particularly useful when the application needs to connect to different databases, services, or endpoints based on the deployment environment.

  In a Node.js application, the **NODE_ENV** environment variable can be used to specify the current environment (e.g., development, production). Based on the value of **NODE_ENV**, the application can load the appropriate configuration file (e.g., **config/ development.js** or **config/production.js**) that contains environment-specific settings.

- **Security**: Sensitive information, such as API keys or database credentials, should not be hardcoded in the application code or version control system. Storing these secrets in the environment helps keep them secure and prevents accidental exposure.

  In a containerized application deployed using Docker, sensitive configuration values can be passed as environment variables during container creation. The Docker Compose file or Kubernetes secrets can be used to securely provide these values to the containers without exposing them in the codebase.

- **Flexibility and portability**: By externalizing configuration, the application becomes more flexible and portable across different environments. The same codebase can be deployed in various environments without modifications, as the configuration is provided externally.

  A Python application that relies on a third-party API can store the API endpoint URL as an environment variable. This allows the application to be easily deployed in different environments (e.g., staging, production) with different API endpoints without modifying the code.

Best practices for storing configuration in the environment are as follows:

- Use environment variables to store configuration values. Most programming languages and frameworks provide easy access to environment variables.

- Keep sensitive information, such as secrets and credentials, out of version control systems. Use secure mechanisms, like encrypted config files or secrets management tools to store and manage them.

- Provide default configuration values in the codebase for fallback purposes but allow them to be overridden by environment-specific settings. For example, Spring Boot simplifies this pattern through its externalized configuration philosophy. You might define a default database connection pool size in **application.properties**:

```
# Default configuration (src/main/resources/application.properties)
app.datasource.pool-size=10
```

  This value can then be overridden in production using **application-prod.properties**:

```
# src/main/resources/application-prod.properties
app.datasource.pool-size=50
```

- Use configuration management tools or platforms, such as *Ansible, Puppet*, or *Kubernetes ConfigMaps*, to manage and distribute configuration across different environments consistently.

  In a *Ruby* on *Rails* application, the **config/database.yml** file can be configured to read database settings from environment variables, as follows:

```yaml
yaml
production:
adapter: postgresql
host: <%= ENV['DB_HOST'] %>
port: <%= ENV['DB_PORT'] %>
database: <%= ENV['DB_NAME'] %>
username: <%= ENV['DB_USERNAME'] %>
password: <%= ENV['DB_PASSWORD'] %>
```

By storing configuration in the environment, developers can create more adaptable and maintainable distributed systems. It promotes separation of concerns, enables environment-specific settings, enhances security, and improves the portability of the application.

Continuous integration and continuous delivery

Netflix's engineering team offers a compelling example of CI/CD's transformative power. By implementing a fully automated pipeline using tools like Spinnaker, they achieved over 5,000 deployments per day across their distributed streaming platform. Before CI/CD, deploying changes to their microservices architecture required hours of manual coordination between teams, often leading to version mismatches and outages. With automated canary deployments and chaos testing integrated into their pipeline, Netflix reduced production rollback times from 45 minutes to under 60 seconds. This shift not only accelerated feature delivery (e.g., rolling out A/B-tested UI changes globally in hours) but also improved system resilience critical for a service serving 250 million+ users. Such scalability would be unthinkable in a distributed system without CI/CD's ability to enforce consistency across thousands of interdependent components.

CI/CD are essential practices in designing distributed systems for speed and efficiency. CI/CD enables teams to automate and streamline the process of building, testing, and deploying applications, allowing for faster iterations and improved reliability.

CI involves frequently merging code changes from multiple developers into a central repository and automatically building and testing the application. This practice ensures that code changes are regularly integrated and that any issues or conflicts are detected early in the development cycle.

In a CI setup using *Jenkins*, developers push their code changes to a *Git* repository. *Jenkins*, a CI server, is configured to monitor the repository and automatically triggers a build process whenever new changes are detected. The build process includes compiling the code, running unit tests, and generating artifacts, such as binaries or container images.

The CD takes the automation further by ensuring that the application is always in a deployable state. CD pipelines automate the deployment process, enabling the application to be easily and reliably deployed to various environments, such as staging or production.

In a CD pipeline using *GitLab*, the pipeline is triggered after a successful CI build. The pipeline includes stages for deploying the application to a staging environment, running integration tests, and then promoting the deployment to the production environment. Each stage is automated, and the pipeline can be configured to require manual approvals before proceeding to critical stages like production deployment.

Key components and benefits of CI/CD pipelines

A typical CI/CD pipeline consists of several key components, as follows:

- **Source code management (SCM)**: The SCM system, such as *Git*, serves as the central repository for storing and managing the application's codebase. It enables version control, branching, and collaboration among developers.

- **Build automation**: Tools, such as *Maven* for *Java* or *npm* for Node.js, are used to compile the code, resolve dependencies, and generate executable artifacts. These tools ensure consistent and repeatable builds across different environments.

- **Testing automation**: Automated tests, including unit tests, integration tests, and acceptance tests, are executed as part of the CI/CD pipeline. Test automation helps catch bugs early, ensures the application's stability, and provides confidence in the deployments.

- **Artifact repository**: The generated artifacts, such as binaries, libraries, or container images, are stored in an artifact repository. Tools like *JFrog Artifactory* or *Docker Registry* act as central storage for these artifacts, making them accessible for deployment.

- **Deployment automation**: Tools, such as *Ansible, Kubernetes,* or *AWS CodeDeploy,* are used to automatically deploy the application to target environments. These tools ensure consistent and reliable deployments, reducing the risk of manual errors.

Implementing CI/CD pipelines offers several benefits, as follows:

- **Faster feedback loop**: CI/CD enables quick feedback on code changes. Developers can identify and fix issues early in the development cycle, reducing the overall time and effort required for debugging and troubleshooting.

- **Improved collaboration**: CI/CD promotes collaboration among team members. With automated builds and tests, developers can integrate their changes frequently, avoiding long-lived feature branches and reducing merge conflicts.

- **Increased reliability**: Automated testing and consistent deployment processes reduce the risk of human errors and ensure the application's reliability. CI/CD pipelines help catch bugs, ensure the application's stability, and provide confidence in the deployments.

- **Faster time to market**: By automating the build, test, and deployment processes, CI/CD enables faster delivery of features and updates to end-users. It reduces the time required for manual tasks and allows teams to focus on delivering value to customers.

Suppose an organization implements a CI/CD pipeline using *Jenkins* and *Kubernetes*. Developers push their code changes to a Git repository, triggering a *Jenkins* job. The job builds the code, runs unit tests, and creates a *Docker* container image. If the tests pass, the container image is pushed to a *Docker Registry*. The CD pipeline then deploys the container image to a staging environment using *Kubernetes*. After successful integration tests, the pipeline promotes the deployment to the production environment. This automated process ensures consistent and reliable deployments, reducing the time and effort required for manual deployments.

CI/CD for enhanced speed and efficiency

In order to implement CI/CD effectively and enhance the speed and efficiency of distributed systems, consider the following best practices:

- **Automation**: Automate as much of the build, test, and deployment processes as possible. Automation reduces manual errors, saves time, and ensures consistency across different environments.

- **Use version control**: Utilize a version control system like Git to manage the application's codebase. Version control enables collaboration, branching, and tracking of changes, making it easier to manage and roll back if needed.

- **Implement comprehensive testing**: Include comprehensive automated tests in the CI/CD pipeline. Write unit tests, integration tests, and acceptance tests to cover different aspects of the application. Automated tests catch bugs early and provide confidence in the deployments.

- **Establish consistent environments**: Ensure consistency across development, staging, and production environments. Use **infrastructure as code (IaC)** tools, like *Terraform* or *CloudFormation* to define and provision environments consistently.

- **Monitor and log**: Implement monitoring and logging mechanisms to track the health and performance of the application in different environments. Monitoring helps identify issues quickly, and logging provides valuable insights for troubleshooting and optimization.

- **Continuously improve**: Continuously measure and improve the CI/CD pipeline. Collect metrics, such as build times, test coverage, and deployment frequency, to identify bottlenecks and optimize the process. Regularly review and update the pipeline to incorporate new tools and best practices.

For example, a team implements a comprehensive CI/CD pipeline using GitLab. They define a **`.gitlab-ci.yml`** file that specifies the stages and jobs in the pipeline. The pipeline includes stages for building, testing, and deploying the application. Each stage has multiple jobs, such as linting, unit tests, integration tests, and deployment to different environments. The team uses *GitLab Runners to* execute the jobs in parallel, speeding up the pipeline. They also integrate tools, like *SonarQube* for code quality analysis and Prometheus for monitoring. By continuously measuring and optimizing the pipeline, the team improves the speed and efficiency of their distributed system development process.

By adopting CI/CD practices and implementing automated pipelines, distributed system development teams can significantly enhance the speed and efficiency of their development and deployment processes. CI/CD enables faster feedback, improves collaboration, increases reliability, and reduces the time to market for new features and updates.

Stateless application processes

In distributed systems, designing application processes to be stateless is a fundamental principle for achieving scalability, fault tolerance, and efficient resource utilization. Stateless processes do not maintain any persistent state within the process itself, making them easier to scale horizontally and recover from failures.

When designing distributed systems, it is important to architect the application as a set of stateless processes. Each process should be independent and self-contained, without relying on any internal state that persists across requests or transactions.

Consider a web application that processes user requests. Instead of maintaining user session data within the application process, the session data is stored in an external database or a distributed cache like Redis. When a request comes in, the application process retrieves the necessary session data from the external store, processes the request, and returns the response. The process itself does not store any session data internally.

Stateless processes in distributed systems

Stateless processes offer several advantages in distributed systems, as follows:

- **Scalability**: Stateless processes can be easily scaled horizontally by adding more instances of the process. Since each process is independent and does not maintain an internal state, requests can be distributed across multiple instances without any coordination or state synchronization.

  In a stateless web application, multiple instances of the application can be deployed behind a load balancer. The load balancer distributes incoming requests evenly across the instances, allowing the system to handle a higher volume of traffic without any single instance becoming a bottleneck.

- **Fault tolerance**: Stateless processes are more resilient to failures. If a process crashes or becomes unavailable, it can be seamlessly replaced by spinning up a new instance. Since the process does not maintain any internal state, there is no need for complex state recovery mechanisms.

In a microservices architecture, each microservice is designed as a stateless process. If a microservice instance fails, a new instance can be quickly provisioned to replace it. The system can continue processing requests without any data loss or interruption.

- **Efficient resource utilization**: Stateless processes have a smaller footprint and consume fewer resources compared to stateful processes. They do not need to allocate memory or storage to maintain an internal state, making them lightweight and efficient.

Serverless computing platforms, such as *AWS Lambda* or *Google Cloud Functions,* leverage stateless functions to execute code in response to events. These functions are short-lived and do not maintain any state between invocations, allowing for efficient resource utilization and automatic scaling based on demand.

Stateless application architectures

To design and implement stateless application architectures, consider the following best practices:

- **Externalize state**: Move any state that needs to persist across requests or transactions to external storage systems, such as databases, distributed caches, or message queues. This allows the application processes to remain stateless while still having access to necessary data.

- **Use stateless communication protocols**: Employ stateless communication protocols, such as HTTP or gRPC, for inter-process communication. Stateless protocols ensure that each request contains all the necessary information and does not rely on any prior context or state.

- **Implement idempotency**: Design operations to be idempotent, meaning that multiple identical requests should have the same effect as a single request. Idempotency ensures that the system remains consistent even if requests are retried or replayed due to failures.

- **Leverage caching**: Utilize caching mechanisms to store frequently accessed data in memory or distributed caches. Caching reduces the need for expensive database or external service calls, improving performance and reducing latency.

Suppose a stateless e-commerce application is designed using a microservices architecture. Each microservice, such as the product catalog, shopping cart, and order processing, is implemented as a stateless process. The product catalog microservice stores product data in a database and uses a distributed cache, like *Redis* to cache frequently accessed product information. The shopping cart microservice stores cart data in a NoSQL database like MongoDB, allowing for high scalability and availability. The order processing microservice receives orders through a message queue and processes them asynchronously, ensuring idempotency and fault tolerance.

Scaling and fault tolerance considerations

When designing stateless application processes, it is important to consider scaling and fault tolerance aspects.

Following are a list of considerations that one must explore:

- **Horizontal scaling**: Stateless processes enable horizontal scaling by allowing multiple instances of the process to run concurrently. Use load balancing techniques to distribute requests evenly across the instances, ensuring optimal resource utilization and high availability.

- **Auto-scaling**: Implement auto-scaling mechanisms to automatically adjust the number of process instances based on the incoming load. Auto-scaling helps optimize resource allocation and ensures that the system can handle varying levels of traffic efficiently.

- **Fault detection and recovery**: Implement robust fault detection and recovery mechanisms to identify and handle process failures. Use health checks to monitor the status of processes and automatically restart or replace failed instances. Employ techniques, like circuit breakers and retry mechanisms to handle temporary failures gracefully.

- **Stateless session management**: If session management is required, use stateless session techniques, like **JSON Web Tokens (JWT)** or session IDs stored in cookies. Store session data in external storage systems rather than relying on process memory, allowing for seamless session handling across multiple instances.

A video streaming platform built using stateless application processes can handle a large number of concurrent users. The video processing and encoding microservices are designed as stateless processes, allowing them to scale horizontally based on the incoming video uploads. The video-serving microservice is also stateless, enabling it to scale based on the number of active viewers. Auto-scaling policies are configured to automatically adjust the number of instances based on CPU utilization or request rate. Health checks are implemented to detect and replace failed instances automatically, ensuring high availability and fault tolerance.

By designing application processes to be stateless, distributed systems can achieve better scalability, fault tolerance, and resource utilization. Stateless processes enable horizontal scaling, simplify failure recovery, and allow for efficient resource allocation. By externalizing state and leveraging stateless communication protocols, distributed systems can handle a large volume of requests and adapt to changing demands effectively.

Concurrency and horizontal scaling

In distributed systems, concurrency and horizontal scaling are fundamental concepts that enable improved performance, scalability, and efficient resource utilization. By leveraging concurrency and scaling out via the process model, distributed systems can handle a large volume of requests and adapt to varying workloads effectively.

Scaling out process model

The process model is a key principle in designing distributed systems for scalability. It involves running the application as a set of independent processes that can be scaled out horizontally. Each process is responsible for handling a subset of the workload, and multiple processes can run concurrently to distribute the load.

Consider a web application that receives a high volume of requests. Instead of handling all the requests in a single process, the application is designed to run as multiple processes, each handling a portion of the requests. As the load increases, additional processes can be spawned to scale out the application horizontally. This approach allows for better resource utilization and improved performance.

Concurrency for improved performance

Concurrency is the ability to execute multiple tasks simultaneously. By leveraging concurrency, distributed systems can achieve better performance and utilize system resources more efficiently. Concurrency can be applied at different levels, such as process-level concurrency and thread-level concurrency.

In a distributed system that processes large amounts of data, concurrency can be employed to parallelize the processing tasks. Instead of processing the data sequentially, the system can split the data into smaller chunks and process them concurrently using multiple processes or threads. This approach reduces the overall processing time and allows for efficient utilization of available computing resources.

Horizontal partitioning strategies for scalability

Horizontal partitioning, also known as **sharding**, is a technique used to distribute data across multiple nodes or instances in a distributed system. By partitioning the data horizontally, the system can scale out to handle a larger volume of data and requests.

Consider a distributed database system that stores user profile information. As the number of users grows, the system can employ horizontal partitioning to distribute the user data across multiple database instances. Each instance is responsible for storing and serving a subset of the user data. This approach allows the system to scale horizontally by adding more database instances as the data volume increases.

Load balancing for distributed processing

In order to effectively leverage concurrency and horizontal scaling, distributed systems need to implement load balancing and distributed processing mechanisms. Load balancing ensures that the incoming requests are evenly distributed across the available processes or nodes, while distributed processing enables the system to parallelize and coordinate tasks across multiple nodes.

In a distributed system that processes real-time data streams, load balancing can be implemented using a message queue or a pub-sub system, like *Apache Kafka*. The data streams are partitioned and distributed across multiple consumer processes, each handling a subset of the data. The consumer processes can process the data concurrently and scale horizontally based on the volume of incoming data.

Considerations for stateful and stateless services

When designing distributed systems for concurrency and horizontal scaling, it is important to consider the stateful and stateless nature of the services. Stateless services are easier to scale horizontally since they do not maintain any internal state and can handle requests independently. Stateful services, on the other hand, require additional coordination and synchronization mechanisms to ensure data consistency and integrity.

In a microservices architecture, stateless services like API Gateways or authentication services can be easily scaled out by running multiple instances behind a load balancer. Stateful services, such as user session management or shopping cart services, may require additional considerations like distributed caching or state replication to ensure data consistency across instances.

Monitoring and scaling strategies

In order to effectively manage concurrency and horizontal scaling in distributed systems, monitoring, and scaling strategies are crucial. Monitoring helps track the performance, resource utilization, and health of the system while scaling strategies determine when and how to adjust the number of processes or nodes based on the workload.

For example, a distributed system can use metrics like CPU utilization, request rate, and response times to monitor the performance of individual processes or nodes. Auto-scaling policies can be defined based on these metrics to automatically scale out or scale in the number of processes or nodes. If the CPU utilization exceeds a certain threshold, additional processes can be spawned to handle the increased load.

By embracing concurrency and horizontal scaling, distributed systems can achieve better performance, scalability, and resource utilization. The process model allows for scaling out the application by running multiple independent processes concurrently. Leveraging concurrency helps parallelize tasks and improve overall performance. Horizontal partitioning strategies enable the system to distribute data and requests across multiple nodes. Implementing load balancing and distributed processing ensures efficient utilization of resources and fair distribution of workload.

When designing distributed systems for concurrency and horizontal scaling, it is important to consider the stateful and stateless nature of the services and implement appropriate coordination and synchronization mechanisms. Monitoring and scaling strategies help manage the system's performance and automatically adjust the resources based on the workload.

Ephemeral processes and disposability

In distributed systems, designing processes to be ephemeral and disposable is a key principle for achieving fault tolerance, resilience, and easier management. Ephemeral processes are short-lived and can be easily replaced or terminated without affecting the overall system's functionality. Disposability ensures that processes can be quickly started and stopped, allowing for efficient resource utilization and fast recovery from failures.

When designing distributed systems, it is important to treat processes as disposable units. Disposable processes are designed to be easily replaceable and have a minimal impact on the system when they are terminated or replaced. This approach enables better fault tolerance and simplifies the management of the system.

In a microservices architecture, each microservice is designed as a disposable process. If a microservice instance fails or becomes unresponsive, it can be quickly terminated and replaced with a new instance. The system can continue operating without any significant disruption, as other microservice instances can handle the incoming requests.

Benefits of ephemeral processes

Ephemeral processes offer several benefits in distributed systems, as follows:

- **Fault tolerance**: Ephemeral processes enhance fault tolerance by minimizing the impact of individual process failures. If a process fails, it can be quickly replaced without affecting the overall system's availability or functionality.

  In a distributed data processing system, if a worker process fails while processing a task, the task can be reassigned to another available worker process. The system can continue processing tasks without any data loss or interruption.

- **Scalability**: Ephemeral processes enable easier scalability by allowing the system to dynamically adjust the number of processes based on the workload. Processes can be quickly started or terminated to match the current demand.

In a web application that experiences fluctuating traffic, ephemeral processes can be used to scale the application dynamically. During peak hours, additional processes can be spawned to handle the increased load, and during low-traffic periods, excess processes can be terminated to conserve resources.

- **Resource efficiency**: Ephemeral processes promote efficient resource utilization by allowing processes to be started and stopped as needed. Resources can be allocated to processes only when they are actively required, reducing wastage and optimizing resource consumption.

In a serverless computing environment, ephemeral processes are used to execute functions in response to events or requests. The processes are started when a function is invoked and terminated once the function execution is complete. This approach ensures that resources are consumed only during the actual execution of the function.

Process disposability and fault tolerance

In order to implement process disposability and fault tolerance in distributed systems, consider the following techniques:

- **Stateless design**: Processes should be stateless whenever possible. Stateless processes do not maintain any internal state and can be easily replaced or restarted without losing any critical data. State should be externalized and stored in distributed storage systems or databases.

  In a stateless API server, each request is handled independently without relying on any previous state. The server can be easily scaled by adding or removing instances, and if an instance fails, it can be replaced without any data loss or consistency issues.

- **Graceful shutdown**: Implement graceful shutdown mechanisms for processes to ensure proper cleanup and resource release. When a process needs to be terminated, it should first complete any in-progress tasks, release held resources, and then shut down cleanly.

  In a message processing system, when a consumer process receives a shutdown signal, it should finish processing the current message, acknowledge its completion, and then gracefully terminate. This ensures that no messages are lost or left in an inconsistent state.

- **Health monitoring and self-healing**: Implement health monitoring and self-healing mechanisms to detect process failures and automatically recover from them. Use health checks to periodically assess the status of processes and restart or replace them if they become unresponsive or fail.

In a *Kubernetes* cluster, liveness and readiness probes can be configured for each container. The liveness probe checks if the container is running and restarts it if it becomes unresponsive. The readiness probe determines if the container is ready to serve requests and removes it from the load balancer if it fails the probe.

Resilience and recovery strategies

In order to enhance the resilience and recovery capabilities of distributed systems, consider the following strategies:

- **Replication and redundancy**: Implement replication and redundancy mechanisms to ensure high availability and fault tolerance. Replicate critical components and data across multiple nodes or regions to minimize the impact of failures.

  In a distributed database system, data can be replicated across multiple nodes using techniques like master-slave replication or multi-master replication. If a node fails, the system can continue serving requests from the replicated nodes without any data loss.

- **Automatic failover**: Implement automatic failover mechanisms to seamlessly switch to backup or standby components in case of failures. Detect failures quickly and automatically redirect requests to healthy instances to minimize downtime.

  In a load-balanced web application, if a server instance fails, the load balancer can automatically detect the failure and route incoming requests to the remaining healthy instances. This ensures continuous availability and minimizes the impact of individual server failures.

- **Disaster recovery**: Develop a comprehensive disaster recovery plan to handle major failures or outages. Define **recovery time objectives** (**RTO**) and **recovery point objectives** (**RPO**) based on business requirements. Regularly test and practice disaster recovery procedures to ensure readiness.

  In a cloud-based system, implement cross-region replication and failover mechanisms. In case of a regional outage, the system can automatically switch to a backup region and continue serving requests with minimal downtime and data loss.

By designing processes to be ephemeral and disposable, distributed systems can achieve better fault tolerance, scalability, and resource efficiency. Ephemeral processes can be easily replaced or terminated without affecting the overall system's functionality, enabling quick recovery from failures. Implementing process disposability, fault tolerance techniques, and resilience strategies helps build robust and reliable distributed systems.

Leveraging serverless architectures

Serverless architectures have emerged as a powerful paradigm for designing and building distributed systems. Serverless computing allows developers to focus on writing code and building applications without worrying about the underlying infrastructure management. By leveraging serverless architectures, distributed systems can achieve enhanced efficiency, scalability, and cost-effectiveness.

While serverless models eliminate upfront infrastructure costs, they are not universally cheaper than traditional architectures. For example, a high-throughput API handling sustained traffic might incur higher long-term expenses on AWS Lambda (pay-per-execution model) compared to provisioning dedicated servers. Similarly, poorly optimized functions with excessive memory allocation can erode cost savings. The true cost-effectiveness of serverless depends on workload patterns it shines for sporadic or event-driven tasks (e.g., image processing pipelines) but may falter under predictable, constant loads. Architects must weigh tradeoffs like vendor lock-in and debugging complexity to determine if serverless aligns with their system's operational profile.

Serverless computing

Serverless computing is a cloud computing model where the cloud provider manages the infrastructure and automatically allocates resources to execute code in response to events or requests. Developers can write and deploy individual functions or small pieces of code, and the cloud provider takes care of scaling, provisioning, and managing the underlying servers.

The advantages of serverless computing are as follows:

- **Simplified infrastructure management**: Serverless platforms abstract away the complexities of infrastructure management, such as server provisioning, scaling, and maintenance. Developers can focus on writing code and business logic without worrying about the underlying infrastructure. For example, when using AWS Lambda you don't need to worry about these activities. AWS takes care of these tasks, allowing you to focus on writing code.

- **Automatic scaling**: Serverless platforms automatically scale the execution of functions based on the incoming workload. The system can handle a large number of concurrent requests without the need for manual scaling or resource management. Talking about AWS Lambda as a specific serverless option, it automatically scales your code execution and can handle a large number of concurrent requests.

- **Pay-per-use pricing**: With serverless computing, you only pay for the actual execution time and resources consumed by your functions. This pricing model can lead to significant cost savings compared to maintaining always-on servers or provisioning resources upfront.

- **Rapid development and deployment**: Serverless architectures enable faster development and deployment cycles. Developers can quickly write and deploy individual functions, reducing the time and effort required to build and release new features or updates. AWS Lambda seamlessly integrates with other AWS services, such as *Amazon S3, Amazon DynamoDB, Amazon API Gateway,* and *Amazon CloudWatch*. This integration allows you to build serverless applications that leverage the power of these services quickly without worrying about provisioning capacity.

In our e-commerce application, a serverless function can be used to process order payments. When a customer places an order, it triggers more of the payment processing function. The function can handle the payment transaction, update the order status, and send a confirmation email to the customer. The serverless platform automatically scales the function to handle multiple concurrent payment requests during peak shopping periods.

Implementing serverless functions and services

When designing and implementing serverless functions and services, consider the following best practices:

- **Function granularity**: Design functions to be small, focused, and single-purpose. Each function should perform a specific task and have a clear responsibility. This granular approach allows for better scalability, reusability, and maintainability.

- **Event-driven architecture**: Embrace an event-driven architecture where functions are triggered by events or messages. Use event sources like message queues, storage events, or HTTP requests to invoke functions asynchronously.

- **Stateless functions**: Design functions to be stateless and idempotent. Functions should not maintain any internal state between invocations. Any required state should be stored in external services like databases or caches.

- **Performance optimization**: Optimize functions for fast startup times and efficient execution. Minimize the initialization overhead by keeping function packages small and avoiding unnecessary dependencies.

- **Error handling and retries**: Implement proper error handling and retry mechanisms within functions. Handle transient failures gracefully and use exponential backoff or retry policies to handle temporary errors.

In our e-commerce application, a serverless function can be responsible for generating personalized product recommendations for users. The function can be triggered whenever a user visits their profile page. It can retrieve the user's purchase history and browsing behavior from a database, apply a recommendation algorithm, and return personalized product suggestions. The function can be optimized for fast execution and handle any errors gracefully.

Integrating serverless components

Serverless architectures can be seamlessly integrated into distributed systems to enhance efficiency and scalability.

Consider the following approaches:

- **Microservices decomposition**: Decompose monolithic applications into smaller, loosely coupled microservices. Implement each microservice as a set of serverless functions that collaborate to provide the desired functionality.

- **Event-driven workflows**: Use serverless functions to orchestrate and coordinate event-driven workflows. Functions can be triggered by events from various sources, such as message queues, storage services, or external APIs.

- **API composition**: Leverage serverless functions to compose and aggregate data from multiple services or APIs. Functions can act as a facade layer, providing a unified interface to clients while internally interacting with different backend services.

- **Data processing pipelines**: Implement data processing pipelines using serverless functions. Functions can be triggered by data events, such as new file uploads or database updates, and perform tasks like data transformation, enrichment, or aggregation.

In our e-commerce application, serverless functions can be used to implement the order fulfillment workflow. When an order is placed, it can trigger a series of serverless functions. One function can validate the order details, another can update the inventory levels, and another can generate the shipping labels. These functions can be orchestrated using a serverless workflow service, such as *AWS Step Functions*, to ensure the correct sequence of execution and handle any errors or retries.

Best practices

When deploying and managing serverless functions and services, consider the following best practices:

- **IaC**: Use IaC tools and frameworks to define and manage serverless infrastructure. Tools like *AWS CloudFormation*, *Serverless Framework*, or *Terraform* allow you to define your serverless resources as code and automate the deployment process.

- **Function versioning and aliases**: Implement versioning and aliases for your serverless functions. Versioning allows you to manage and deploy different versions of a function, while aliases provide a way to reference specific versions or environments.

- **Monitoring and logging**: Implement comprehensive monitoring and logging for your serverless functions. Use platform-provided tools or third-party services to monitor function invocations, performance metrics, and error rates. Centralize logs for easier troubleshooting and analysis.

- **Security best practices**: Follow security best practices when deploying serverless functions. Use the principle of least privilege, restrict access to resources, and protect sensitive data. Implement authentication and authorization mechanisms to control access to functions and APIs.

In our e-commerce application, the serverless functions can be deployed using the Serverless Framework. The framework allows you to define the functions, their triggers, and the required resources (e.g., databases, storage buckets) in a configuration file. You can use the framework's command line interface to deploy the functions to the cloud provider, manage different environments (e.g., development, staging, production), and monitor the functions' performance and logs. Security best practices can be followed by using API Gateway to control access to the functions and by encrypting sensitive data stored in databases or storage services.

By leveraging serverless architectures, our e-commerce application can achieve enhanced efficiency, scalability, and cost-effectiveness. Serverless computing abstracts away the complexities of infrastructure management, enabling developers to focus on building and deploying application logic. Integrating serverless components into our e-commerce system allows for event-driven workflows, microservices decomposition, and efficient data processing pipelines.

When designing and implementing serverless functions and services for our e-commerce application, it is important to follow best practices such as designing granular and stateless functions, optimizing performance, and handling errors effectively. Deploying and managing serverless applications requires the use of IaC tools, versioning and aliases, monitoring and logging, and adherence to security best practices.

Environment parity

Environment parity is a crucial concept in designing and deploying distributed systems consistently across different environments, such as development, staging, and production. It ensures that the application behaves predictably and reliably regardless of the environment it is running in. Cloud providers offer various services and tools to help achieve environment parity for serverless applications.

Maintaining consistency across different environments is essential for the following reasons:

- **Predictability**: Environment parity ensures consistent application behavior across all environments. Tools like Docker Compose enforces this by allowing developers to mirror production services, for example, Redis, PostgreSQL in lightweight local containers. For example, defining a **docker-compose.yml** ensures developers test against the same database engine used in production, eliminating discrepancies like SQLite locally vs. MySQL in production. This containerized consistency reduces **works on my machine** failures, a critical safeguard in distributed systems where configuration drift can cascade into outages.

- **Easier debugging**: When the environments are consistent, it becomes easier to debug and troubleshoot issues. If a problem arises in the production environment, it can be reproduced and investigated in the development or staging environment with greater confidence.

- **Smooth deployments**: Environment parity facilitates smoother deployments. When the application is deployed to production, there is a lower risk of encountering environment-specific issues or surprises. This reduces the chances of deployment failures and improves the overall deployment process.

- **Collaboration and reproducibility**: Environment parity enables better collaboration among team members. Developers can work on their local environments with the assurance that their changes will behave consistently when deployed to other environments. It also enhances reproducibility, allowing team members to reproduce and investigate issues independently.

In our e-commerce application, environment parity ensures that the application behaves consistently across the development, staging, and production environments. For example, if a new feature for processing orders is developed and tested in the development environment, it should work seamlessly when deployed to the staging and production environments. This consistency reduces the risk of unexpected issues and ensures a smooth deployment process.

Achieving environment parity

Cloud providers offer several techniques and services to help achieve environment parity for serverless applications, as follows:

- **IaC**: Use infrastructure provisioning tools or cloud-specific templates to define and manage your serverless infrastructure as code. By version controlling your infrastructure code, you can ensure that the same infrastructure is provisioned consistently across different environments.

- **Environment variables**: Utilize environment variables to store environment-specific configuration values. Serverless platforms allow you to define environment variables for your functions, which can be used to provide different values for each environment. This enables you to parameterize your application and easily switch between environments.

- **Serverless frameworks**: Consider using serverless frameworks that simplify the deployment and management of serverless applications. These frameworks provide a consistent and declarative way to define your serverless resources and support multiple cloud providers.

- **Configuration management**: Use configuration management systems or secret management services provided by cloud providers to securely store and manage configuration data and secrets. These services provide a centralized store for storing environment-specific values, such as database connection strings or API keys, which can be easily accessed by your serverless functions.

- **Automated deployment pipelines**: Implement automated deployment pipelines using CI/CD tools. These pipelines can automatically build, test, and deploy your serverless application across different environments, ensuring consistency and reducing manual errors.

In our reference e-commerce application, you can achieve environment parity by using infrastructure as code to define the serverless resources, such as the function for processing orders and the database for storing order information. The infrastructure code can include parameters for environment-specific values, such as the database connection strings or API endpoints. These parameters can be provided with different values for each environment using configuration files or secret management services. Serverless frameworks can be used to simplify the deployment process and manage serverless resources consistently across environments. Automated deployment pipelines can be set up to automatically deploy the application to different environments based on the defined stages and approval processes.

Best practices for maintaining environment parity

In order to maintain environment parity effectively, consider the following:

- **Centralized configuration management**: Use a centralized configuration management system or secret management service to store and manage environment-specific configuration values. This ensures that the configuration is consistent across environments and can be easily updated.

- **Automated testing**: Implement automated testing as part of your deployment pipeline. Run unit tests, integration tests, and end-to-end tests in each environment to verify the functionality and consistency of the application. Automated tests help catch environment-specific issues early in the deployment process.

- **Monitoring and alerting**: Set up comprehensive monitoring and alerting for your serverless application. Monitor key metrics, logs, and events in each environment to identify any discrepancies or anomalies. Configure alerts to notify the team of any deviations from the expected behavior.

- **Immutable infrastructure**: Embrace the principle of immutable infrastructure, where you treat your infrastructure as disposable and replaceable. Instead of modifying existing resources, create new versions of your infrastructure and deploy them as separate instances. This approach reduces the risk of configuration drift and ensures consistency across environments.

In our e-commerce application, you can maintain environment parity by using a centralized configuration management system to store environment-specific values, such as the API endpoints or database connection strings. Automated tests can be implemented using testing frameworks to verify the functionality of the serverless functions in each environment. Monitoring and alerting can be set up to track the application's performance and notify the team of any issues. The immutable infrastructure approach can be applied by creating new versions of the infrastructure stack for each deployment and managing the stack instances separately.

Continuous delivery and infrastructure as code

CD and IaC are key practices that complement environment parity in serverless deployments.

CD enables frequent and automated deployments of the application to different environments. By automating the deployment process, it reduces the risk of manual errors and ensures consistency across environments. CI/CD tools and pipelines provided by cloud providers or third-party solutions can be used to set up CD for serverless applications.

IaC allows you to define and manage your serverless infrastructure using declarative configuration files. By version controlling your infrastructure code, you can track changes, collaborate with team members, and ensure that the same infrastructure is provisioned consistently across environments. Cloud providers offer templating languages and tools for implementing IaC for serverless applications.

In our e-commerce application, you can implement continuous delivery using a CI/CD pipeline. The pipeline can be triggered automatically whenever changes are pushed to the source code repository. It can include stages for building the application, running automated tests, and deploying to different environments based on the defined approval processes. IaC can be implemented using cloud-specific templating languages or tools, where the serverless resources, such as functions, databases, and API gateways, are defined in configuration files. The configuration files can be version-controlled and used to consistently provision and update the infrastructure across environments.

By combining environment parity, continuous delivery, and IaC, you can create a robust and reliable deployment process for your serverless e-commerce application. Environment parity ensures consistency and predictability across environments, CD enables frequent and automated deployments, and IaC provides a declarative and version-controlled way to manage the serverless infrastructure.

Applying SOLID design principles

SOLID is an acronym that represents five design principles for writing maintainable, scalable, and flexible software. These principles, when applied to the design and development of a serverless application, help in creating a modular, extensible, and loosely coupled architecture.

Let us explore each of the SOLID principles and their application in the context of the serverless e-commerce application.

Single Responsibility Principle

The **Single Responsibility Principle** (SRP) states that a class or module should have only one reason to change. In serverless architectures, this principle applies to individual functions or microservices, where each should encapsulate a single, well-defined task. Adhering to SRP ensures that components remain focused, testable, and resilient to cascading failures.

Consider our e-commerce application where order processing is split into discrete functions, as follows:

- **Validate order details**: Checks item availability and customer data.
- **Process payment**: Handles transaction authorization and charging.
- **Update inventory**: Adjusts stock levels post-purchase.

This modular approach simplifies debugging, scaling, and updates. For instance, modifying payment gateways affects only the **process_payment** function, leaving other components untouched.

A frequent violation of SRP occurs when a function combines business logic with infrastructure operations.

Following is an example:

```
def process_payment(order):
    # Business logic: Validate transaction
    if order.amount > account_balance(order.customer_id):
        raise InsufficientFundsError()


    # Database operation: Log transaction
    db.execute("INSERT INTO payments VALUES (?, ?)", order.id, order.
amount)
```

Here, payment validation and database writes are entangled. If the database schema changes or logging requirements evolve, the payment logic itself risks unintended breakage.

Refactoring the above into two distinct functions resolves the issue, as follows:

- **Business logic**: **authorize_payment()** handles transaction validation.
- **Data layer**: **log_transaction()** manages database writes.

This separation ensures that the payment logic remains unaffected by storage changes. Any database failures do not block core transaction flows. Each component can scale independently (e.g., adding retries for DB writes).

By enforcing SRP, teams avoid brittle designs where a single change triggers widespread rework, while enabling granular monitoring and deployment.

Open-Closed Principle

The **Open-Closed Principle (OCP)** states that software entities (classes, modules, functions) should be open for extension but closed for modification. In a serverless architecture, this principle can be applied by designing functions and microservices in a way that allows them to be extended without modifying their core functionality.

Consider the payment processing function in our e-commerce application. If the application needs to support multiple payment gateways, the payment processing function can be designed to be open for extension. The function can define an interface for payment processors and allow new payment gateways to be added as separate implementations of that interface. This way, the core payment processing logic remains closed for modification, while new payment gateways can be easily added.

Liskov Substitution Principle

The **Liskov Substitution Principle (LSP)** states that objects of a superclass should be replaceable with objects of its subclasses without affecting the correctness of the program. In a serverless context, this principle can be applied to the design of function interfaces and the interaction between different services.

Suppose our e-commerce application has a notification service that sends order confirmation emails to customers. The notification service can define an interface for different notification channels, such as email, SMS, or push notifications. Each notification channel can be implemented as a separate function that adheres to the common interface. This allows the notification service to be extended with new channels without affecting the existing functionality.

Interface Segregation Principle

The **Interface Segregation Principle (ISP)** states that clients should not be forced to depend on interfaces they do not use. In a serverless architecture, this principle can be applied by designing function interfaces that are focused and specific to the needs of the clients consuming them.

In our e-commerce application, the product catalog microservice may expose different interfaces for various clients, such as the web frontend, mobile app, or admin dashboard. Instead of having a single, monolithic interface that includes all possible operations, the microservice can provide separate interfaces tailored to the specific needs of each client. This allows clients to depend only on the functionality they require, making the system more maintainable and less coupled.

Dependency Inversion Principle

The **Dependency Inversion Principle (DIP)** states that high-level modules should depend on abstractions, not on concrete implementations. In a serverless context, this principle can be applied by designing functions and microservices to depend on abstractions or interfaces rather than concrete implementations.

Consider the inventory management function in our e-commerce application. Instead of directly depending on a specific database or storage service, the function can depend on an abstract repository interface. The concrete implementation of the repository can be provided through dependency injection or configuration. This allows the inventory management function to be decoupled from the specific storage implementation, making it more flexible and easier to test.

Applying SOLID principles in serverless development

In order to effectively apply SOLID principles in serverless development, consider the following practices:

- **Modular function design**: Design functions to be modular, focused, and single-purpose. Each function should have a clear responsibility and encapsulate its own logic and dependencies.

- **Loose coupling**: Strive for minimal dependencies between functions and microservices. Use event-driven architectures and message queues (e.g., AWS SQS, RabbitMQ) to decouple services, enabling asynchronous communication and reducing ripple effects from failures.

  For complex workflows, orchestration tools like **AWS Step Functions** help maintain loose coupling while coordinating serverless components. For instance, in an order fulfillment process, Step Functions can manage the sequence of tasks such as payment processing, inventory checks, and shipping by invoking Lambda functions via events. Each task runs independently, and the workflow itself acts as a state machine that handles retries, errors, and transitions *without* hardcoding dependencies between services. If the payment service changes, the shipping service remains unaffected, as they interact only through events. This approach keeps services decoupled, scalable, and focused on their specific responsibilities.

  By prioritizing loose coupling, systems gain resilience to change and flexibility to evolve components in isolation.

- **Abstraction and interfaces**: Define abstractions and interfaces for cross-cutting concerns, such as logging, error handling, and data access. This allows for easier extension and substitution of implementations.

- **Composition over inheritance**: Favor composition over inheritance when designing serverless components. Compose functions and microservices using event-driven patterns and choreography to create flexible and scalable architectures.

- **Dependency injection**: Use dependency injection techniques to provide concrete implementations of dependencies to functions. This can be achieved through serverless frameworks or by leveraging container-based serverless platforms.

In a large distributed system like our e-commerce application, SOLID principles can be applied as follows:

- Split the order processing functionality into separate functions, following the single responsibility principal.

- Design the payment processing function to be open for extension, allowing new payment gateways to be added without modifying the core logic thus following the open-close principal.

- Define a common interface for notification channels and implement each channel as a separate function adhering to that interface which helps follow the LSP.

- Consider an application supporting SMS, email, and Slack notifications. While most channels share the same send method, edge cases may arise. For instance:

- SMS might require character limits (e.g., truncating messages beyond 160 characters).

- Push notifications may need device token validation before sending.

- A poorly designed interface might force all channels to support unnecessary parameters (e.g., **device_token** in the base send method), violating LSP.

Let us refactor the interface to handle unique requirements gracefully:

```
class NotificationChannel(ABC):
    @abstractmethod
    def send(self, message: str, **kwargs):
        """Base method with extensible keyword arguments"""


class SMSChannel(NotificationChannel):
    def send(self, message: str, **kwargs):
        truncated = message[:160]  # Handle SMS-specific logic
        sms_provider.send(truncated)
```

```
class PushChannel(NotificationChannel):
    def send(self, message: str, **kwargs):
        device_token = kwargs.get("device_token")
        if not device_token:
            raise ValueError("Device token required for push
notifications")
        push_service.send(message, device_token)
```

- Here, the **kwargs** parameter allows channels to declare their unique needs without altering the core interface. Clients invoking send must provide channel-specific arguments (e.g., **device_token** for push), preserving substitutability while accommodating edge cases.

- By designing interfaces to anticipate variability, teams avoid interface pollution and ensure LSP compliance, even when channels evolve independently.

- Provide focused interfaces for the product catalog microservice based on the needs of different clients.

- Use an abstract repository interface for the inventory management function, decoupling it from the specific storage implementation.

By applying SOLID principles, the serverless e-commerce application can achieve a modular, maintainable, and scalable architecture. The principles promote separation of concerns, loose coupling, and extensibility, making the application more adaptable to changes and easier to evolve over time.

Conclusion

In this chapter, we explored the key principles and practices for designing distributed systems optimized for speed and efficiency. By adhering to the twelve-factor app principles, developers can create resilient, scalable, and easily maintainable systems. Maintaining a single codebase in version control, implementing explicit dependency management and isolation, and storing configuration in the environment promote consistency, portability, and flexibility.

CI/CD practices automate and streamline the deployment process, enabling faster iterations and improved reliability. Designing stateless application processes enhances scalability and fault tolerance while embracing simplicity in execution simplifies deployment and maximizes robustness.

Leveraging concurrency and horizontal scaling techniques allows distributed systems to handle increased loads and achieve better performance. Ephemeral processes and disposability enable quick recovery from failures and efficient resource utilization. Serverless architectures offer simplified infrastructure management, automatic scaling, and cost-effectiveness.

Maintaining environment parity ensures consistent behavior across development, staging, and production environments, facilitating smooth deployments and easier debugging. Applying SOLID design principles promotes modularity, extensibility, and loose coupling, making the system more adaptable to changes.

By understanding and applying these principles and practices, developers can design distributed systems that are fast, efficient, and capable of handling the demands of modern applications. The knowledge gained from this chapter equips readers with the tools and insights necessary to build high-performance distributed systems that deliver exceptional user experiences and meet the challenges of today's digital world.

In the next chapter, we will look into how event-driven systems help enable vastly scalable distributed systems. Armed with the knowledge we have so far gained, it will help understand the various design choices that are made to help a system scale well.

Join our book's Discord space

Join the book's Discord Workspace for Latest updates, Offers, Tech happenings around the world, New Release and Sessions with the Authors:

https://discord.bpbonline.com

CHAPTER 6

Event-driven Systems

Introduction

In the fast-paced world of modern software development, building scalable, resilient, and loosely coupled systems has become a necessity. As architectures evolve and applications grow in complexity, traditional request-response models often fall short in meeting the demands of today's distributed environments. This is where event-driven systems help provide a welcome shift in how we design and build software systems.

Imagine that you are the architect behind a popular e-commerce platform that is gearing up for a massive *Black Friday* sale. You know that the sudden surge of traffic could bring your system to its knees, causing frustrated customers and lost revenue. But with an Event-driven architecture in place, you are better prepared. Event-driven systems work at a pace that the system is designed to handle, adapting dynamically to varying workloads and maintaining performance during peak traffic. In an event-driven system, the different components or microservices work together by sending and receiving messages through a central hub (event broker). This decoupled approach allows each component to focus on its own responsibilities, completely unaware of the others' existence. It is a choreography of asynchronous communication and eventual consistency.

As with any architectural style, event-driven systems come with their own set of challenges and considerations. Architects and developers are always looking for solutions optimized for their specific use case like ensuring message ordering and exactly-once processing or design for scaling the system for handling millions of events per second.

In this chapter, we will explore the world of event-driven systems, exploring the concepts, patterns, and tools that will help you build robust and scalable applications. From the fundamentals of message queues and event streaming to the intricacies of Kafka and its ecosystem.

Structure

The chapter covers the following topics:

- Synchronous and asynchronous systems
- Publish and subscribe model
- Fundamentals of event-driven systems
- Exploring message queues
- Event streaming with Apache Kafka
- Event streaming use case considerations

Objectives

By the end of this chapter, readers will explore event-driven systems. We will also learn how event-driven systems are different from synchronous request-response systems and how they help distributed systems. We will learn when to use one to scale the system you are designing or want to improve. We will also look at various technologies and tools, and understand some common terminologies used in event/messaging world.

Synchronous and asynchronous systems

When designing a system, one should have certain considerations to decide whether a use case is fit for synchronous or asynchronous systems.

Let us look at these considerations to always keep in mind the primary factors, as follows:

- **Loose coupling and scalability**: If your system consists of multiple services or components that need to communicate with each other but can operate independently, an event-driven architecture can provide loose coupling and scalability.

  Event-driven systems allow services to publish events to a broker or topic and subscribe to receive them without direct dependencies to other services, enabling them to evolve and scale independently.

- **Asynchronous processing**: When you have long-running tasks or operations that do not require immediate responses, an event-driven approach can be beneficial.

  Event-driven systems allow for asynchronous processing, where the sender of an event does not need to wait for the receiver to complete its processing before continuing.

This can improve performance, responsiveness, and resource utilization, especially in scenarios with high concurrency or variability in processing times. For example, when a user uploads a video to a streaming platform, the system might emit a *VideoUploaded* event, triggering asynchronous tasks like transcoding, thumbnail generation, and metadata indexing. The frontend need not wait for these backend processes decoupling allows the system to prioritize responsiveness for the user while efficiently managing resource-heavy workflows in the background.

- **Resilience and fault tolerance**: Event-driven systems can provide better resilience and fault tolerance compared to synchronous systems.

  If a service or component fails or becomes unavailable, other parts of the system can continue to operate independently by processing events from a queue or message broker.

  This decoupling allows for graceful degradation and easier recovery from failures.

- **Real-time and reactive systems**: If you are building real-time or reactive systems that need to respond to events or changes in near real-time, an event-driven architecture can be a good fit.

  Event-driven systems can efficiently handle high volumes of events and enable real-time processing, updates, and notifications.

  The same decoupled foundation enables real-time capabilities when low latency is critical. Consider a collaborative document editor: when one user edits a paragraph, a *TextUpdated* event propagates through a high-speed message broker (e.g., Apache Kafka or WebSocket channels), ensuring other users see changes within milliseconds. Here, the architecture prioritizes event propagation speed over deferred processing, often using in-memory brokers and pre-allocated resources to meet strict SLAs.

  > **Note: Asynchronous processing defers non-urgent work to optimize scalability, while real-time subsystems use the same event backbone with tighter latency controls. A well-designed system might even combine both: an e-commerce platform could process payments asynchronously (seconds) while emitting inventory updates in real time (milliseconds) to prevent overselling. The key is architecting event pathways with purpose, choosing durable queues for deferred tasks and low-latency channels for immediate reactions, all within a unified event-driven paradigm.**

- **Complex workflows and orchestration**: When you have complex workflows or business processes that involve multiple steps and interactions between services, an event-driven approach can simplify orchestration.

  Events can trigger subsequent actions and workflows, allowing for decoupled and flexible coordination of activities.

On the other hand, synchronous systems may be more suitable in the following situations:

- o **Immediate response and consistency**: If your application requires immediate responses and strong consistency, a synchronous system may be a better choice.

  Synchronous communication ensures that the sender waits for the receiver to complete its processing and receives a response before proceeding.

- o **Tight coupling and simple interactions**: When you have tightly coupled services or components with simple and well-defined interactions, a synchronous approach can be simpler to implement and reason about.

  Synchronous communication can be suitable for systems with limited complexity and straightforward request-response patterns.

- o **Transactional consistency**: If your system requires transactional consistency and **Atomicity, Consistency, Isolation, Durability (ACID)** properties, synchronous communication can ensure that operations are completed in a single transaction.

  Synchronous systems can maintain data integrity and consistency more easily compared to event-driven systems, which may introduce eventual consistency.

Ultimately, the choice between an event-driven system and a synchronous system depends on the specific requirements, scalability needs, fault tolerance considerations, and the nature of the interactions within the application. It is common for systems to employ a combination of both approaches, using event-driven communication for certain parts and synchronous communication for others, based on the specific needs of each component or service.

Publish and subscribe model

The **publish and subscribe (pub/sub)** model is a fundamental messaging pattern that forms the backbone of event-driven systems. In this model, message senders, called publishers, do not directly send messages to specific receivers. Instead, they publish messages to abstract categories called topics or channels. Similarly, subscribers express interest in one or more topics and receive messages that are published to those topics.

Let us understand this through our e-commerce application example. When a customer places an order, the order service does not need to know about all the different services that might be interested in this event such as inventory management, shipping, customer notifications, analytics, etc. Instead, it simply publishes an OrderCreated event to an order-related topic. Any service interested in new orders can subscribe to this topic and process the event according to its specific requirements.

The pub/sub model consists of three main components, as follows:

- **Publishers**: These are the components that generate events or messages. In our e-commerce example, the order service, inventory service, and user management service are all potential publishers. Publishers are decoupled from subscribers and have no knowledge of who will consume their messages.

- **Topics/Channels**: These are the categories or channels through which messages are distributed. Topics provide a way to organize and categorize different types of events. For instance, our e-commerce system might have topics like OrderEvents, InventoryUpdates, and UserActivity.

- **Subscribers**: These are the components that receive and process messages from topics they're interested in. A subscriber can listen to multiple topics, and multiple subscribers can listen to the same topic. For example, both the notification service and analytics service might subscribe to the OrderEvents topic.

Figure 6.1 describes how publishers and subscribers interact via topics. Notice that a single subscriber may be consuming events from multiple topics.

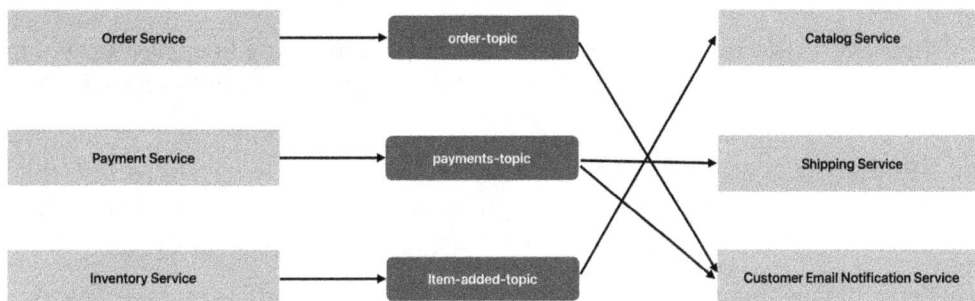

Figure 6.1: *Illustration of producer, subscriber interaction*

Message delivery patterns

Messages are the data that is passed via the topic or channel to subscribers by the publisher. The pub/sub model supports different message delivery pattern, as follows:

- **Fan-out**: When a message is published to a topic, it is delivered to all active subscribers. This is particularly useful for broadcasting events. For example, when a price change occurs, all services interested in pricing (display, analytics, cache) receive the update.

- **Content-based filtering**: Subscribers can filter messages based on their content. For instance, the fraud detection service might only want to receive order events where the order value exceeds a certain threshold.

- **Topic-based filtering**: Subscribers receive messages published to the topics they explicitly subscribe to. This allows for coarse-grained message filtering based on message categories.

Benefits and considerations

The pub/sub model provides benefits and also come with their own considerations that one should be familiar, as follows:

- **Loose coupling**: Publishers and subscribers are independent of each other. This independence allows for easier system evolution and maintenance. Publishers do not need to know about their subscribers as long as they agree on a common data structure for sending and receiving messages.

- **Scalability**: New subscribers can be added without modifying publishers or other subscribers. This makes it easy to extend system functionality.

- **Flexibility**: The model supports different communication patterns and can adapt to changing business requirements. If a subscribing service is later discarded or modified, no other part of the overall system needs to necessarily change to allow for this.

However, there are also important considerations, as follows:

- **Message ordering**: In distributed systems, maintaining message order across multiple subscribers can be challenging. Some subscribers might process messages faster than others.

- **Message delivery guarantees**: Different pub/sub implementations offer various delivery guarantees (at-least-once, at-most-once, exactly-once). Understanding these guarantees is crucial for system design.

- **State management**: Subscribers need to handle scenarios like message duplication and missed messages, especially after downtime.

The pub/sub model's ability to decouple publishers from subscribers while maintaining reliable message delivery makes it a cornerstone of modern distributed systems. As we will explore in later sections, this pattern becomes especially powerful when combined with other event-driven architectural patterns and technologies.

Fundamentals of event-driven systems

Event-driven systems are built on three key components: event producers, event consumers, and event brokers. Event producers are entities that are responsible for generating events within the system. An event producer could be a microservice, a user interface component, or an external system that detects and publishes significant occurrences or state changes. For example, in an e-commerce application, an event producer might be the order placement service that emits an *OrderPlaced* event when a customer completes a purchase. Event consumers on the other end of the spectrum are the components that subscribe to and react to the events generated by producers. Event consumers are typically microservices or functions that perform specific actions based on the received events. In our e-commerce example, an event consumer could be the inventory management service that listens for *OrderPlaced* events and updates the stock levels accordingly. Event brokers act as the intermediary between event producers and consumers. They provide a centralized platform for event distribution and ensure reliable delivery of events to the appropriate consumers. Event brokers can be message queues, publish-subscribe systems, or event streaming platforms like Apache Kafka. They decouple producers from consumers, allowing for loose coupling and asynchronous communication within the system.

Let us use an example to illustrate an event driver system further using our favorite ecommerce application. When a customer completes a purchase, the *OrderService* produces an *OrderPlaced* event with details like orderId, userId, items, and totalAmount. The inventory service registers itself with the event broker to listen to a topic where it listens to the *OrderPlaced* event. When an order is placed, the *InventoryService* receives the event and updates its inventory accordingly. In this process, neither the *OrderService* nor the *InventoryService* are aware of each other's existence. Such an event-driven system can accommodate a large no of services interdependent on each other without being aware of each other's existence as long as they have a known structure for the event's messages. Such event-based interdependent systems are called choreographed systems. Choreography is an important architectural pattern in event-driven systems that helps in coordinating complex processes across multiple services without relying on a central orchestrator. Let us dive into the concept and see how it works in practice.

Choreography architectural pattern

In event-driven choreography, each service or component in the system operates independently, reacting to events produced by other services. Instead of having a central controller dictating the workflow, services decide for themselves when and how to react to events. This approach promotes loose coupling, scalability, and flexibility in distributed systems.

Following are some common aspects and features of choreographed systems:

- **Decoupled services**: Each service or component operates independently and is responsible for its own logic and data. Services are loosely coupled and communicate through events.

- **Event publishing**: When a service performs an action or undergoes a state change, it publishes an event to a message broker or event bus. The event typically contains relevant data about the action or state change.

- **Event subscription**: Services interested in specific events subscribe to those events through the message broker or event bus. They receive and react to the events they have subscribed to.

- **Reactive behavior**: Upon receiving an event, a subscribed service reacts by performing its own logic or updating its own state. It may also publish new events as a result of its processing.

- **Emergent behavior**: The overall behavior of the system emerges from the collective interactions and collaborations among the services. No central control or orchestration dictates the flow of events or the actions of services.

- **Scalability and resilience**: Choreography allows for scalability and resilience as services can be deployed, scaled, and maintained independently. Failures in one service do not necessarily impact the entire system.

- **Eventual consistency**: Due to the asynchronous nature of event-driven communication, data consistency is typically achieved through eventual consistency. Services may have temporary inconsistencies, but they eventually converge to a consistent state.

Choreography is suitable for systems where services are highly autonomous, loosely coupled, and can operate independently. It enables flexibility, scalability, and the ability to evolve services independently. However, it requires careful design and handling of event ordering, consistency, and error handling.

Message IDs and correlation IDs

In distributed event-driven systems, tracking message flows and understanding relationships between different events is crucial. Two key concepts help achieve this: message IDs and correlation IDs.

Message IDs

A message ID is a unique identifier assigned to each event or message when it is created.

This identifier serves several critical purposes, as follows:

- **Message deduplication**: In distributed systems, the same message might be sent multiple times due to network issues or retry mechanisms. Message IDs help identify and filter out duplicate messages.

- **Message tracking**: Message IDs enable tracking of individual messages as they flow through the system. This is particularly valuable for debugging and monitoring.

- **Message reference**: They provide a way to reference specific messages in logs, debugging sessions, and customer support scenarios.

In our e-commerce system, consider an order placement event, as follows:

```
{
    "messageId": "msg_2024120912345",
    "eventType": "OrderPlaced",
    "timestamp": "2024-12-09T14:30:00Z",
    "data": {
```

```
        "orderId": "ORD-98765",
        "customerId": "CUST-12345",
        "items": [...]
    }
}
```

Correlation IDs

While message IDs identify individual messages, correlation IDs help track related messages across a business transaction or process. A correlation ID is passed along with all events that are part of the same logical operation, enabling us to trace the entire flow of a business process across multiple services.

Key uses of correlation IDs are as follows:

- **Transaction tracing**: Following the complete path of a business transaction across multiple services and events.

- **Debugging complex workflows**: Understanding how different services interact during a business process.

- **Root cause analysis**: Identifying the origin of issues in distributed transactions.

Let us see how correlation IDs work in our e-commerce system, as follows:

```
// Initial Order Placement Event
{
    "messageId": "msg_2024120912345",
    "correlationId": "corr_2024120967890",
    "eventType": "OrderPlaced",
    "data": {
        "orderId": "ORD-98765"
    }
}


// Subsequent Inventory Check Event
{
    "messageId": "msg_2024120912346",
    "correlationId": "corr_2024120967890",  // Same correlation ID
    "eventType": "InventoryChecked",
    "data": {
        "orderId": "ORD-98765",
        "status": "AVAILABLE"
```

```
    }
}


// Payment Processing Event
{
    "messageId": "msg_2024120912347",
    "correlationId": "corr_2024120967890",  // Same correlation ID
    "eventType": "PaymentProcessed",
    "data": {
        "orderId": "ORD-98765",
        "status": "SUCCESS"
    }
}
```

Implementation best practices

When implementing message and correlation IDs, consider the following best practices:

- **ID generation**: Use a reliable ID generation strategy (UUID, timestamp-based IDs, or sequential IDs). Always ensure that IDs are unique within your system's scope and consider including useful information in the ID format, for example, timestamp, service identifier.

- **Correlation ID propagation**: Passing correlation IDs in all service-to-service communications.

  And including the correlation IDs in logs and monitoring data helps track end to end event processing and tracking the business objective was fulfilled or not when there are several microservices across multiple hosts running them. It is important to maintain the same correlation ID across async operations.

- **Header vs. payload**: Storing IDs in message headers rather than the payload, when possible, helps ensure implementation is system-wide for tracking and monitoring.

Logging and monitoring

Effective use of message and correlation IDs enables powerful logging and monitoring capabilities. A structured logging approach allows you to trace all events related to a specific transaction and monitor processing times across services. During errors, it helps identify bottlenecks and failures in distributed processes by facilitating generation of detailed transaction timelines for debugging. When an error occurs, correlation IDs help maintain context across error boundaries. Understanding and implementing proper message and correlation ID strategies is crucial for building maintainable and debuggable event-driven systems. These IDs form the backbone of distributed tracing and monitoring, enabling teams to understand and troubleshoot complex distributed transactions effectively.

Message queues and event streaming

Message queues provide a reliable and persistent way to store and deliver events. Producers send events to a message queue, and consumers pull events from the queue for processing. They ensure that events are not lost and can be processed in a **first-in, first-out (FIFO)** manner. Messages are usually stored until consumed or until they expire. Message queues are designed for high throughput but may face challenges with extremely high volumes. Once a message is consumed, it is usually removed from the queue. Message queues are typically point to point, messages are typically sent from one producer to one consumer. As a developer implementing code to consume messages from a message queue, they are easy to understand and implement basic use cases and well suited for task queues and job processing. They are often used in microservices for asynchronous communication. Examples of message queue systems include RabbitMQ, Apache ActiveMQ, and cloud-based offerings like AWS **Simple Queue Service (SQS)**.

Event streaming platforms, such as Apache Kafka, offer a more real-time and scalable approach to event distribution. In event streaming, producers publish events to a stream, and consumers subscribe to the stream and process events as they arrive. Event streaming enables low-latency processing, allows multiple consumers to read from the same stream, and provides the ability to replay events if needed. Events are typically stored for a configurable retention period, allowing for replay. These systems are designed for extremely high-volume event processing by dividing topics into partitions for parallel processing. Event consumers keep track of their position (offset) in the event stream. As a developer, consuming event streams is more complex to set up and manage, but offers greater flexibility and scalability. It helps to enable the building real-time data pipelines and stream processing applications.

Some key differences between message queues and event streams can be divided into the following categories:

- **Data retention:**
  - **Message queues**: Messages are typically deleted after consumption.
  - **Event streaming**: Events are retained for a set period, allowing for replay and multiple consumers.

- **Consumption model:**
  - **Message queues**: Usually one consumer per message.
  - **Event streaming**: Multiple consumers can read the same event stream.

- **Scalability:**
  - o **Message queues**: Can handle high throughput but may face limitations with extreme volumes.
  - o **Event streaming**: Designed for massive scalability and parallel processing.

- **Use cases:**
  - o **Message queues**: Task processing, workload distribution, decoupling services.
  - o **Event streaming**: Real-time analytics, event sourcing, complex event processing, building data pipelines.

- **Developer experience:**
  - o **Message queues**: Simpler to set up and use for basic scenarios.
  - o **Event streaming**: More complex but offers greater flexibility and power for advanced use cases.

- **State management:**
  - o **Message queues**: Typically, stateless; once a message is processed, it's gone.
  - o **Event streaming**: Maintains state (offsets) for each consumer group, allowing for more complex processing patterns.

In summary, while both message queues and event streaming systems facilitate asynchronous communication, they serve different purposes and excel in different scenarios. Message queues are often simpler and well-suited for task processing and basic inter-service communication. Event streaming systems, on the other hand, provide a more robust foundation for building real-time, scalable data pipelines and event-driven architectures, at the cost of increased complexity.

Benefits and challenges of event-driven architecture

Event-driven architecture offers several compelling benefits for building scalable and resilient systems, are as follows:

- **Loose coupling**: By communicating through events, components in an event-driven system are decoupled from each other. This loose coupling allows for independent development, deployment, and scaling of services.

- **Scalability**: Event-driven systems can easily scale horizontally by adding more event producers, consumers, or brokers as needed. Each component can be scaled independently based on its specific workload requirements.

- **Fault tolerance**: Event brokers provide built-in fault tolerance mechanisms, such as event persistence and replication, to ensure that events are not lost in case of failures. Consumers can also be designed to handle failures gracefully and retry event processing if needed.

However, event-driven architecture also comes with its own set of challenges, as follows:

- **Eventual consistency**: Since events are processed asynchronously, there may be temporary inconsistencies between different parts of the system. Designing for eventual consistency and handling race conditions becomes crucial.

- **Message ordering**: Ensuring the correct order of event processing can be challenging, especially in distributed systems. Techniques like event versioning and sequence numbers may be needed to maintain ordering guarantees.

- **Error handling**: Dealing with failed event processing requires careful consideration. Strategies like dead-letter queues, retry mechanisms, and compensating actions need to be implemented to handle errors gracefully.

Understanding these fundamentals is essential for effectively designing and implementing event-driven systems. In the upcoming sections, we will explore these concepts in more detail and discuss best practices for building robust and scalable event-driven architectures.

Next, we will explore the message queues, exploring polling mechanisms, FIFO queues, and handling message failures.

Exploring message queues

Message queues are a fundamental component of event-driven systems, providing a reliable and persistent mechanism for event distribution. In this section, we will explore the intricacies of message queues, including polling mechanisms, message ordering, and error handling.

Polling mechanisms

Polling is the process by which consumers retrieve messages from a message queue. There are two primary polling mechanisms: short polling and long polling.

Short polling

In short polling, consumers periodically send requests to the message queue to check for new messages. If messages are available, they are retrieved and processed. If the queue is empty, the consumer waits for a short interval before polling again. Short polling is straightforward to implement but can result in increased latency and unnecessary network traffic.

The short polling process follows a simple, cyclical pattern, as follows

- The client sends a request to the server.
- The server immediately responds with available data or an empty response.
- The client waits for a predetermined interval.
- The cycle repeats from *Step 1*.

This process creates a loop of regular check-ins between the client and server, allowing for updates to be delivered with minimal delay.

Short polling is suitable for various scenarios where periodic updates are beneficial, as follows:

- Chat applications (checking for new messages)
- News feeds or social media timelines
- Stock price or sports score updates
- Progress monitoring for long-running processes

Short polling is easy to implement and understand. It works with standard web technologies and protocols like standard HTTP methods, avoiding issues with restrictive firewalls. There are no persistent connections with each request-response cycle being independent of the other. They can be inefficient and waste resources if updates are infrequent. So, one has to be careful when using them. It is important to consider your use case carefully. It can also add to server load, frequent requests can strain server resources. It is important to consider the polling interval to ensure the server load, use case, and latency of updates.

Long polling

Long polling addresses the limitations of short polling by allowing consumers to wait for messages to become available. When a consumer sends a long polling request, the message queue holds the request open until a message arrives or a timeout occurs. This approach reduces latency and eliminates the need for frequent polling. Long polling is more efficient than short polling but requires careful management of timeouts and connection handling.

The long polling process follow these steps:

1. The client sends a request to the server.
2. The server does not immediately respond. Instead, it holds the request open and waits for data to become available.
3. When new data is available, the server sends a response to the client.
4. The client immediately sends a new request to the server after receiving a response.

This process creates a cycle where the client always has an outstanding request to the server, allowing for quicker data transmission once it becomes available.

Long polling is most suitable for various scenarios where updates may not be predetermined or periodic but when an update is available it must be immediately consumed. For example:

- Collaborative tools, for example, shared document editing
- Some sporting events
- Notification systems

Push-based delivery

Push-based delivery is a communication model in which the server proactively sends data to the client without the client explicitly requesting it. This approach is in contrast to pull-based models like polling, where the client repeatedly asks the server for updates. Push-based delivery aims to provide real-time or near-real-time data transfer with minimal latency and reduced network overhead.

The push-based delivery process typically follows these steps:

1. The client establishes a connection with the server.

2. The client registers or subscribes to certain types of updates or channels.

3. The server maintains this connection.

4. When new data is available, the server immediately sends it to the client without waiting for a request.

5. The client receives and processes the data in real-time.

This process allows for instant delivery of information as soon as it becomes available on the server side.

Figure 6.2 Illustrates a push-based model:

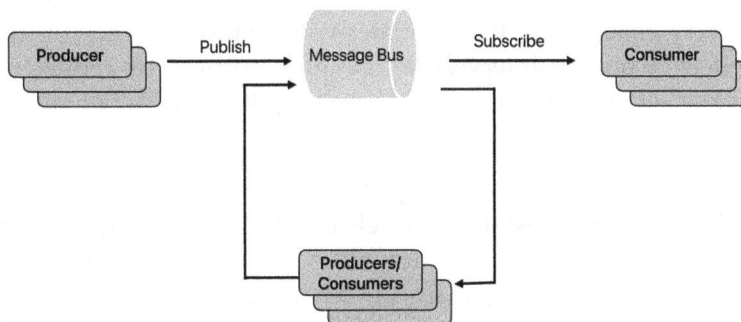

Figure 6.2: *Illustration of a push-based model*

There are several technologies and protocols that enable push-based delivery, some are as follows:

- **WebSockets**: It provides a Full-duplex, bidirectional communication channel over a single network connection allowing real-time data transfer between client and server. WebSockets are supported by most modern web browsers.

- **Server-sent events (SSE)**: These provide unidirectional channel from server to client over HTTP. It is simpler than WebSockets but limited to server-to-client communication only. There is native support in most modern browsers for this technology.

- **HTTP/2 server push**: This allows the server to proactively push resources to the client along with the response to the original request. It is primarily used for pushing web assets rather than real-time data.

- **Push notifications**: Used in mobile and web applications to deliver notifications even when the app is not actively running. These are often implemented using platform-specific services, for example, Firebase Cloud Messaging, Apple Push Notification Service.

Push-based delivery is ideal for scenarios requiring real-time updates as follows:

- Live chat and messaging applications
- Real-time collaboration tools
- Live sports scores and stock tickers
- IoT device updates
- Social media feeds
- Gaming (for real-time game state updates)
- Notification systems

Push-based delivery enables real-time updates with reduced latency by eliminating the delay associated with polling intervals. It is highly efficient by reducing unnecessary network traffic and server load compared to polling. It can be more energy-efficient on mobile devices compared to constant polling.

There are some downsides to this technology though, it is more complex to implement and maintain than simple request-response models due to the requirement to manage long-lived connections, which can be resource-intensive. With a large no of clients, it can create scalability challenges, as maintaining many open connections can be resource-intensive for server infrastructure. Some firewalls may block persistent connections, requiring fallback mechanisms.

When compared to pull-based methods, push-based delivery offers several advantages over pull-based methods like short polling and long polling, some are as follows:

- **Latency**: Push methods deliver updates instantly, while polling introduces delays.

- **Efficiency**: Push reduces unnecessary network traffic and server load.

- **Real-time capability**: Push provides true real-time communication, which polling approximates.

Pull-based methods may be simpler to implement and may work better in certain network environments.

When considering a push-based implementation, developers should consider the following points:

- **Fallback mechanisms**: Implement fallbacks (e.g., long polling) for environments where the push is not supported.

- **Connection management**: Handle connection drops and reconnections gracefully.

- **Security**: Ensure proper authentication and authorization for push connections.

- **Scalability**: Design the server architecture to handle many concurrent connections.

- **Message ordering and delivery guarantees**: Implement mechanisms to ensure correct message ordering and delivery.

Message ordering and exactly-once processing

Maintaining the correct order of messages and ensuring exactly-once processing are critical requirements in many event-driven systems.

Let us explore how message queues handle these aspects.

First-in, first-out queues

First-in, first-out (**FIFO**) queues guarantee that messages are delivered to consumers in the same order they were sent by producers. This is crucial for scenarios where the order of events matters, such as in a sequence of financial transactions. Message queue systems like Amazon SQS and Apache Kafka provide FIFO ordering guarantees. So does **Java Messaging Specification** (**JMS**) compliant implementations like Active MQ.

Figure 6.3 illustrates a typical message queue. Messages are enqueued from the back while messages in the queue are dequeued from the front, the earliest message is dequeued first.

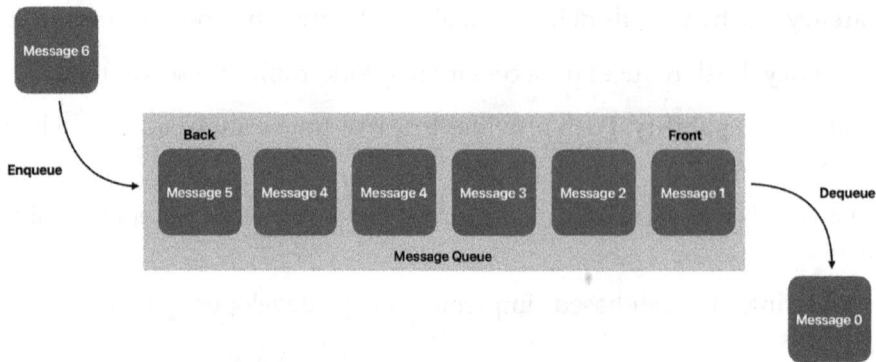

Figure 6.3: *An illustration of a FIFO message queue*

Message groups

Message groups allow you to group related messages and ensure that they are processed in a specific order. By assigning a group ID to messages, you can enforce ordering within a group while allowing parallel processing across different groups. Additionally, message queues often provide deduplication mechanisms to prevent the same message from being processed multiple times.

Figure 6.4 illustrates how messages assigned to two different message groups 1 and 2 will be available in the message queue. Notice that the messages assigned to group 1 and to group 2 are each independently ordered in FIFO. Here the assumption is that messages 0,2,4,6,8,10 and 12 are assigned to group 1 while messages 1,3,5,7,9,11,13 are assigned to group 2.

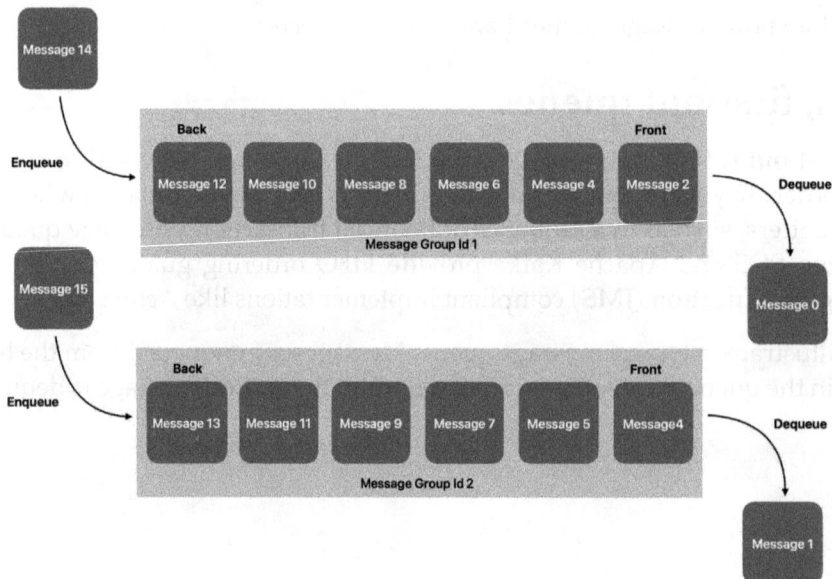

Figure 6.4: *An illustration of a FIFO message queues with multiple message groups*

Deduplication keys

A deduplication key serves as a unique identifier for each event to prevent processing the same event multiple times. This is crucial for maintaining data consistency and avoiding unintended duplicate actions. They are especially important in distributed systems where events might be sent multiple times due to network issues or retry mechanisms. They help ensure exactly-once processing semantics in scenarios where this is critical. For example, in a payment processing system, you would not want to charge a customer twice for the same transaction if an event is accidentally duplicated. A deduplication key based on the transaction ID would prevent this.

Following is how deduplication keys typically work in event-driven architectures:

- **Generation**: When an event is created, a unique deduplication key is assigned to it. This could be based on various factors like event content, timestamp, or a combination of attributes.

- **Storage**: The system maintains a record of processed deduplication keys, often in a fast-access data store like Redis.

- **Checking**: Before processing an incoming event, the system checks if its deduplication key already exists in the store.

- **Action**: If the key is new, the event is processed, and the key is recorded. If the key exists, the event is typically discarded as a duplicate.

- **Expiration**: Keys may have a **time-to-live** (**TTL**) to manage storage and allow for reprocessing after a certain period.

Note that the choice of what constitutes a deduplication key can vary based on business requirements. Sometimes, natural business identifiers (like order IDs) can serve as deduplication keys. In other cases, you might need to generate a composite key from multiple event attributes.

Handling message failures and retries

Despite the reliability provided by message queues, failures can still occur during message processing.

It is essential to have mechanisms in place to handle these failures gracefully, as follows:

- **Visibility timeout**: When a consumer retrieves a message from a queue, it becomes invisible to other consumers for a specified duration called the visibility timeout. During this time, the consumer processes the message. If the consumer fails to process the message within the visibility timeout, the message becomes visible again and can be picked up by another consumer. This ensures that messages are not lost due to consumer failures.

- **Dead-letter queues**: In case of repeated processing failures, message queues provide **dead-letter queues (DLQs)** to store problematic messages. If a message exceeds a specified number of retries or fails to process within a certain time limit, it is moved to the DLQ for further analysis and manual intervention. DLQs prevent failed messages from blocking the main queue and allow for separate error handling.

Scaling and performance considerations

Message queues offer several features and best practices to optimize scaling and performance in event-driven systems.

Partitioning and parallel processing

Message queues support partitioning, which allows you to distribute messages across multiple queues or partitions. Each partition can be processed independently by different consumers, enabling parallel processing and improved throughput. Partitioning also helps to distribute the workload evenly and scale the system horizontally.

Batching and prefetching

In order to reduce the overhead of individual message retrieval, message queues often support batching and prefetching. Batching allows consumers to retrieve multiple messages in a single request, reducing the number of round trips to the queue. Prefetching enables consumers to retrieve messages in advance, keeping a buffer of messages ready for processing. These techniques can significantly improve performance and reduce latency.

Understanding the intricacies of message queues is crucial for designing efficient and reliable event-driven systems. By leveraging the right polling mechanisms, ensuring message ordering, handling failures gracefully, and optimizing for performance, you can build robust and scalable systems that can handle high volumes of events.

In the next section, we will explore another critical component of event-driven systems: *Apache Kafka*. We will explore the Kafka's architecture, its pub/sub messaging model, and its powerful stream processing capabilities. Get ready to unleash the full potential of event streaming.

Event streaming with Apache Kafka

Apache Kafka has emerged as a leading platform for event streaming and real-time data processing. Its scalable and fault-tolerant architecture has made it a go-to choice for building Event-driven systems. In this section, we will explore Kafka's architecture, its pub/sub-messaging model, and its stream processing capabilities

Kafka's architecture is designed for high throughput, low latency, and fault tolerance.

Let us break down the key components of Kafka, as follows:

- **Brokers**: Kafka clusters consist of one or more server called **brokers**. Each broker is responsible for storing and serving partitions of topics. Brokers are designed to be highly scalable and can handle a large number of producers and consumers.

- **Topics and partitions**: In Kafka, messages are organized into topics. A topic is a category or feed name to which messages are published. Topics are further divided into partitions, which are the basic units of parallelism in Kafka. Each partition is an ordered, immutable sequence of messages that is continually appended to.

- **Producers**: They are the entities that publish messages to Kafka topics. They send messages to the appropriate partition based on a partitioning key or a round-robin strategy. Producers can choose to receive acknowledgments for message delivery to ensure reliability.

- **Consumers**: They are the entities that subscribe to topics and read messages from Kafka. They are responsible for keeping track of their position (offset) in each partition they consume from. Consumers can be part of consumer groups, allowing multiple consumers to share the workload of processing messages from a topic.

Figure 6.5 Illustrates the relationship between consumers, consumer groups, partitions and topics:

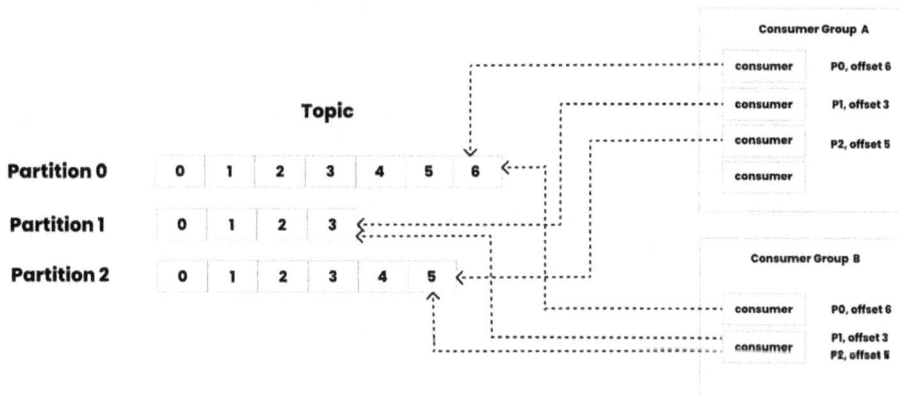

Figure 6.5: Illustration representing relationship between various entities within Kafka

Kafka follows a **publish-subscribe (pub/sub)** messaging model, which enables loose coupling between producers and consumers. Let us explore the key aspects of Kafka's pub/sub model:

- **Message retention and durability**: Kafka retains messages on disk for a configurable period of time, even after they have been consumed. This allows consumers to reprocess messages if needed and enables use cases like event sourcing and data replay. Kafka's log-based storage provides excellent performance and durability.

- **Consumer groups and offset management**: Kafka allows multiple consumers to form a consumer group and share the workload of processing messages from a topic. Each consumer in a group is assigned a subset of partitions to consume from. Kafka keeps track of the offset (position) of each consumer within a partition, enabling fault-tolerant and scalable message consumption.

Kafka streams

Kafka Streams is a powerful stream-processing library built on top of Kafka. It allows you to build real-time data processing applications and perform complex transformations on streams of data.

Let us discuss the key concepts of Kafka Streams, as follows:

- **Stream processing topology**: In Kafka Streams, you define a processing topology that describes how data flows and is transformed. A topology consists of a set of stream processors, which are basic processing units that consume input streams, apply operations, and produce output streams. Processors can be connected to form complex processing pipelines.

- **Stateful operations and aggregations**: Kafka Streams supports stateful operations, allowing you to maintain and update state across multiple input records. This enables powerful use cases like windowed aggregations, joins, and stateful transformations. Kafka Streams transparently handles the fault tolerance and scalability of stateful operations.

Kafka Connect is a framework for scalably and reliably streaming data between Kafka and other systems. It provides a set of connectors that simplify the integration of Kafka with external data sources and sinks.

Let us explore the key components of Kafka Connect, as follows:

- **Source and sink connectors**: Kafka Connect includes a wide range of pre-built connectors for popular data sources (e.g., databases, filesystems) and sinks (e.g., Elasticsearch, HDFS). These connectors handle the specifics of reading from or writing to the external system, allowing you to focus on data movement and transformation.

- **Fault-tolerant data pipelines**: Kafka Connect ensures fault tolerance and reliability in data pipelines. It supports features like automatic offset management, distributed work coordination, and error handling. Connectors can be scaled horizontally to handle increased data volumes and provide high availability.

By leveraging Kafka's pub/sub messaging model, Kafka Streams for real-time processing, and Kafka Connect for data integration, you can build powerful and scalable event-driven systems. Kafka's architecture enables you to handle high-volume data streams, perform complex transformations, and integrate with a wide range of external systems.

Event streaming use case considerations

Let us imagine a use case with our e-commerce platform, with millions of users browsing and purchasing products daily. You want to enhance the user experience by providing personalized product recommendations and targeted ads based on each user's recent browsing history.

Following is how you can achieve this using Kafka-based event streaming:

- **Capturing user events**: Every time a user interacts with a product on your e-commerce platform, for example, viewing a product page, adding an item to the cart, an event is generated and published to a Kafka topic called **user-interactions**. The event contains information such as the user ID, product ID, and the type of interaction.

- **Real-time event processing with Kafka Streams**: A Kafka Streams application consumes the **user-interactions** topic and processes the events in real-time. It maintains a state store that keeps track of each user's recently browsed products. As new events arrive, the application updates the state store and applies business logic to generate personalized product recommendations and ads.

- **Serving recommendations and ads**: The Kafka Streams application publishes the generated recommendations and ads to separate Kafka topics, such as *product-recommendations* and *targeted-ads*. These topics are consumed by the e-commerce platform's frontend application, which displays the recommendations and ads to the user in real-time.

- **Scaling and fault tolerance**: Kafka's distributed architecture allows you to scale the event processing pipeline horizontally by adding more instances of the Kafka Streams application. It ensures fault tolerance by replicating data across multiple brokers and automatically handling failover in case of node failures.

Now, let us see how this implementation enhances the user experience.

Imagine you are a fashion enthusiast browsing an e-commerce platform for the latest trends. As you navigate through various product pages, the platform captures your interactions as events and processes them in real-time using Kafka Streams. Based on your recently viewed products, such as a floral summer dress and a pair of sunglasses, the platform generates personalized recommendations for complementary items like sandals, handbags, and fashion accessories. These recommendations are seamlessly displayed on your screen, enticing you to explore more products that match your style.

The platform also leverages your browsing history to display targeted ads that align with your interests. As you continue to browse, you see ads for upcoming fashion sales, discount codes for your favorite brands, and exclusive offers tailored just for you. These real-time recommendations and ads enhance your shopping experience, making it more engaging, personalized, and likely to result in a purchase.

By leveraging Kafka-based event streaming, the e-commerce platform can process vast amounts of user interactions in real-time, generate valuable insights, and deliver a highly personalized experience to each user. This not only improves customer satisfaction but also drives increased sales and customer loyalty.

As you can see, Apache Kafka's event streaming capabilities, combined with the power of Kafka Streams for real-time processing, enable businesses to unlock the potential of their data and deliver exceptional user experiences. By harnessing the power of event-driven architectures, companies can stay ahead of the competition and meet the ever-growing expectations of today's digital consumers.

Conclusion

Event-driven systems have emerged as a powerful architectural paradigm for building scalable, resilient, and loosely coupled distributed applications. Throughout this chapter, we have explored the fundamental concepts, patterns, and technologies that enable effective event-driven architectures.

We began with the distinction between synchronous and asynchronous systems, followed by the publish-subscribe model that enables loose coupling between services. Through our e-commerce application example, we examined how event-driven patterns facilitate complex business processes while maintaining system flexibility.

Our exploration of message queues revealed different polling mechanisms, message ordering, and failure handling strategies, while our study of Apache Kafka demonstrated how modern event streaming platforms handle massive scale while providing powerful features for real-time data processing.

The practical examples showed how event-driven architectures solve real business problems, from enabling personalized user experiences to powering real-time analytics.

In the next chapter, we will explore how effective design of traffic management can make your system resilient to failures and errors caused by external factors like network or hardware failures. We will also explore how one can manage traffic for extremely large distributes system covering thousands of hosts.

Join our book's Discord space

Join the book's Discord Workspace for Latest updates, Offers, Tech happenings around the world, New Release and Sessions with the Authors:

https://discord.bpbonline.com

CHAPTER 7
Traffic Routing Strategies

Introduction

In the world of distributed systems, efficiently managing and routing traffic is crucial for ensuring high availability, scalability, and performance. This chapter explores various traffic routing strategies, exploring both architectural patterns and specific techniques used in modern distributed systems. We will use examples that would suit a large-scale online retail platform to illustrate these concepts in real-world scenarios.

At the core of traffic routing are multiple important considerations for an architect or developer building such a system, they must plan to ensure that traffic is well distributed across the hosts that serve the traffic, when a failure is detected among the hosts, how will the system be resilient to those failures and continue serving traffic. In the event of traffic surges, how could the system scale to meet those demands.

Structure

The chapter covers the following topics:
- Enabling resiliency
- Failover strategies
- Internal service traffic management
- Traffic shaping and load management

- Event-based system architecture
- Consistent hashing
- AWS implementation patterns
- Single node patterns in distributed systems
- Request processing protocols

Objectives

By the end of this chapter, readers will have a comprehensive understanding of traffic routing strategies in distributed systems, focusing on both theoretical foundations and practical implementations. Through real-world examples from e-commerce platforms, we will explore essential concepts including resilient routing architectures, failover strategies, and internal traffic management. You will learn about various load balancing techniques, leverage event-based architectures, and ways to utilize consistent hashing for distributed data management. The chapter covers both traditional approaches and modern cloud-native solutions, with particular emphasis on AWS implementations. We will examine when to use specific routing patterns, how to choose appropriate protocols for different scenarios, and how to implement effective service discovery mechanisms. By understanding these concepts and their practical applications, you will be equipped to design and implement robust traffic routing solutions for large-scale distributed systems. Special attention is given to maintaining system reliability through proper failover strategies, ensuring optimal performance through sophisticated load balancing, and managing complexity through appropriate architectural choices. The knowledge gained will enable you to make informed decisions about traffic routing strategies in your own distributed system implementations.

Enabling resiliency

Resiliency of a distributed system depends on its ability to tolerate failure conditions due to self-inflicted ones like deploying an erroneous code, handling errors due to dependencies it does not control and even catastrophic ones, like when a geographic partition completely goes down. Suppose our ecommerce application runs from a cloud service provider in the east coast and parts of it also run in the west coast. If for some reason the eastern region is down, the west region could take up the load and carry on so that external customers are still able to browse the catalog, checkout and place orders. Non-essential parts may still be down, like updating addresses or sending real-time email notifications. However, architects must consider challenges such as increased latency for users geographically closer to the failed region, potential replication delays for synchronized data, for example, inventory or cart contents, or temporary inconsistencies during failover. Making these tradeoffs accepting short-term limitations to ensure core functionality helps a system become resilient.

Active-Active architecture

In an Active-Active architecture, multiple nodes or data centers are simultaneously active to handle incoming traffic.

This approach offers several advantages as follows:

- **High availability**: If one node fails, others continue to serve traffic.

- **Load distribution**: Traffic is distributed across multiple nodes, improving overall system performance.

- **Scalability**: Easy to add more nodes to handle increased load.

Following is an example:

Following from previous example of a global online ecommerce retail platform, let us assume the platform uses an Active-Active architecture for its product catalog service. Multiple instances of the service run across different data centers, each capable of handling read and write requests. For illustration perspective, let us assume the platform is run from two regions, one located in the US east coast while the other is in the US west coast. In an Active-Active architecture, both regions are able to service traffic simultaneously. If one region is not available, the traffic meant for that region can follow the failover path and be directed to the other region. In an Active-Active system, the traffic is generally forwarded to one region versus another depending on their proximity to the region. For example, a client in New York City will be routed to east region, while one in Seattle will be routed to the west region data center.

Figure 7.1 illustrates an Active-Active architecture of a product catalog service:

Note: The primary database is in the east region, meaning all data updates first occur in the eastern database before being asynchronously replicated to the west. This replication delay introduces eventual consistency in the west region. If concurrent updates occur in both regions during replication (e.g., simultaneous inventory adjustments), conflicts may arise. These can be resolved through strategies like conflict-free replicated data types (CRDTs), Last-Write-Wins policies, or application-level reconciliation logic. This tradeoff between availability and immediate consistency is inherent to distributed Active-Active systems.

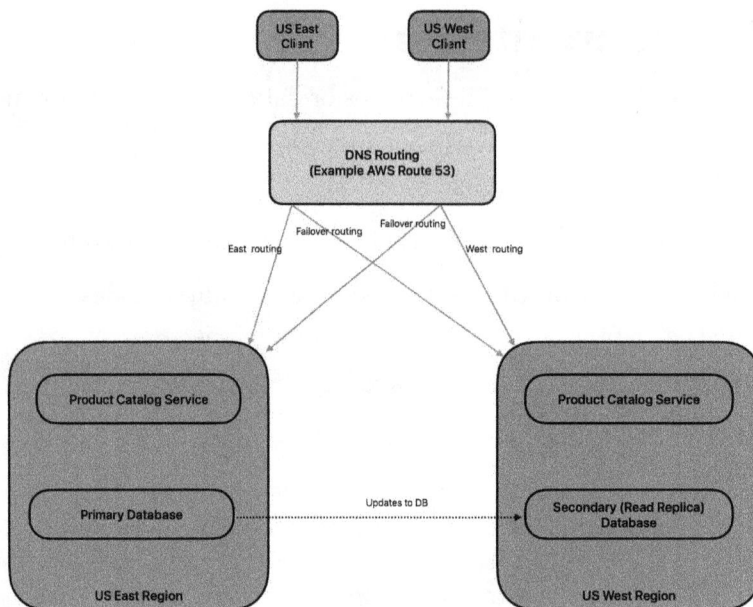

Figure 7.1: Active-Active architecture of a product catalog service

Active-Passive architecture

In an Active-Passive setup, one node (the active node) handles all the traffic while the other nodes (passive nodes) stand by as backups.

Following are the key characteristics:

- **Simplicity**: Easier to manage as only one node is active at a time.

- **Consistency**: Reduces the complexity of maintaining data consistency across nodes.

- **Resource efficiency**: Passive nodes can be used for other tasks when not needed.

Following is an example:

Our platform's payment processing system uses an Active-Passive architecture to ensure data consistency and simplify transaction management.

Figure 7.2 explains illustrates an Active-Passive architecture:

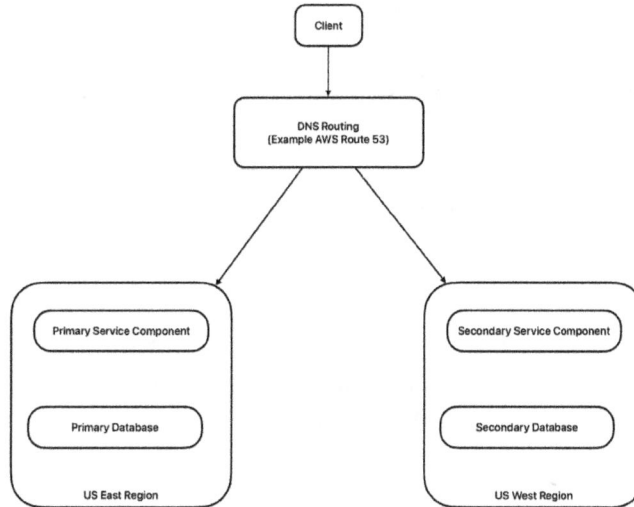

Figure 7.2: *Active-Passive architecture of a payment processing system*

Choosing Active-Active or Active-Passive

Every architectural pattern comes with their own tradeoffs and cost. A pattern may be more suitable for specific requirements. It is important to consider what behavior is most important for a service to preserve when making a choice of architecture while also identifying whether it is possible to preserve those behavior with the architecture, as follows:

- **Consistency requirements**: Consistency is the ability of the system to keep data across the system to be consistent across. If data is duplicated across hosts, all hosts should have the same data within a stipulated and pre-defined time. If strong consistency is crucial, for example, for financial transactions, Active-Passive might be preferred. This is because, the secondary database could be a read replica of the primary. In an eventuality that the primary goes down, the secondary can take the role of the primary database.

- **Scale of operations**: Scale pertains to the ability to work with increased load. For high-traffic services, for example, product catalog, Active-Active provides better scalability.

- **Complexity tolerance**: Complexity arises when systems have to be developed to consider technical requirements which are challenging to develop and maintain. Active-Active systems are more complex to manage and maintain since both partitions need to keep each other in synch with the other.

- **Resource utilization**: Resource utilization pertains to the cost of ensuring a system to address the challenge with additional resources. Active-Active makes better use of available resources but will be costlier since such a system requires some redundancy across geographically separated regions.

In our online retail platform, we may use a mix of both architectures as follows:

- Active-Active for high-traffic, read-heavy services like product catalogs and search.

- Active-Passive for critical, write-heavy services like payment processing and inventory management.

Failover strategies

Failover strategies are crucial for maintaining system availability in the face of failures. Let us explore some key strategies and their implementation in our online ecommerce platform.

Automatic failover mechanisms

Automatic failover involves detecting failures and redirecting traffic without manual intervention. In order to do that, we first need a mechanism to be able to periodically check if the system is functioning correctly or there are failures being encountered.

We do this by health checks as follows:

- **Health checks**: Regular monitoring of system components to detect failures. For example, modern platforms like Kubernetes use liveness probes (checking if a container needs restarting) and readiness probes (verifying when a container can accept traffic), typically through HTTP calls to endpoints like `/healthz`, for web services, this could be a simple HTTP GET to a health endpoint, for example, `/status` returning `200 OK`.

- **Decision making**: Determining when to initiate failover based on health check results. This is generally implemented via pre-determined rules, for example, call health every 30 seconds, if no response for the next three calls, that is, for 90 seconds, assume the service is unhealthy.

- **Traffic redirection**: Once it is determined that the service is unhealthy, automatically route traffic to healthy nodes or move the traffic to another region or partition or logical grouping of service cluster.

Following is an example:

In the product catalog service, we can implement automatic failover using AWS Route 53 health checks and DNS failover. We can create an Active-Active architecture, so that when one of the regions is down, then the traffic is redirected to the other region.

Figure 7.3 illustrates this example visually:

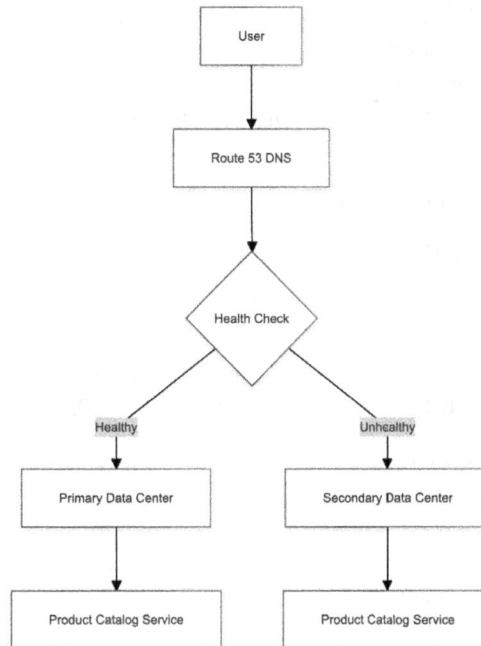

Figure 7.3: Illustrating the health check pattern to failover to secondary datacenter

Recovery processes

After a failover, systems must be restored carefully to avoid cascading failures or data corruption.

This section discusses the critical steps with implementation insights.

Data synchronization

When a failed node recovers, it must reconcile data changes that occurred during its downtime. This requires mechanisms for replay/catch-up, as follows:

- **Database replication**: PostgreSQL uses logical replication to sync specific tables, while MySQL employs binary logs to replay write operations chronologically. This ensures the recovered node mirrors the active node's state before accepting writes.

- **Event log replay**: Apache Kafka retains event streams, for example, order placed events, allowing the recovered node to reprocess missed transactions from the log. This maintains business process continuity, for example, ensuring no orders are lost.

- **Change data capture (CDC)**: Tools like *Debezium* monitor database transaction logs and streams changes to the recovered node. This enables near-real-time sync without impacting source database performance.

- **Conflict resolution**: If both nodes processed writes during the outage, for example, a customer updated their address in the west region while the east was down, conflicts arise. We can use version vectors to track timestamps/sequence numbers to auto-resolve conflicts, for example, **last write wins**.

Gradual traffic restoration

Flooding a recovered node with 100% traffic immediately risks overloading it. Instead we can use the following techniques:

- **Weighted routing**: AWS Route 53 can shift traffic incrementally, for example, 5% → 20% → 50% → 100% over 30 minutes. This allows the node to **warm up** (caches, connection pools) while monitoring metrics like CPU or error rates.

- **Circuit breakers** like *Istio* service mesh can halt traffic to the node if its error rate exceeds 10%. This prevents a partially healthy node from destabilizing the entire system.

Root cause analysis

Failures are inevitable, but resilient systems learn from them, we can use the strategies mentioned in the following cases:

- **Diagnostic tools**: Distributed Tracing tools like OpenTelemetry or AWS X-Ray map how a request flowed through services before the failure to investigate questions like was the timeout in the payment service or database

- **Log aggregation**: Centralized platforms like Elasticsearch or Datadog correlate logs from all nodes to reconstruct timelines.

- **Preventive actions**: Chaos Engineering helps proactively test recovery processes by simulating failures like using Gremlin to randomly terminate EC2 instances.

- **Post-mortems**: We must document findings in a blameless report (e.g., Primary DB failed due to disk I/O saturation; mitigation: add read replicas). Use of the five techniques to investigate issues helps identify deeper system problems.

Recovery is not just about **fixing** a failure; it is about ensuring the system stays resilient and matures with time. With the right processes in mind as mentioned above, not only can systems mature but also teams maintaining them grow and mature about understanding their own systems better as those systems become bigger and more complex with multiple feature enhancements and wider usage.

Ensuring consistency during failovers

Maintaining data consistency during failovers is critical, especially for systems handling financial transactions or inventory. Strategies are as follows:

- **Write-ahead logging**: Ensuring all operations are logged before being applied.

- **Quorum-based systems**: Requiring a minimum number of nodes to agree on the current state.

- **Eventual consistency with conflict resolution**: Allowing temporary inconsistencies but providing mechanisms to resolve conflicts.

Internal service traffic management

In modern distributed systems, managing traffic between internal services is as crucial as handling external requests. Consider an e-commerce platform processing millions of orders daily. Each order triggers a cascade of internal communications: inventory checks, payment processing, shipping calculations, and customer notifications. An effective solution will need to ensure these internal communications remain reliable, efficient, and scalable.

The foundation of effective internal traffic management lies in three key components, that is, service discovery, communication patterns, and partition handling. Let us explore how these elements work together to create robust distributed systems.

Communication patterns, for example, synchronous REST vs. asynchronous event-driven flows) and partition handling (via circuit breakers or retries with exponential backoff) complete the trifecta. Together, these components enable resilient systems where services dynamically locate one another, adapt to failures, and scale under load.

Service discovery

Imagine you are building a microservices architecture where services need to locate and communicate with each other dynamically. Service discovery acts as the system's directory, maintaining an up-to-date registry of available services and their locations. This becomes particularly important when services are frequently scaled up, down, or replaced.

Modern service discovery systems like *Consul* or *etcd* provide more than simple lookup functionality. They offer health checking, configuration management, and even basic coordination between services. For example, when a new instance of product catalog service starts up, it automatically registers itself with the service registry. Other services, like the shopping cart or recommendation engine, can then discover and begin routing requests to this new instance without any manual intervention.

Let us look at some of the tools and their strengths, as follows:

- **HashiCorp Consul**: Ideal for multi-cloud or hybrid environments, offering strong consistency, health checks, and service mesh integration.

- **etcd**: A lightweight, highly consistent key-value store popular in Kubernetes-native systems for its simplicity and CNCF-backed reliability.

- **AWS Cloud Map**: A fully managed option optimized for AWS ecosystems, tightly integrated with ECS, EKS, and Lambda, but less portable across clouds.

Communication patterns

Internal service communication has to be tailored for the specific use case. Different scenarios call for different communication patterns, each with its own strengths and trade-offs.

Let us examine the three primary patterns in this section.

Synchronous communication with REST and gRPC

REST APIs remain popular for their simplicity and familiarity. They work well for simple CRUD operations and when immediate responses are needed. However, modern distributed systems often require more efficient protocols for internal communication.

This is where gRPC shines, offering benefits as follows:

- Efficient binary serialization
- Strong typing with protocol buffers
- Built-in streaming support
- Lower latency and higher throughput

Consider a product inventory system. While external clients might interact with it through REST APIs, internal services could use gRPC for real-time inventory updates and high-performance batch operations.

Asynchronous communication with message queues

Not all operations need immediate responses. For many scenarios, asynchronous communication through message queues provides better scalability and reliability. Imagine a user placing an order: while the order confirmation should be immediate, secondary processes like updating analytics, sending confirmation emails, or adjusting inventory levels can happen asynchronously.

Modern message queue systems like Apache Kafka or RabbitMQ offer the following:

- Decoupled communication between services
- Built-in persistence and replay capabilities
- Ability to handle traffic spikes through buffering
- Support for different consumption patterns (pub/sub, queue, etc.)

Event-driven architecture

Event-driven architecture takes asynchronous communication further by making events the primary mechanism for service interaction. Services emit events when their state changes, and other services react to these events accordingly.

This pattern excels in scenarios requiring the following:

- Complex workflows with multiple steps
- Real-time updates across services
- Loose coupling between services
- Audit trails of system changes

Traffic shaping and load management

Managing traffic flow between services is crucial for system stability and performance. Modern distributed systems employ several strategies to achieve this.

Rate limiting and circuit breaking

Just as we protect external APIs, internal services need safeguards against overwhelming traffic. Rate limiting prevents service degradation by controlling request rates commonly implemented using tools like Istio's adaptive throttling or token-bucket algorithms in NGINX. Circuit breakers halt cascading failures by blocking requests to unhealthy services popularized by libraries like Netflix Hystrix (now deprecated) and its modern successor Resilience4j, or infrastructure-layer solutions like Envoy's circuit breaking.

For example, If the product recommendation service becomes sluggish, a Resilience4j circuit breaker in dependent services can trip after a failure threshold, for example, 50% errors in 10 seconds, temporarily disabling recommendations rather than letting retries cripple the system.

Load balancing strategies

Internal load balancing goes beyond simple round-robin distribution.

Modern systems use sophisticated strategies as follows:

- **Adaptive load balancing**: Systems dynamically adjust traffic distribution based on real-time metrics like response times, error rates, and resource utilization. This ensures optimal resource usage and better overall system performance.

- **Content-aware routing**: Requests are routed based on their content or context. For instance, premium customer requests might be routed to dedicated service instances with higher resources and priority.

Load balancing

Load balancing is a cornerstone of distributed system architecture, but its effectiveness lies in the details of implementation. Let us explore how different load balancing approaches work together to create resilient, high-performance systems.

Request distribution

Load balancing is more than simply distributing requests across servers. Modern systems require sophisticated algorithms that consider multiple factors to make intelligent routing decisions.

Following are the most effective approaches:

- **Evolution of round robin**: While simple round robin distribution might seem basic, its weighted variant offers surprising sophistication. Consider an e-commerce platform where some service instances run on more powerful hardware. Weighted round robin automatically routes more traffic to these higher-capacity instances, maximizing resource utilization while maintaining system stability.

- **Connection-based intelligence**: The least connections method takes a more dynamic approach, routing requests to servers with the fewest active connections. This becomes particularly valuable in scenarios with varying request processing times. For instance, in a product catalog service, some product details might require complex permission checks or real-time inventory calculations, leading to longer connection times. Least Connections balancing naturally adapts to these variations.

- **Smart routing with IP hash**: Session persistence becomes crucial for certain types of applications. IP hash-based routing ensures that requests from the same client consistently reach the same server, which is essential for maintaining session state or implementing sticky sessions. However, this approach needs careful monitoring to prevent uneven load distribution, especially when dealing with traffic from large corporate networks or proxy servers.

Layer 4 versus Layer 7 load balancing

The choice between network-layer (L4) and application-layer (L7) load balancing significantly impacts system architecture and performance.

Each approach serves different needs as follows:

- **Network-layer excellence**: L4 load balancing excels in raw performance, operating at the TCP/UDP level. It is particularly effective for handling high-throughput scenarios where deep packet inspection is not necessary. For example, a video streaming service might use L4 balancing to efficiently distribute connection requests across edge servers.

- **Application-layer intelligence**: L7 load balancing, while more resource-intensive, enables sophisticated request routing based on application-specific attributes. Consider an API gateway that routes requests based on URL paths, HTTP headers, or even request body content. This level of intelligence enables the following:
  - o Feature-based routing for A/B testing
  - o Content-based distribution for microservices
  - o Smart caching strategies
  - o Request transformation and manipulation

Event-based system architecture

Event-based architectures have become increasingly important in modern distributed systems. They offer unique advantages in handling complex workflows, maintaining system state, and ensuring data consistency.

Event sourcing and CQRS

Event sourcing and **Command Query Responsibility Segregation (CQRS)** work together to provide a robust foundation for managing system state and operations. Instead of storing just the current state, event sourcing maintains a complete history of changes through events.

This approach offers several benefits as follows:

- Complete audit trail of all changes
- Ability to reconstruct system state at any point in time
- Natural support for event-driven architectures
- Easier debugging and system analysis

CQRS complements event sourcing by separating read and write operations, allowing each to be optimized independently. This separation is particularly valuable in systems with complex domain models or significant differences between read and write patterns.

Message queue management

Effective message queue management is crucial for event-based systems. Modern distributed systems often implement sophisticated patterns for queue management.

Dead letter queues and Message replay handle different aspects of message queue management, as follows:

- **Dead letter queues**: Failed messages are automatically moved to separate queues for analysis and potential reprocessing, preventing data loss and enabling better error handling.

- **Message replay**: Systems maintain the ability to replay events from any point in time, crucial for recovery scenarios or data corrections.

Consistent hashing

In distributed systems, efficient data distribution and lookup mechanisms are crucial for scalability. **Distributed hash tables** (**DHTs**) and consistent hashing provide elegant solutions to these challenges. Let us try to understand why consistent hashing is useful.

Imagine you are building a distributed caching system for an e-commerce platform that needs to store millions of product details across multiple cache servers.

Following is why consistent hashing becomes crucial:

Let us take an example that leverages traditional hashing techniques, let us say we have 4 cache servers and use a simple hash approach: server = hash(key) % no_of_servers, suppose we have a thousand products, where we look at a sample of product ids and how they are mapped to the servers using this hashing technique hash(Product Id) % no_of_servers, let us take a very simple example for illustrative purposes only, as follows:

- Product 10 → Server 2 (hash →10%4 = 2)
- Product 3 → Server 3 (hash →3%4 = 3)
- Product 5 → Server 1 (hash →5%4 = 1)
- Product 4 → Server 0 (hash →4%4 = 0)

When Server 2 fails, we only have 3 servers available, which means the hash calculations for the products will now have to change, as follows:

- Product 10 → Server 1 (hash →10%3 = 1) (result data does not move)
- Product 3 → Server 2 (hash →3%3 = 0 (result data has to be moved)
- Product 5 → Server 0 (hash →5%3 = 2, result data has to be moved)
- Product 4 → Server 0 (hash →4%3 = 1, result data has to be moved)

This means most of your cached data needs to be remapped and moved when server count changes.

When you have thousands of servers in a distributes systems, you have failures in your system quite often, moving data across when a server fails is an added overhead. Server addition or removal causes massive data redistribution. It also causes bad customer experience as cache misses spike dramatically in case of the above example, networks become congested with data movement, system performance degrades significantly. All these add to higher costs.

When using consistent hashing, both servers and data items are mapped to positions on a circular hash ring. When looking up which server should store a particular data item, we move clockwise on the ring from the data items hash position until we find the first server.

When a server is removed, only the data items that were mapped to that server need to be remapped, and they will move to the next server found clockwise on the ring. This means that only the data that was originally between the failed server and its predecessor needs to be redistributed, rather than having to remap all data as would happen with traditional modulo-based hashing. Similarly, when adding a new server, only the data items that fall between the new server and its predecessor in the ring need to be redistributed to the new server.

Figure 7.4 illustrates a simple consistent hashing ring with multiple servers and how data is mapped on failure:

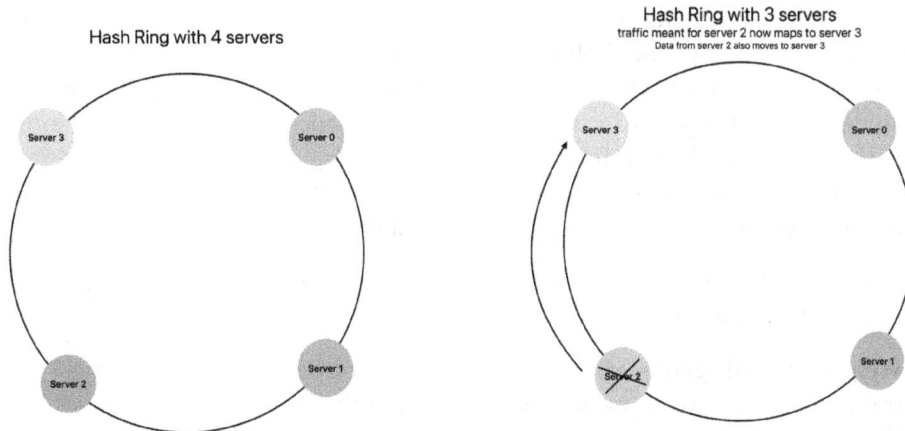

Figure 7.4: Illustration of a consistent hashing ring and behavior when a server fails

There are additional benefits of consistent hashing, we have more predictable effects when scaling up or down, we can better handle hot spots by using virtual nodes. Virtual node in consistent hashing are multiple hash positions on the ring representing a single physical server. Using these virtual nodes, we achieve better distribution of data and load balancing, as each server is responsible for multiple segments of the hash ring instead of just one. We also lower costs due to minimized data movement and making capacity planning more predictable.

Consistent hashing is particularly important in. Distributed caches like Memcached, Redis clusters, **content delivery networks** (**CDNs**), load balancers, distributed databases and distributed storage systems. Without consistent hashing, scaling distributed systems would be significantly more complex and costlier. It is one of those fundamental algorithms that has made modern large-scale distributed systems practical to operate and maintain.

AWS implementation patterns

Modern cloud platforms like AWS provide powerful tools for implementing traffic routing strategies. Let us explore practical implementations using AWS services in this section.

Route 53 global traffic management

Route 53 extends beyond simple DNS services to become a global traffic management solution. Its routing policies enable sophisticated traffic distribution, though understanding both their capabilities and limitations is crucial for robust system design.

Refer to the following:

- **Latency-based routing**: This routing strategy serves as a powerful tool for optimizing user experience. Consider a global e-commerce platform where Route 53's latency-based routing automatically directs users to the closest regional deployment, ensuring optimal response times. This becomes particularly valuable during flash sales or holiday shopping seasons when milliseconds matter. However, architects should account for scenarios where latency-based routing alone might not provide the best user experience. During regional outages or periods of degraded performance, the physically closest region might not be the best choice. In such cases, implementing health checks and failover configurations becomes essential to maintain service reliability.

   To address these challenges, Route 53 offers complementary routing policies that can work in conjunction with latency-based routing.

- **Weighted and geolocation routing**: This routing strategy enables advanced traffic management scenarios that enhance both reliability and business flexibility. Organizations can implement gradual rollouts of new features using weighted routing, ensuring controlled deployment and risk mitigation. Geolocation routing supports region-specific content delivery, enabling compliance with data sovereignty requirements while optimizing costs by directing traffic to regions with better pricing structures.

A comprehensive traffic management strategy often combines multiple routing policies. For example, an application might use geolocation routing as the primary mechanism to ensure compliance, while incorporating latency-based routing within allowed regions and weighted routing for controlled feature deployment. This layered approach helps maintain both performance and reliability even when individual regions experience issues.

Application load balancer

AWS provides ALB to enable sophisticated application-layer routing. In context of Web based traffic, the application layer routing will be based on Http protocol specific attributes that are part of the traffic content and thus called **content-based routing,** as follows:

- **Content-based routing**: ALBs can route requests based on the following:
   - URL paths (**/api/v1/*** vs. **/api/v2/***)
   - HTTP headers (for A/B testing)

- o Query parameters
- o Source IP ranges

This flexibility enables microservices architectures where different services handle different aspects of the application.

Single node patterns in distributed systems

While distributed systems emphasize decentralization, certain scenarios benefit from centralized coordination. Single node patterns, when properly implemented, can enhance system reliability and simplicity. In a single node pattern, one node serves as the primary or leader, while other nodes adopt secondary roles in serving the system. A common implementation involves the leader handling all writes, updates, and state changes, while follower nodes serve read requests. Since leader nodes can fail, the system must incorporate mechanisms to elect new leaders when needed.

Leader election ensures that exactly one node coordinates critical activities in distributed systems. To understand this concept practically, let us examine how Apache ZooKeeper implements leader election in production environments. ZooKeeper uses a protocol called **Fast Leader Election** (**FLE**), which ensures consensus even in complex distributed environments. When a ZooKeeper ensemble starts up or loses its leader, each server enters a candidate state and proposes itself as the new leader. The servers then exchange vote messages containing two crucial pieces of information: their transaction ID (representing how up-to-date they are) and server ID. The candidate with the highest transaction ID typically wins the election, ensuring the most up-to-date server becomes the leader.

This leader election mechanism supports various critical operations, as follows:

- **Scheduled job execution**: For instance, in a distributed cron system, the leader ensures jobs run exactly once across the cluster

- **Configuration management**: The leader maintains and distributes consistent configuration updates

- **Global rate limiting**: The leader coordinates resource usage across the entire system

- **Distributed lock management**: The leader arbitrates access to shared resources

Successfully implementing single node patterns requires careful attention to several factors, as follows:

- **High availability through automatic failover**: Using ZooKeeper as our example, the system maintains a constant watch on the leader's health through periodic heartbeat messages. If the leader fails to send heartbeats within a configured timeout period, the remaining servers automatically initiate a new election process. This approach ensures minimal downtime during leader transitions.

- **Consistency during leader transitions**: When a new leader takes over, it must ensure consistency with previous operations. ZooKeeper achieves this through its **ZooKeeper Atomic Broadcast (ZAB)** protocol, which guarantees that all pending transactions from the previous leader are either completed or rolled back before the new leader begins accepting new operations.

- **Network partition handling**: In the event of a network partition, ZooKeeper prevents the split-brain problem by requiring a quorum (majority) of servers to be available for leader election. This ensures that only one leader can exist at any time, maintaining system consistency even during network failures.

- **Performance optimization**: Since the leader node handles all write operations, it can become a bottleneck. ZooKeeper addresses this by implementing an efficient, in-memory operation model with disk-based transaction logs. Additionally, read operations are distributed across follower nodes to reduce the load on the leader.

Request processing protocols

The choice of communication protocols significantly impacts system performance and capabilities. Modern distributed systems often employ multiple protocols to meet different requirements. Understanding the evolution and characteristics of these protocols helps architects make informed decisions for their specific use cases.

HTTP/2 and gRPC

HTTP/2 and gRPC represent significant advancements in request processing protocols, each bringing distinct advantages to distributed systems.

To understand their roles clearly, let us examine their key differences and use cases, as follows:

- **Communication model**: HTTP/2 builds upon the traditional request-response paradigm while introducing significant improvements. It maintains backwards compatibility with HTTP/1.x while adding features like multiplexing and server push. For example, when loading a web page, HTTP/2 can simultaneously transfer multiple resources over a single connection, dramatically reducing page load times.

  gRPC, built on top of HTTP/2, takes a different approach by implementing remote procedure calls. Instead of thinking in terms of resources and representations, gRPC allows developers to call remote functions as if they were local. This becomes particularly powerful in microservices architectures where services need to communicate efficiently.

Table 7.1 compares both across key dimensions:

Feature	HTTP/2	gRPC
Protocol format	Binary framing over text-based HTTP	Binary Protocol Buffers
API contract	OpenAPI/Swagger specifications	Protocol Buffer service definitions
Service definition	Resource-oriented (URLs)	Function-oriented (Methods)
Payload size	Larger due to JSON/XML	Smaller due to Protocol Buffers
Language support	Universal web standard	Requires language-specific runtime
Browser support	Native	Requires proxy for browser clients
Learning curve	Familiar to web developers	Steeper due to Protocol Buffers
Use case fit	Public APIs, web applications	Internal microservices, performance-critical

Table 7.1: Feature comparison between HTTP/2 and gRPC

- **Protocol selection strategy**: The choice between these protocols should align with specific system requirements. HTTP/REST remains ideal for public APIs and browser interactions due to its universal support and developer familiarity. For instance, a public-facing e-commerce API would benefit from HTTP/REST's wide tooling support and cache-friendly nature.

  gRPC excels in internal service communication where performance and strict contracts are crucial. Consider a recommendation engine that needs to process millions of user interactions quickly, gRPC's efficient binary protocol and strong typing would provide significant advantages.

WebSocket and real-time communication

When systems require real-time features, WebSocket provides crucial capabilities through its bidirectional communication model. This protocol enables natural event-driven architectures and efficient real-time updates without the overhead of repeated polling.

Implementation patterns

Successful implementations require careful attention to several key aspects, as follows:

- **Connection management at scale**: Systems must efficiently handle thousands of concurrent connections. This involves proper load balancing, connection pooling, and resource allocation strategies.

- **Heartbeat mechanisms**: Regular heartbeat messages help detect connection health and network issues early. Implementing appropriate heartbeat intervals requires balancing between timely failure detection and unnecessary network traffic.

- **Reconnection strategies**: Robust systems implement exponential backoff with jitter for reconnection attempts, preventing thundering herd problems during service recovery.

- **Message delivery guarantees**: Different scenarios require different delivery guarantees. Some systems might need exactly-once delivery with persistent storage, while others can tolerate at-least-once delivery for better performance.

Conclusion

Throughout this chapter, we explored the multifaceted world of traffic routing in distributed systems, examining how different strategies work together to create resilient and scalable architectures. From the foundational concepts of Active-Active and Active-Passive architectures to sophisticated implementations of consistent hashing and event-based systems, we have seen how each approach serves specific needs while contributing to overall system reliability. The key lesson is that there is no one-size-fits-all solution in traffic routing. Instead, successful distributed systems often combine multiple strategies. We have seen how Active-Active architectures excel for high-traffic, read-heavy services, while Active-Passive setups better serve scenarios requiring strong consistency. The choice of load balancing techniques, from simple round-robin to sophisticated content-aware routing, depends heavily on specific use cases and requirements.

Modern cloud platforms like AWS have simplified the implementation of many routing strategies, but understanding the underlying principles remains crucial. Whether implementing failover mechanisms, managing internal service traffic, or choosing between different protocols, the fundamental goal remains the same: ensuring reliable, efficient, and scalable system operation.

Looking ahead, traffic routing will continue to evolve as distributed systems face new challenges from edge computing, increased real-time processing demands, and stricter privacy regulations. Success in this field requires not just understanding current patterns but maintaining the flexibility to adapt as requirements change. The best traffic routing strategy is one that aligns with your specific system requirements, operational capabilities, and business needs while providing room for future growth and adaptation. Traffic routing is a part of building resilient systems, however there are many other considerations to ensure stable, fault tolerant resilient systems.

In the next chapter, we will look at how do we build resilient systems by looking right from design stage to observability aspects to gather insights in real time.

CHAPTER 8

Building Resilient Systems

Introduction

In today's digital landscape, system failures can trigger cascading effects that impact millions of users and result in substantial business losses. When a major e-commerce platform experiences downtime during peak shopping seasons, it is not just about lost sales, it is about eroded customer trust, damaged brand reputation, and potential long-term business impact. Building resilient systems is therefore not merely a technical consideration but a fundamental business imperative.

A resilient system maintains its core functionality and essential services even under adverse conditions. Unlike traditional high-availability systems that focus primarily on uptime, resilient systems adapt to changing conditions, gracefully degrade services when necessary, and maintain data consistency throughout disruptions. Think of resilience as your system's immune system, it must detect, respond to, and recover from threats while keeping critical business functions operational.

Structure

The chapter covers the following topics:

- Distributed systems, practical considerations
- Recovery strategies and business continuity

Objectives

By the end of this chapter, readers will have a comprehensive understanding of building resilient distributed systems. We will explore fundamental concepts starting with the key challenges and fallacies in distributed computing, focusing on practical considerations in network reliability, latency, and security. The chapter delves into essential patterns like circuit breakers, CQRS, and rate limiting strategies that form the backbone of resilient architectures. We examine critical aspects of system recovery through RTO/RPO frameworks and explore how modern practices like chaos engineering contribute to system resilience. Through real-world examples from e-commerce platforms, we demonstrate how these concepts apply in practice. The goal is to equip architects and developers with the knowledge needed to design and maintain systems that can withstand failures, adapt to changing conditions, and maintain core functionality under stress.

Distributed systems, practical considerations

Some essential truths when dealing with distributed systems are that we need to factor in for multiple constraints and failure scenarios for them to work reliably. We cannot assume that the system has network access at all times, or that they will have infinite bandwidth, latencies exists and are a reality. We need to factor in security from ground up while designing components. When we do not factor in these, we end up with systems that fail often that can cause catastrophic results.

Designing for unreliable networks

Network failures are not exceptional events, they are an inherent part of distributed systems. Consider an e-commerce platform's order processing workflow, a single order completion might require communication between order, inventory, payment, shipping, and notification services. Each of these interactions represents a potential point of failure.

Following is a naive Java implementation of a product service:

```java
public ProductDetails getProductDetails(String productId) {
    // DON'T DO THIS
    ProductBasicInfo basic = productService.getBasicInfo(productId);
    PricingInfo pricing = pricingService.getCurrentPrice(productId);
    InventoryStatus inventory = inventoryService.getStatus(productId);

    return new ProductDetails(basic, pricing, inventory);
}
```

This code will fail if any service is unavailable, leading to complete failure of the product detail page.

Following is a more resilient approach:

```java
public ProductDetails getProductDetails(String productId) {
    ProductDetails details = new ProductDetails();

    // Use CompletableFuture for parallel execution
    CompletableFuture<ProductBasicInfo> basicInfoFuture = CompletableFuture
        .supplyAsync(() -> getBasicInfoWithRetry(productId))
        .exceptionally(ex -> getFallbackBasicInfo(productId));

    CompletableFuture<PricingInfo> pricingFuture = CompletableFuture
        .supplyAsync(() -> getPricingWithRetry(productId))
        .exceptionally(ex -> getFallbackPricing(productId));

    CompletableFuture<InventoryStatus> inventoryFuture = CompletableFuture
        .supplyAsync(() -> getInventoryWithRetry(productId))
        .exceptionally(ex -> getFallbackInventory(productId));

    // Combine results with timeouts
    try {
        details.setBasicInfo(basicInfoFuture.get(1, TimeUnit.SECONDS));
        details.setPricing(pricingFuture.get(1, TimeUnit.SECONDS));
        details.setInventory(inventoryFuture.get(1, TimeUnit.SECONDS));
    } catch (TimeoutException e) {
        // Handle timeouts gracefully
        handleTimeout(details);
    }

    return details;
}

private ProductBasicInfo getBasicInfoWithRetry(String productId) {
    return new RetryTemplate()
        .withExpBackoff(100, 3) // Start at 100ms, try 3 times
        .withCircuitBreaker(5, 60000) // Break after 5 failures, reset
after 60s
        .execute(() -> productService.getBasicInfo(productId));
}
```

This implementation includes the following:

- Parallel execution of requests
- Retry logic with exponential backoff
- Circuit breaker pattern
- Fallback mechanisms
- Timeout handling

Modern architectures must embrace this reality. In our e-commerce example, this means implementing patterns, as follows:

- Circuit breakers to prevent cascade failures when services become unresponsive
- Retry mechanisms with exponential backoff for transient failures
- Asynchronous processing for operations that do not require immediate consistency
- Compensation mechanisms for partial failures

The goal is not to eliminate network failures, it is to design systems that can operate effectively despite them.

Designing for unpredictable latency

In distributed systems, latency is not just present, it is variable and significant. A request that takes 10ms in a development environment might take 200ms in production, and potentially seconds during peak loads or network congestion.

Consider a product recommendation system for an e-commerce application. What appears as a single operation to the user might involve multiple service calls, as follows:

- User profile data
- User purchase history
- Current trending products
- Personalized recommendations
- Similar products based on purchase history

```
// DON'T DO THIS
public List<Recommendation> getRecommendations(String userId) {
    UserProfile profile = userService.getProfile(userId);  // ~100ms
    List<Purchase> history = orderService.getHistory(userId);  // ~200ms
    List<Product> trending = analyticsService.getTrending();   // ~150ms
    List<Product> similar = similarityService.findSimilar(history);  //
~300ms

    // Total time: ~750ms + processing time
```

```
    return calculateRecommendations(profile, history, trending, similar);
}
```

Each of these operations introduces latency, and the cumulative effect can significantly impact over performance. Effective latency management requires the following:

- Concurrent processing of independent operations
- Prioritization of critical paths over optional features
- Caching strategies at multiple levels
- Dynamic timeout management based on system conditions
- Graceful degradation of non-essential features

Following is how to handle latency properly:

```java
public List<Recommendation> getRecommendations(String userId) {
    // Use caching for relatively static data
    List<Product> trending = cache.get("trending", () ->
        analyticsService.getTrending(), Duration.ofMinutes(5));

    // Parallel execution of necessary real-time calls
    CompletableFuture<UserProfile> profileFuture = CompletableFuture
        .supplyAsync(() -> userService.getProfile(userId));

    CompletableFuture<List<Purchase>> historyFuture = CompletableFuture
        .supplyAsync(() -> orderService.getHistory(userId));

    // Wait for all data with timeout
    try {
        UserProfile profile = profileFuture.get(200, TimeUnit.MILLISECONDS);
        List<Purchase> history = historyFuture.get(200, TimeUnit.
MILLISECONDS);

        // Calculate recommendations asynchronously
        return CompletableFuture
            .supplyAsync(() -> calculateRecommendations(profile, history,
trending))
            .get(500, TimeUnit.MILLISECONDS);
    } catch (TimeoutException e) {
        return getFallbackRecommendations(userId);
    }
```

```
}
// Implement a circuit breaker for external service calls
@CircuitBreaker(name = "similarityService", fallbackMethod =
"getFallbackSimilar")
private List<Product> getSimilarProducts(List<Purchase> history) {
    return similarityService.findSimilar(history);
}


private List<Product> getFallbackSimilar(List<Purchase> history, Exception
e) {
    return cache.get("default_recommendations");
}
```

Designing for limited and costly bandwidth

While network bandwidth has increased dramatically since these fallacies were first articulated, so have the demands we place on our systems. Modern applications, especially those dealing with media-rich content, must carefully manage their bandwidth usage.

In an e-commerce context, consider product image delivery. A single product might have multiple high-resolution images, 360-degree views, and video content. Efficient bandwidth usage requires sophisticated strategies.

Following is a Naïve Java implementation:

```
// DON'T DO THIS
@GetMapping("/products/{id}/images")
public List<ProductImage> getProductImages(@PathVariable String id) {
    return productImageRepository.findAllByProductId(id);
}
```

This simple implementation has several problems as follows:
- It returns all images at full resolution
- There is no pagination
- No consideration of client capabilities
- No optimization for network conditions

Following is a more network-aware implementation:

```
public class ProductImageService {
    private final ImageOptimizer imageOptimizer;
    private final NetworkQualityDetector networkDetector;
```

```java
    private final ClientCapabilityAnalyzer clientAnalyzer;

    @GetMapping("/products/{id}/images")
    public ProductImageResponse getProductImages(
            @PathVariable String id,
            @RequestParam(required = false) ImageQuality quality,
            @RequestParam(required = false) Integer page,
            @RequestParam(required = false) Integer size,
            HttpServletRequest request) {

        // Analyze client capabilities and network conditions
        ClientCapabilities clientCaps = clientAnalyzer.analyze(request);
        NetworkQuality networkQuality = networkDetector.
detectQuality(request);

        // Determine optimal image parameters
        ImageParameters params = ImageParameters.builder()
            .quality(determineQuality(quality, networkQuality))
            .format(selectOptimalFormat(clientCaps))
            .dimensions(calculateOptimalDimensions(clientCaps))
            .build();

        // Implement pagination
        Pageable pageable = PageRequest.of(
            Optional.ofNullable(page).orElse(0),
            Optional.ofNullable(size).orElse(10)
        );

        // Fetch and optimize images
        Page<ProductImage> imagePage = productImageRepository
            .findByProductId(id, pageable)
            .map(image -> optimizeImage(image, params));

        return ProductImageResponse.builder()
            .images(imagePage.getContent())
            .totalPages(imagePage.getTotalPages())
```

```
            .hasNext(imagePage.hasNext())
            .optimizationParams(params)
            .build();
    }


    private ImageQuality determineQuality(ImageQuality requested,
NetworkQuality network) {
        if (requested != null) {
            return requested;
        }

        return switch(network) {
            case POOR -> ImageQuality.LOW;
            case MEDIUM -> ImageQuality.MEDIUM;
            case GOOD -> ImageQuality.HIGH;
            default -> ImageQuality.MEDIUM;
        };
    }


    private ProductImage optimizeImage(ProductImage original,
ImageParameters params) {
        // Implement caching for optimized images
        String cacheKey = generateCacheKey(original.getId(), params);

        return imageCache.get(cacheKey, () ->
            imageOptimizer.optimize(original, params));
    }
}
```

The above implementation carefully considers the following:

- Dynamic content optimization based on client capabilities
- Progressive loading of content
- **Content delivery network (CDN)** utilization
- Format and compression optimization
- Intelligent caching strategies

This is just a sample of varied solutions depending on the problem domain at hand. One should consider implementation based on these factors.

Designing with security considerations

The fallacy that the network is secure has become particularly dangerous in today's threat landscape. Security breaches can compromise not just data but system resilience itself. Modern systems must implement security at every layer, as follows:

- **Network level**: Encryption, firewalls, intrusion detection
- **Application level**: Authentication, authorization, input validation
- **Data level**: Encryption at rest, secure backup, access controls
- **Operational level**: Audit logging, anomaly detection, incident response

Dynamic nature of network topology

Modern distributed systems operate in an environment of constant change. The traditional assumption of stable network topology has been completely upended by cloud computing and containerization. Today's systems must handle infrastructure that expands, contracts, and transforms based on demand and conditions.

In a large-scale e-commerce platform, this dynamic nature becomes particularly evident during high-traffic events like Black Friday sales. The system might begin with a modest baseline of services, but as traffic increases, new instances are automatically provisioned across different availability zones or regions. This elastic scaling introduces complexity far beyond simple capacity addition. Each new instance must be discovered by other services, added to load balancing pools, granted appropriate security credentials, and integrated into the monitoring system. Meanwhile, existing connections must be maintained or gracefully terminated, cached data must remain coherent, and database connections must be managed without overwhelming the underlying systems.

This dynamism requires a fundamental shift in how we design our systems. Service discovery becomes not just a convenience but a critical requirement. Hard-coded endpoints or static configuration files give way to dynamic service registries and real-time configuration management. Load balancers must continuously adjust their routing decisions based on instance health, capacity, and location. The entire system must operate more like a living organism, constantly adapting to changes in its environment, rather than a static, unchanging structure.

Cross administrative domain challenges

The complexity of modern distributed systems extends beyond technical considerations into organizational and administrative realms. The notion of a single administrator managing all system components has become as outdated as physical server rooms. Today's systems span multiple administrative domains, each with its own constraints, requirements, and objectives.

Consider a global e-commerce platform's payment processing system. It must integrate with payment providers across different geographic regions, each operating under different regulatory frameworks. In the European Union, payment processing must comply with PSD2 requirements for strong customer authentication. In contrast, North American operations might prioritize frictionless checkout experiences. Asian markets might require integration with completely different payment systems like *Alipay* or *WeChat Pay*. Each of these integrations operates under different administrative control, with its own release cycles, maintenance windows, and operational procedures.

This administrative complexity manifests in numerous ways. API versions must be managed across different providers, each potentially operating on different upgrade cycles. Security policies must adapt to regional requirements while maintaining a consistent user experience. Performance monitoring must account for different SLAs and reporting requirements. The system must handle situations where one provider undergoes maintenance while others remain operational, all while maintaining consistent business operations.

Real cost of data movement

When architects discuss the cost of moving data in distributed systems, the conversation often focuses on bandwidth. However, the true cost encompasses many more factors that can significantly impact system performance and operational expenses. In cloud environments, data transfer between regions or availability zones incurs direct monetary costs that can quickly become substantial. Beyond these obvious costs lie numerous hidden expenses in terms of processing overhead, time delays, and system complexity.

Data movement in a distributed system involves multiple stages of processing. Data must be serialized from its internal format, possibly compressed, transmitted across the network, then decompressed and deserialized at its destination. Each of these steps consumes CPU cycles and adds latency. Security requirements add another layer of complexity, as data often needs to be encrypted before transmission and decrypted upon receipt. Connection management itself requires resources, from establishing secure connections to maintaining connection pools and handling network timeouts.

In the context of our e-commerce platform, consider the seemingly simple task of maintaining product catalog consistency across multiple geographic regions. Each product update must be propagated to all regions, but doing this naively could result in excessive data transfer costs and unnecessary network load. A more sophisticated approach might involve differential updates, intelligent caching strategies, and careful consideration of data locality. Critical product data like pricing and inventory might need near-real-time synchronization, while less critical data like product descriptions or images might be updated on a more relaxed schedule.

Building truly resilient systems

Understanding these fundamental challenges leads us to a more nuanced approach to building resilient systems rather than treating resilience as a collection of individual techniques or patterns, we must view it as an integral part of the system's architecture. Resilience is not achieved through any single mechanism but through the careful orchestration of multiple strategies working in concert.

A resilient system acknowledges that failures are normal and plans for them accordingly. Instead of treating failures as exceptional cases, they become part of the standard operating model. This means moving beyond simple redundancy or failover mechanisms to create systems that can operate effectively even when impaired. For instance, when a product recommendation service becomes slow or unresponsive, the system should not only detect this but automatically adjust its behavior perhaps falling back to cached recommendations or even eliminating recommendations temporarily to maintain core shopping functionality.

Implementing resilience through service design

The journey from understanding distributed system challenges to implementing resilient solutions requires careful consideration of service design and interaction patterns. This goes beyond mere technical implementation to encompass how services communicate, handle failures, and maintain system integrity under varying conditions.

Art of asynchronous communication

Asynchronous communication patterns form the backbone of resilient service design. In our e-commerce context, consider the order processing workflow. When a customer places an order, multiple actions need to occur, inventory must be reserved, payment must be processed, shipping labels need to be generated, confirmation emails must be sent, and analytics need to be updated. A synchronous implementation would require all these operations to complete in sequence before responding to the customer, creating multiple points of potential failure and unnecessarily increasing response times.

Instead, a resilient design separates these operations into essential synchronous operations and deferrable asynchronous tasks. The system might immediately process payment and confirm inventory availability synchronously, as these directly affect the customer's ability to complete their purchase.

However, generating shipping labels, sending confirmation emails, and updating analytics can be handled asynchronously through message queues or event streams. This separation serves multiple purposes as follows:

- It reduces the system's vulnerability to individual component failures
- Improves response times
- Allows for better resource utilization during peak loads

Graceful degradation in practice

The concept of graceful degradation takes on particular importance in modern distributed systems rather than a binary state of working or failed, systems should be designed with multiple service levels that can be dynamically adjusted based on system health and load. This approach requires careful consideration of feature criticality and user experience impact.

Consider the product detail page of our e-commerce platform. Under normal conditions, it might display real-time inventory levels, personalized recommendations, dynamic pricing, customer reviews, and social proof indicators. As system load increases or components fail, the page should degrade gracefully. Real-time inventory might fall back to periodic updates, personalized recommendations might be replaced with popular items, and non-essential features like social proof indicators might be temporarily disabled. The key is maintaining core functionality, the ability to view and purchase products, while selectively reducing features that could impact system stability.

State management and system awareness

A sophisticated understanding of system state becomes crucial in building resilient systems. This goes beyond simple health checks to encompass a holistic view of system capacity, performance, and operational status. Modern distributed systems must maintain this awareness across multiple dimensions while avoiding the pitfalls of distributed state management.

In the e-commerce context, consider inventory management across multiple warehouses and regions. The system must maintain consistent views of inventory levels while handling concurrent orders, returns, and stock updates. Traditional approaches might attempt to maintain strong consistency across all nodes, but this can lead to reduced availability and increased latency. A more resilient approach might employ eventual consistency with careful conflict resolution strategies, for example, the system might maintain local inventory caches that are periodically reconciled with a master record, with business rules for handling temporary inconsistencies.

Recovery automation and self-healing

The scale and complexity of modern distributed systems make manual recovery procedures increasingly impractical. Automated recovery mechanisms become not just a convenience but a necessity for maintaining system reliability. This automation must extend beyond simple restart procedures to encompass sophisticated healing and recovery strategies.

For instance, when a service instance fails in our e-commerce platform, the recovery process must orchestrate multiple actions as follows:

- Redirecting traffic away from the failed instance
- Starting a new instance

- Ensuring proper initialization
- Verifying the new instance's health
- gradually restoring traffic

This process must happen automatically and safely, without human intervention. The system should learn from these failures, adjusting its behavior to prevent similar issues in the future. This might involve automatically adjusting resource allocations, modifying retry parameters, or updating routing policies based on observed failure patterns.

Data resilience and state recovery

While much attention in resilient system design focuses on service availability and communication patterns, data resilience deserves special consideration. Data represents the system's state and business value, making its protection and recovery crucial to system resilience. This extends beyond simple backup and restore procedures to encompass sophisticated strategies for maintaining data availability and consistency.

Consider the shopping cart service in our e-commerce platform. Cart data must be highly available (customers expect to see their cart contents immediately), consistent (items added on one device should be visible on others), and durable (cart contents should persist even through system failures). A resilient implementation might use a multi-tiered approach, in-memory caches for performance, distributed databases for durability, and event sourcing for auditability and state reconstruction. The system must handle scenarios like partial failures, network partitions, and data center outages while maintaining data integrity and availability.

Protection mechanisms in resilient systems

Modern distributed systems face challenges not just from internal failures but from external pressures and malicious actors. Understanding and implementing proper protection mechanisms becomes crucial for maintaining system resilience under various forms of stress.

Rate limiting and throttling strategies

Every system has finite capacity, and exceeding these limits can lead to cascading failures that affect all users. Rate limiting and throttling serve as crucial protective mechanisms, but their implementation requires careful consideration of business priorities and user experience. In our e-commerce context, consider how different types of requests might require different throttling strategies.

Search queries, for instance, place significant load on the system but are less critical than checkout operations. During peak periods, the system might reduce the complexity of search results, limit autocomplete suggestions, or increase the minimum time between searches while maintaining full capacity for checkout operations. This selective degradation preserves core business functions while managing system load.

More sophisticated approaches might implement adaptive throttling based on user behavior and business value. A customer with items in their cart might receive higher priority than one merely browsing. Similarly, wholesalers or premium customers might receive higher rate limits than regular users. The key is implementing these restrictions in a way that maintains system stability while minimizing impact on valuable business operations.

Understanding rate limiting dimensions

Rate limiting must consider multiple dimensions beyond simple request counts. In our e-commerce platform, different operations have varying impacts on system resources. A product search query might consume significant CPU and memory resources, while an API call to check shipping rates might stress external service quotas. An effective rate limiting strategy must account for these different resource constraints.

For instance, during a flash sale event, the platform might need to manage the following:

- Overall requests per user
- Concurrent sessions per account
- Database operations per service
- External API calls per minute
- Compute-intensive operations per time window
- Network bandwidth per client

Each of these dimensions might require different rate limiting approaches and thresholds based on their impact on system stability and business objectives, as follows:

- **Token Bucket algorithm**: Token Bucket algorithm stands out for its flexibility and effectiveness in handling burst traffic while maintaining long-term rate limits. The algorithm is particularly valuable in e-commerce scenarios where legitimate users might have burst patterns of activity, such as adding multiple items to cart quickly then being inactive.

  In practice, Token Bucket implementation requires careful tuning of two key parameters as follows:

  o **Bucket size**: Determines maximum burst capacity
  o **Refill rate**: Controls sustained request rate

  For example, a product catalog service might implement a Token Bucket that allows for brief bursts of rapid page views (larger bucket size) but enforces stricter limits on sustained high-volume access (lower refill rate). This approach accommodates natural user behavior while preventing abuse.

- **Leaky Bucket Algorithm**: Leaky Bucket algorithm provides a more stringent approach to rate limiting, enforcing a consistent outflow rate. This makes it particularly suitable for protecting downstream services that have fixed processing capacity. Unlike the Token Bucket, the Leaky Bucket smooths out bursts, which can be advantageous when managing access to critical resources.

  Consider a payment processing service that can handle a maximum of 1000 transactions per second. Leaky Bucket implementation would ensure that requests are processed at a steady rate, queueing excess requests (up to a configurable limit) rather than rejecting them immediately. This helps maintain system stability while maximizing throughput.

Adaptive rate limiting

Static rate limits often prove insufficient in dynamic distributed systems. Adaptive rate limiting adjusts thresholds based on system conditions, resource availability, and observed patterns. This approach is particularly valuable in cloud environments where resource capacity can change dynamically.

Key factors in adaptive rate limiting are as follows:
- System load metrics
- Error rates
- Response times
- Resource utilization
- Business priorities

For instance, during periods of high system load, the rate limiting system might dynamically reduce limits for lower-priority operations while maintaining higher limits for critical business functions like checkout processes.

Distributed rate limiting

Implementing rate limiting in distributed systems introduces additional complexity. Multiple service instances must coordinate to enforce global limits while maintaining acceptable performance. This typically requires a shared state store like Redis and careful consideration of consistency requirements.

Consider rate limiting for an API gateway serving multiple regions as follows:
- Local rate limits can be enforced immediately at each gateway instance
- Global limits require coordination through a shared state store
- Cached limit states reduce latency but may allow brief limit violations
- Network partitions must be handled gracefully

Backpressure management

Backpressure represents a more nuanced approach to system protection than simple rate limiting. While rate limiting focuses on restricting incoming requests, backpressure provides feedback mechanisms that allow the system to self-regulate under load. This becomes particularly important in microservice architectures where different services have different processing capabilities and scaling characteristics.

Consider the order processing pipeline in our e-commerce platform. The order ingestion service might be capable of accepting hundreds of orders per second, but downstream services like payment processing or fraud detection might operate at lower capacities. Without proper backpressure mechanisms, this mismatch could lead to queue buildup and eventual system failure. Instead, the system should communicate capacity limitations upstream, allowing for flow control at multiple levels.

Effective backpressure implementation might involve multiple strategies working in concert. At the API level, response codes can indicate when a service is approaching capacity. At the messaging level, queue depth monitoring can trigger temporary request rejection. At the system level, load balancers can redirect traffic based on service health metrics. The goal is maintaining system stability through controlled request management rather than allowing requests to accumulate until failure occurs.

Defence against distributed denial-of-service

Distributed denial-of-service (**DDoS**) attacks represent a particular challenge for distributed systems, as they can exploit the very mechanisms designed for legitimate user access. Modern DDoS protection requires a multi-layered approach that begins at the network edge and extends through all system layers. However, the challenge lies in distinguishing between malicious traffic and legitimate high-load scenarios, such as a successful marketing campaign or sales event.

A comprehensive DDoS protection strategy must consider both technical and business impacts. At the network level, traffic pattern analysis can identify and filter obvious attack patterns. At the application level, request characteristics and user behavior patterns can help identify potentially malicious activity. However, these protections must be carefully tuned to avoid impacting legitimate users.

Consider an e-commerce flash sale scenario. The sudden spike in traffic might resemble a DDoS attack, with thousands of simultaneous requests targeting specific product pages. The protection system must be sophisticated enough to distinguish this legitimate business event from an attack, perhaps by considering factors like user authentication, historical patterns, and request characteristics.

Circuit breaking and fault isolation

The circuit breaker pattern, while conceptually simple, requires careful consideration in implementation to effectively protect distributed systems. Unlike electrical circuit breakers that simply cut power, software circuit breakers must manage complex state transitions and recovery procedures.

In our e-commerce platform, circuit breakers might protect various system integrations payment processors, shipping carriers, or external service providers. The challenge lies in configuring appropriate thresholds and recovery strategies. Too-sensitive circuit breakers might unnecessarily disable critical functionality, while too-lenient ones might allow system degradation to progress to failure.

Modern implementations might employ adaptive circuit breakers that adjust their behavior based on observed patterns. For instance, a circuit breaker protecting an external payment processor might become more sensitive during known maintenance windows, or adjust its thresholds based on historical performance patterns. The goal is protecting system stability while maximizing available functionality.

Recovery strategies and business continuity

Recovery in distributed systems extends beyond simple restart procedures. It encompasses a comprehensive strategy for maintaining business operations during failures and restoring full functionality in a controlled manner. This becomes particularly critical when different parts of the system have different recovery requirements and capabilities.

Recovery time objective and recovery point objective

Recovery time objective (RTO) and **recovery point objective (RPO)** form the foundation of any recovery strategy, but their implementation in modern distributed systems requires careful consideration of service dependencies and data consistency requirements. In our e-commerce context, different services may have vastly different recovery requirements. The shopping cart service might require near-instant recovery (low RTO) with no data loss (zero RPO), while the recommendation engine might tolerate longer recovery times and some data loss without significantly impacting the business.

The challenge lies in managing these different requirements within an interconnected system. For instance, the order processing service might depend on multiple other services, each with its own RTO and RPO characteristics. A comprehensive recovery strategy must account for these dependencies while ensuring that critical business functions remain available. This might mean maintaining redundant paths for critical operations, implementing fallback mechanisms for dependencies, and carefully managing state recovery across service boundaries.

Static stability and system initialization

Static stability represents a crucial but often overlooked aspect of system resilience. A statically stable system should maintain its last known good state during failure scenarios, rather than attempting to transition to new states that might introduce additional instability. This principle becomes particularly important during system initialization and recovery procedures.

Consider a product catalog service that depends on multiple data sources and configuration settings. A naive implementation might attempt to refresh all its data and reconfigure itself during startup, potentially introducing points of failure if any dependency is unavailable. A statically stable implementation would instead start with its last known good state and gradually refresh its data as dependencies become available. This approach ensures that the service can provide basic functionality even if some of its dependencies are temporarily unavailable.

The concept extends to configuration management as well. Rather than requiring all configuration to be present at startup, services should fall back to sensible defaults when specific configuration values are unavailable. This allows the system to maintain basic functionality even during configuration service outages or during partial system recovery scenarios.

Chaos engineering practices

Chaos engineering has evolved from simple failure injection testing to a sophisticated practice of systematic resilience verification. However, implementing chaos engineering in a production environment requires careful consideration of business risk and system capabilities. The goal is not merely to create chaos but to build confidence in the system's resilience through controlled experimentation.

In an e-commerce context, chaos experiments might start with simple scenarios like simulating instance failures or network latency increases. As confidence grows, more complex scenarios can be introduced, that is, partial database failures, configuration service outages, or regional network partitions. The key is conducting these experiments in a way that validates system resilience while maintaining safety boundaries that protect business operations.

Modern chaos engineering practices often employ automated safety checks and experiment verification. For instance, before injecting a failure into the payment processing system, the experiment framework might verify that alternate payment paths are available and functioning correctly. During the experiment, key business metrics are monitored to ensure that the system's response matches expected behavior. If unexpected conditions arise, the experiment can be automatically terminated and the system restored to its normal state.

Event-driven recovery patterns

Event-driven architectures provide powerful tools for implementing resilient recovery procedures, but they also introduce their own complexities that must be carefully managed. The ability to replay events for state reconstruction, while powerful, requires careful consideration of event ordering, idempotency, and consistency requirements.

Consider a scenario where the order processing service needs to recover from a failure. Simply replaying all missed events might not produce the correct system state if events have complex interdependencies or if external systems have continued to process requests during the outage. The recovery process must consider these dependencies and ensure that the recovered state is consistent with both the internal system state and any external systems.

Modern event-driven systems often implement sophisticated recovery patterns such as event sourcing with snapshots, **Command Query Responsibility Segregation** (**CQRS**), and compensating transactions. These patterns allow for more flexible recovery strategies but require careful design to maintain system consistency and prevent unintended side effects during recovery procedures.

Command Query Responsibility Segregation

CQRS represents more than just a design pattern, it is a fundamental approach to building resilient systems that can maintain high availability while managing complex data operations. By separating read and write operations, CQRS allows systems to scale and evolve each aspect independently, but this separation introduces its own challenges and considerations.

In our e-commerce platform, consider the product inventory management system. Traditional approaches might use a single model for both updating inventory levels (commands) and checking current stock levels (queries). However, these operations have fundamentally different characteristics and requirements. Stock updates must be strictly consistent and serialized to prevent overselling, while stock level queries need to be fast and highly available to support the shopping experience.

CQRS addresses the different expectations by maintaining separate models for commands and queries. The command model might use a strongly consistent database to handle inventory updates, ensuring that each sale correctly decrements the available stock. Meanwhile, the query model could use a denormalized, eventually consistent view optimized for rapid reads. This separation allows the system to maintain strict consistency where necessary while providing high performance and availability for read operations. *Figure 8.1* illustrates a typical CQRS design:

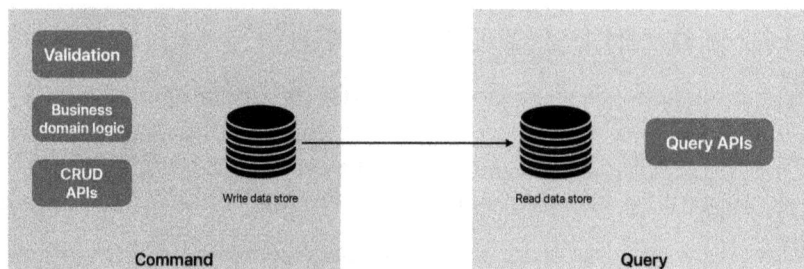

Figure 8.1: Illustration of CQRS architecture

The challenge lies in maintaining consistency between these models. The system must propagate changes from the command model to the query model while handling scenarios like network partitions, service failures, and concurrent updates. This often involves implementing sophisticated event processing pipelines with guaranteed delivery and idempotency guarantees.

Scale inversion and system evolution

Scale inversion occurs when components designed for different scales interact, potentially leading to system instability. This phenomenon becomes particularly relevant as systems evolve and usage patterns change. Understanding and managing scale inversion is crucial for maintaining system resilience over time.

Consider a product recommendation service that was initially designed to handle moderate traffic levels. As the platform grows, this service might become a bottleneck during high-traffic periods, not because it is poorly implemented, but because its design assumptions no longer match current usage patterns. The challenge is particularly acute when such services are deeply integrated into critical user journeys.

Addressing scale inversion requires more than just horizontal scaling. It often necessitates fundamental architectural changes to handle different scales of operation effectively. This might involve implementing caching layers, adopting different data storage strategies, or completely reimagining service interactions. The key is identifying potential scale mismatches before they impact system stability and implementing appropriate architectural adaptations.

Auditing systems in resilient architectures

Auditing in distributed systems extends beyond simple record-keeping to become a crucial component of system resilience. Effective audit systems must capture not just what happened but also the context in which events occurred, while maintaining their own resilience against system failures.

In an e-commerce context, consider the audit requirements for payment processing. The system must maintain detailed records of every transaction, including attempted transactions, for regulatory compliance and dispute resolution. However, this audit system must not impact the performance or availability of the core payment processing functionality.

Modern audit architectures often implement event-sourcing patterns, where every state change is recorded as an immutable event.

This approach provides several benefits as follows:

- Complete audit trails of all system changes
- Ability to reconstruct system state at any point in time
- Support for complex analysis and reporting requirements
- Basis for system recovery and state reconstruction

However, implementing such audit systems requires careful consideration of storage requirements, query patterns, and data retention policies. The system must balance the need for comprehensive audit trails with practical limitations of storage and processing capacity.

Retrying systems and idempotency

In distributed systems, retrying failed operations is essential for resilience, but implementing retry mechanisms requires careful consideration of idempotency and consistency requirements. The challenge lies not just in deciding when to retry operations, but in ensuring that retries do not create unintended side effects or inconsistencies.

Consider a scenario in our e-commerce platform where a customer places an order. The payment service successfully charges the customer's card, but before confirming the order, a network partition occurs. The system must decide whether to retry the order confirmation, but it must do so without risking duplicate charges or inventory updates.

Modern retry systems often implement sophisticated strategies as follows:

- **Progressive backoff to prevent system overload**: This is a technique used in distributed systems where a service gradually increases the delay between retry attempts following a failure. Instead of retrying failed operations immediately or at fixed intervals, the delay between attempts progressively increases, typically exponentially. This approach helps prevent system overload and allows temporary issues to resolve naturally.

- **Retry budgets to limit resource consumption**: This is a rate-limiting mechanism that controls how many retry attempts a system can make within a specific time window. Unlike simple retry limits that cap attempts per request, retry budgets consider the system's overall health and capacity, preventing retry storms that could overwhelm services during recovery periods.

- **Circuit breakers to prevent futile retries**: A circuit breaker is a design pattern that monitors for failures when making remote service calls. Like its electrical counterpart, it trips to prevent cascading failures by stopping requests to failing services

- **Idempotency tokens to prevent duplicate processing**: Idempotency tokens are unique identifiers assigned to operations to ensure they are processed exactly once, even if the same request is sent multiple times. They prevent duplicate processing in distributed systems, particularly crucial for financial transactions. If a request with the same token arrives again, the system returns the original response.

These mechanisms must work together to provide resilience while maintaining system consistency and preventing unintended side effects. The implementation must also consider the business impact of failed retries and provide appropriate fallback mechanisms when operations cannot be completed successfully.

Observability and recovery planning

Observability in resilient systems goes far beyond basic monitoring and logging. It provides the foundation for understanding system behavior, predicting potential issues, and executing effective recovery strategies. This deep system insight becomes particularly crucial as systems grow more complex and interconnected.

Beyond basic monitoring

Traditional monitoring focuses on known failure modes and predefined metrics. However, modern distributed systems require a more sophisticated approach to observability. Consider our e-commerce platform during a major sale event. Simply monitoring individual service health checks and basic metrics might show all systems as **healthy** while customers experience transaction failures or slow response times.

Modern observability requires understanding the relationships between services and their impact on business outcomes. For instance, a slight increase in latency in the inventory service might not trigger any traditional alerts, but could cascade into significant checkout delays during high-traffic periods. Effective observability must capture these subtle interactions and their business impact.

This depth of understanding requires correlating data across multiple dimensions, as follows:

- Service interactions and dependencies
- Resource utilization patterns
- Business transaction flows
- User experience metrics
- System performance characteristics

Disaster recovery in practice

Disaster recovery planning must evolve beyond traditional backup and restore procedures. In modern distributed systems, the concept of disaster has become more nuanced. A disaster might not be a complete system failure, but rather a complex degradation of service capabilities that requires careful orchestration to resolve.

Consider a regional outage affecting one of our e-commerce platform's data centers. The traditional approach might focus on failing over to a backup site. However, in a distributed system, the reality is more complex. Different services might have different recovery requirements and capabilities. Some might automatically redirect traffic to other regions, while others might require careful state synchronization before failover.

The true challenge lies in maintaining business continuity during these complex failure scenarios. This requires the following:

- Understanding service dependencies and recovery priorities
- Managing state transfer and synchronization
- Coordinating recovery across multiple services
- Maintaining data consistency during recovery
- Handling partial failures and degraded operations

Predictive analysis and proactive resilience

Modern resilient systems are moving beyond reactive recovery to predictive analysis and proactive intervention. By analyzing patterns in system behavior, it becomes possible to identify potential issues before they impact service quality. This shift from reactive to proactive resilience requires sophisticated analysis capabilities and automated response mechanisms.

For example, in our e-commerce platform, predictive analysis might identify patterns indicating an impending service degradation as follows:

- Gradually increasing response times in specific API endpoints
- Subtle changes in error rates or retry patterns
- Unusual patterns in resource utilization
- Changes in user behavior patterns
- Variations in data access patterns

The key is not just identifying these patterns but understanding their potential impact and taking appropriate preemptive action. This might involve the following:

- Automatically scaling services before they become overwhelmed
- Redirecting traffic to prevent resource exhaustion
- Preemptively warming caches or provisioning resources

- Adjusting system configurations to handle anticipated load
- Initiating prophylactic maintenance operations

Learning from failures

Perhaps the most crucial aspect of building truly resilient systems is the ability to learn from failures when they do occur. This goes beyond simple post-mortem analysis to create a continuous improvement cycle that enhances system resilience over time.

Consider a significant outrage in our e-commerce platform. Traditional analysis might focus on the immediate technical cause, but building resilience requires a deeper understanding:

- What were the precipitating factors that led to the failure?
- How did our detection and response mechanisms perform?
- What unexpected system interactions were revealed?
- How effective were our recovery procedures?
- What business impact occurred during the incident?

This analysis should lead to both immediate improvements and longer-term architectural evolution. The goal is not just to prevent similar failures but to enhance the system's overall resilience posture. This might involve the following:

- Adjusting system architecture to eliminate discovered weaknesses
- Enhancing monitoring and detection capabilities
- Improving recovery procedures and automation
- Updating capacity planning assumptions
- Evolving architectural patterns and practices

Future considerations in resilient system design

The landscape of distributed systems continues to evolve, bringing new challenges and opportunities for resilient system design. As we look forward, several key areas are emerging that will shape how we build and maintain resilient systems in the coming years.

Edge computing and resilience

The rise of edge computing is fundamentally changing how we think about system resilience. Traditional models of centralized failover and recovery become inadequate when dealing with thousands of edge locations, each with its own processing capabilities and failure modes. Consider our e-commerce platform expanding to include edge-based inventory management and order processing.

In this new paradigm, resilience must be reconsidered from the ground up. Each edge location must be capable of operating autonomously while maintaining some level of coordination with the broader system. Data consistency becomes particularly challenging, an edge location might need to process orders even when disconnected from central systems, then reconcile these transactions when connectivity is restored.

The challenge extends beyond technical implementation to fundamental architecture decisions. How much authority should edge locations have to operate independently? How do we handle conflicts when edge locations make conflicting decisions? How do we maintain security and compliance across a vastly distributed edge network? These questions require us to evolve our understanding of resilience for edge-native architectures.

Artificial intelligence and automated resilience

AI and ML is increasingly being employed not just as business features but as core components of system resilience. The complexity of modern distributed systems has begun to exceed human capacity for real-time analysis and response, making AI-driven resilience mechanisms increasingly important.

Consider how AI might enhance our e-commerce platform's resilience as follows:

- Predictive scaling based on complex pattern recognition
- Automated root cause analysis during incidents
- Dynamic optimization of resource allocation
- Intelligent traffic routing and load balancing
- Anomaly detection and automated response

However, incorporating AI into resilience mechanisms introduces its own challenges. AI systems can have their own failure modes and may make decisions that, while mathematically optimal, might not align with business priorities. The key is finding the right balance between automated and human-guided resilience strategies.

Zero-trust resilience

As systems become more distributed and interconnected, the traditional perimeter-based security model is giving way to zero-trust architectures. This shift has profound implications for system resilience. Every service interaction must now be authenticated and authorized, but this additional security cannot come at the cost of system resilience.

In our e-commerce context, zero-trust principles must be balanced against the need for rapid recovery and failover. To ensure that we maintain strict security controls while allowing for emergency recovery procedures and avoiding the security mechanisms themselves from becoming single points of failure, we have to rely on solutions that lie in designing security controls that are both stringent and resilient, capable of degrading gracefully when necessary while maintaining core security guarantees.

Sustainable resilience

The environmental impact of digital systems is receiving increasing attention, leading to a new consideration in resilient system design: sustainability. Traditional approaches to resilience often rely on redundancy and over-provisioning of resources, which can have significant environmental costs.

Future resilient systems must balance traditional reliability metrics with environmental considerations. This might mean the following:

- More sophisticated resource allocation strategies
- Intelligent use of low-power states
- Optimization of data center locations and cooling
- Careful consideration of backup and redundancy strategies
- Energy-aware routing and processing decisions

Human factor in resilience

As systems become more complex and automated, the role of human operators and developers becomes more critical, not less. The future of resilient systems will require a careful balance between automated systems and human insight. The way we design systems must evolve to support this human-system collaboration. Interfaces must be designed not just for normal operations but for understanding and resolving complex failure scenarios. Documentation must evolve from static references to dynamic, context-aware guidance systems. Training must focus not just on procedures but on building deep system understanding.

Conclusion

Building resilient systems is a journey that requires careful consideration of multiple dimensions, that is, technical, operational, and organizational. Throughout this chapter, we have explored how modern distributed systems must evolve beyond simple fault tolerance to embrace comprehensive resilience strategies that address both anticipated and unexpected challenges.

The key takeaway is that resilience is not achieved through any single pattern or technology, but through the thoughtful combination of multiple strategies working in concert. From the fundamental principles of distributed computing to sophisticated patterns like CQRS and event-driven architectures, each element contributes to the overall resilience posture of the system.

As we look to the future, the challenge of building resilient systems continues to evolve. Edge computing, AI-driven automation, and zero-trust architectures are introducing new complexities and opportunities. The increasing focus on sustainability adds another dimension to consider in our resilience strategies. However, the core principles remain constant: systems must be designed to detect, respond to, and recover from failures while maintaining essential business functions.

Success in building resilient systems ultimately comes from understanding that resilience is not just a technical challenge but a holistic approach that encompasses people, processes, and technology. It requires continuous learning, adaptation, and evolution of our practices as new challenges and technologies emerge.

In the next chapter, we will look at how we can design databases which are performant, scalable and resilient. We will look at how NoSQL databases are providing a compelling option where some of the transaction oriented database features may not be suitable.

Join our book's Discord space

Join the book's Discord Workspace for Latest updates, Offers, Tech happenings around the world, New Release and Sessions with the Authors:

https://discord.bpbonline.com

CHAPTER 9
Data Storage Strategies

Introduction

In the world of distributed systems, data storage forms the bedrock upon which all other functionalities are built. Staying with our e-commerce platform example from previous chapters; every product listing, customer review, order transaction, and inventory update relies on robust and efficient data storage solutions. As the platform grows from serving hundreds of customers to millions, the challenges of storing, retrieving, and managing this data become increasingly complex. The system has to ensure that it provides the same level of performance when it had few thousand users to millions of users while making sure it is reliable. Different parts of the system may have contradicting requirements for functioning optimally for their specific use case. In this chapter, we will dive into exploring some of these aspects. Throughout this chapter, we will try to look at problems through the lens of a globally distributed ecommerce platform and its encounters with various situations to help evolve and mature its design.

Structure

The chapter covers the following topics:

- Evolution of data storage
- Database systems in distributed environments
- Multi-model database approach

- Data partitioning and sharding
- Data protection and disaster recovery
- Real-time data protection in action
- Modern storage solutions

Objectives

By the end of this chapter, readers will have a comprehensive understanding of data storage strategies in distributed systems, focusing on both theoretical foundations and practical implementations. Through the lens of our ecommerce platform example, we explore essential concepts including storage models, database systems, partitioning strategies, and data consistency approaches. The chapter covers traditional and modern storage solutions, examining how different storage types serve various business requirements. Special attention is given to maintaining system reliability through replication strategies, ensuring data consistency, and managing storage performance. By understanding these concepts and their practical applications, readers will be equipped to design and implement effective storage solutions for large-scale distributed systems that meet both technical requirements and business needs.

Evolution of data storage

The journey of data storage in distributed systems mirrors the evolution of our e-commerce platforms. In the early days, a single database server might have been sufficient to handle all our product catalog and order information. The platform might have started with a few thousand products and a manageable number of daily orders. However, as the business grew, this simple approach began to show its limitations.

Consider how our e-commerce platform's storage needs evolved. Initially, product information was stored in a single relational database, with straightforward tables for products, categories, and inventory. Orders were processed sequentially, and data backup was a simple nightly process. but as the platform expanded to include features like real-time inventory tracking, personalized recommendations, and customer reviews, the storage requirements became more complex.

The platform now handles millions of products across multiple sellers, each with their own inventory systems. Customer data includes not just basic profile information but also browsing history, preferences, and interaction patterns. Order processing has become more complex, involving multiple microservices that need to access and update data simultaneously while maintaining consistency.

Understanding modern storage challenges

Let us examine the challenges through the lens of our e-commerce platform. When a customer places an order, multiple data operations occur simultaneously, as follows:

- The order service needs to write the order details to a transactional database
- The inventory service must update stock levels across multiple warehouses
- The analytics service records customer behavior data
- The recommendation engine updates its dataset based on the purchase
- The notification service needs to access customer preferences to send alerts

Each of these operations has different requirements for consistency, durability, and performance. For instance, the order processing requires strong consistency and immediate durability, we cannot afford to lose order information or have inconsistent states. However, the recommendation engine can work with eventually consistent data, as slight delays in updating purchase patterns would not significantly impact the user experience.

Impact of scale

Following the e-commerce platform example, consider our e-commerce platform had now expanded globally, the storage system had to evolve to handle various scenarios. Take the product catalog as an example.

While it started as a simple database table, it grew to include the following:
- Detailed product descriptions in multiple languages
- High-resolution images and videos
- Real-time pricing information that varies by region
- Seller-specific inventory levels
- Customer reviews and ratings
- Related product recommendations

The system now needs to serve this information to customers worldwide with low latency. This requires sophisticated caching strategies, data replication across geographic regions, and careful consideration of consistency models.

Read versus write patterns

Our platform's different services exhibit distinct data access patterns. The product catalog service is primarily read-intensive, millions of customers browse products, but the actual product information updates are relatively infrequent. In contrast, the inventory management service is write-intensive, constantly updating stock levels as orders are placed and items are restocked.

For example, during a flash sale event, the system might experience the following:
- Thousands of customers viewing the same products simultaneously
- Hundreds of concurrent order attempts for popular items

- Real-time inventory updates across multiple warehouses
- Continuous price adjustments based on demand
- Frequent cart updates as customers add and remove items

Understanding these patterns is crucial for choosing the right storage solutions. The product catalog might benefit from a read-optimized database with extensive caching, while the inventory system might require a storage solution optimized for high-frequency writes with strong consistency guarantees.

Storage strategy fundamentals

The success of our e-commerce platform depends on choosing the right storage strategies for different types of data and access patterns.

Following is an example:

The order processing system requires transactional integrity. When a customer places an order, multiple operations must succeed or fail as a unit, as follows:

- Creating the order record
- Updating inventory levels
- Processing payment information
- Reserving items in the warehouse

This necessitates a storage solution that supports **Atomic, Consistent, Isolated and Durable (ACID)** transactions and provides strong consistency guarantees.

In contrast, the product recommendation system can tolerate some latency and inconsistency. If a customer's recent purchase takes a few minutes to influence their recommendations, it does not significantly impact the user experience. This system might benefit from a more scalable, eventually consistent storage solution.

As we dive into more details in this chapter, we will explore how our e-commerce platform implements various storage strategies to meet these diverse requirements. We will examine specific solutions for different components of the system, from the product catalog to the order processing pipeline, and understand how they work together to create a robust, scalable platform.

Storage models and architectures

In our e-commerce platform, different types of data require different storage models. Understanding these models and their appropriate use cases is crucial for building a scalable and efficient system.

Block storage

Before hard drives, data was stored sequentially on tapes, making accessing specific data very slow. The development of hard drives enabled random access to data by dividing it into independent blocks, significantly improving data retrieval speed. Block storage allows for easy expansion by adding more storage units, accommodating growing data needs. This storage serves as the foundation for many of the low-level storage needs. In the e-commerce platform example, we can use block storage for hosting our database files and operating systems. Think of block storage as a virtual hard drive, it divides data into fixed-size blocks, each with its own address. When our order processing service needs to update an order status, the database system reads and writes these blocks directly.

For example, when running a PostgreSQL database for order management, block storage provides the raw storage capacity. The database engine interacts with these blocks directly, offering high performance for transactional operations. This is particularly important when processing thousands of orders during peak shopping periods, where quick access to individual data blocks can significantly impact overall system performance.

However, block storage comes with limitations. It requires careful management of capacity and does not inherently provide features like data replication or geographic distribution. In our platform, we can address these limitations by implementing additional layers of redundancy and management.

Managing unstructured data

Object storage evolved as a response to the need for a more scalable and cost-effective way to manage large volumes of unstructured data, particularly with the rise of cloud computing and the explosion of digital content generated by social media, smartphones, and other sources; it addressed limitations of traditional file systems and block storage by offering a flexible, distributed architecture that can easily store and retrieve massive datasets with rich metadata, making it ideal for big data analytics, archiving, and content delivery services. The cloud infrastructure facilitated the development and deployment of distributed object storage systems like *Amazon S3*, making it accessible to a wide range of users.

A distributed system platform like an one needed to run a large e-commerce platform will need vast amounts of unstructured data like product images, technical documentation, customer and seller uploaded content, and more. This is where object storage shines. Unlike block storage, object storage treats each piece of data as a distinct object, complete with metadata and a unique identifier.

Consider images in a product catalog. When a seller uploads new product photos, we can store them in an object storage system like Amazon S3.

Each image becomes an object with the following:

- The image data itself
- Metadata about the image (dimensions, format, upload date)
- A unique URL for access
- Access control information
- Version history

This approach offers several advantages for our use case, as follows:

- Images can be served directly to web browsers without loading our application servers
- We can easily replicate images across different geographic regions for faster access
- Version control allows us to track changes to product images over time
- Built-in access controls help manage who can view or modify the images

Structured data organization

While object storage excels at handling large, independent files, some parts of our system require a more traditional file system approach. Our application servers, for instance, need a hierarchical structure for storing configuration files, logs, and temporary data.

In our platform, we might use a distributed file system to manage shared resources across multiple services. For example, when generating product reports or processing bulk updates, services need a common area to store and share intermediate files.

A distributed file system provides the following:

- Familiar hierarchical organization
- File-level locking for concurrent access
- Traditional file operations (read, write, append)
- Access control at the directory level

Data co-location strategies

Data co-location becomes crucial when dealing with related data that is frequently accessed together. In our e-commerce platform, this concept significantly impacts performance and user experience.

Consider our product detail pages. Each page displays the following:

- Basic product information
- Current inventory levels
- Pricing details
- Customer reviews
- Related products
- Seller information

Traditional normalized database design would store each of these elements in separate tables or even separate databases. However, this could lead to increased latency as the system needs to gather data from multiple sources for each page view.

To optimize this, we can implement strategic data co-location as follows:

- Frequently accessed product information is denormalized and stored together
- Recent reviews are kept in the same database shard as the product data
- Inventory levels for popular products are cached alongside basic product information

For example, our product service maintains a denormalized view that combines the most frequently accessed product attributes, as follows:

```
CREATE TABLE product_view (
    product_id UUID PRIMARY KEY,
    name TEXT,
    description TEXT,
    base_price DECIMAL,
    current_inventory INTEGER,
    average_rating DECIMAL,
    recent_reviews JSONB,
    category_path TEXT[],
    last_updated TIMESTAMP
);
```

This denormalized approach trades some data redundancy for significantly improved read performance crucial for our high-traffic product pages.

Hybrid storage architectures

In practice, our e-commerce platform employs a hybrid approach, combining different storage models to meet various requirements.

Let us examine how this works for order processing, when a customer places an order, as follows:

- Order details go into a traditional relational database for ACID compliance
- Order confirmation emails and documents are generated and stored in object storage
- Temporary processing files use the local file system
- Session data is kept in a distributed cache
- Order events are published to a message queue for async processing

This hybrid approach allows us to leverage the strengths of each storage model while mitigating their individual limitations. The key is understanding which storage model best serves each specific use case within our system.

Geographic distribution and replication

As our e-commerce platform serves customers globally, we must consider how to distribute and replicate data across different regions.

Our storage architecture implements the following:

- **Regional data centers**: Each major geographic region has its own set of storage systems, including the following:
    - Primary databases for order processing
    - Object storage for static content
    - Caching layers for frequently accessed data
    - Message queues for event processing

- **Cross-region replication**: Different types of data have different replication strategies, as follows:
    - Product catalog data is fully replicated across all regions
    - Customer data is primarily stored in the customer's home region
    - Order data is stored in the region where the order was placed
    - Analytics data is aggregated centrally but processed locally

This architecture helps us maintain performance while complying with data sovereignty requirements and providing disaster recovery capabilities.

Let us now explore how different database systems fit into this storage architecture, examining the specific roles of relational and NoSQL databases in our e-commerce platform.

Database systems in distributed environments

In our e-commerce platform example, different services require different database systems to handle their specific data requirements effectively. Let us explore how various database types serve different needs within our distributed system.

Relational databases

Our platform's order processing system relies heavily on relational databases to maintain transactional integrity. Consider what happens when a customer places an order, multiple related operations must succeed or fail as a unit.

Refer to the following code:

```
BEGIN TRANSACTION;
    -- Create the order record
    INSERT INTO orders (order_id, customer_id, total_amount, status)
    VALUES ('ord_123', 'cust_456', 199.99, 'PENDING');

    -- Add order items
    INSERT INTO order_items (order_id, product_id, quantity, price)
    VALUES ('ord_123', 'prod_789', 2, 99.99);

    -- Update inventory
    UPDATE product_inventory
    SET quantity = quantity - 2
    WHERE product_id = 'prod_789';

    -- Record payment
    INSERT INTO payments (order_id, amount, status)
    VALUES ('ord_123', 199.99, 'AUTHORIZED');
COMMIT;
```

This transaction must maintain ACID properties, as follows:

- **Atomicity**: All operations complete successfully, or none of them do
- **Consistency**: Inventory levels cannot go negative; payments must match order totals
- **Isolation**: Other customers cannot reserve the same inventory
- **Durability**: Once confirmed, the order will not be lost even if systems crash

PostgreSQL, our chosen RDBMS for order processing, excels at maintaining these properties. However, this comes with certain limitations in a distributed environment.

As order volumes grow, we need to implement strategies as follows:

- **Read replicas**: For handling order history queries and reporting
- **Horizontal partitioning**: Sharding orders across multiple database instances
- **Connection pooling**: Managing thousands of concurrent connections efficiently

NoSQL databases

NoSQL databases evolved primarily as a response to the limitations of traditional SQL databases when dealing with massive amounts of data, particularly unstructured data, generated by the internet and web applications, which required greater scalability, flexibility, and faster processing speeds that traditional relational databases struggled to provide; essentially, the rise of **big data** pushed the need for a new database model like NoSQL.

While relational databases excel at transactional operations, our product catalog has different requirements that make NoSQL solutions more appropriate.

Let us examine how we can use MongoDB to store product information, as follows:

```
{
  "product_id": "prod_789",
  "name": "Premium Wireless Headphones",
  "description": "High-fidelity audio with noise cancellation",
  "categories": ["Electronics", "Audio", "Wireless"],
  "specifications": {
    "connectivity": "Bluetooth 5.0",
    "battery_life": "30 hours",
    "features": [
      "Active Noise Cancellation",
      "Touch Controls",
      "Voice Assistant Support"
    ]
  },
  "variants": [
    {
      "color": "Midnight Black",
      "sku": "WH-MB-001",
      "price": 299.99,
      "inventory": {
        "warehouse_1": 150,
        "warehouse_2": 85
      }
    },
    {
      "color": "Arctic White",
```

```
      "sku": "WH-AW-001",
      "price": 299.99,
      "inventory": {
        "warehouse_1": 75,
        "warehouse_2": 120
      }
    }
  ],
  "reviews": [
    {
      "rating": 5,
      "comment": "Excellent sound quality!",
      "user_id": "user_123",
      "date": "2024-02-15"
    }
  ]
}
```

This document structure offers several advantages, as follows:

- Product variations can be stored together with the base product
- The schema can evolve without migrations as new attributes are added
- Related data like recent reviews, can be embedded for faster access
- The document maps naturally to the JSON structure used by our API

Access patterns and indexing strategies

Understanding access patterns is crucial for optimizing database performance. In our product catalog, common access patterns include the following:

- Searching products by name or description
- Filtering by category and specifications
- Checking inventory levels across warehouses
- Retrieving product reviews
- Updating prices and inventory levels

To support these patterns efficiently, we implement carefully chosen indexes, as follows:

```javascript
// Compound index for category-based searches
db.products.createIndex({
```

```
  "categories": 1,
  "name": 1
});


// Text search index
db.products.createIndex({
  "name": "text",
  "description": "text"
});


// Inventory monitoring index
db.products.createIndex({
  "variants.inventory.warehouse_1": 1,
  "variants.inventory.warehouse_2": 1
});
```

These indexes accelerate common queries but come with storage and write performance overhead. We carefully monitor index usage and adjust our strategy based on actual query patterns.

Time series data

Time series data is a collection of data points recorded at consistent intervals over a period of time, where the order of the data points is crucial for understanding trends and patterns as they occur chronologically; essentially, it is a sequence of measurements taken at regular intervals, allowing you to analyze how a variable changes over time. In context of a distributed system like an ecommerce platform, we could gather significant time series data from various sources, as follows:

- Product price history
- Inventory level changes
- Order volumes
- System metrics

For this data, we use a specialized time series database that efficiently handles temporal data, as follows:

```
-- Recording price changes
INSERT INTO price_history (
    product_id,
    timestamp,
    price,
```

```
    currency,
    change_reason
)
VALUES (
    'prod_789',
    NOW(),
    299.99,
    'USD',
    'Seasonal Promotion'
);


-- Analyzing price trends
SELECT
    date_trunc('day', timestamp) as day,
    avg(price) as average_price,
    min(price) as lowest_price,
    max(price) as highest_price
FROM price_history
WHERE product_id = 'prod_789'
    AND timestamp >= NOW() - INTERVAL '30 days'
GROUP BY date_trunc('day', timestamp)
ORDER BY day;
```

The time series database optimizes for the following:

- Efficient storage of temporal data
- Fast range-based queries
- Automatic data retention policies
- Built-in aggregation functions

Multi-model database approach

The complexity of our e-commerce platform requires different database systems working in concert to deliver optimal performance and functionality. Consider a typical customer journey during a busy holiday shopping season. Let us follow a customer of the platform, the customer is looking to purchase wireless headphones during a *Black Friday* sale.

When the customer first lands on our homepage, the system immediately begins interacting with multiple databases. The product recommendation engine pulls data from MongoDB, where we store rich product information including categories, specifications, and customer behavior patterns. These recommendations are not simply random selections, they are based on that individual customer's previous browsing history, purchase patterns, and similar customer profiles, all of which require quick access to unstructured, schema-flexible data that MongoDB handles effectively.

As the customer searches for **wireless headphones**, Elasticsearch comes into play. Unlike a traditional relational database, Elasticsearch excels at full-text search and complex filtering. It processes the customer's search query, considering not just product names and descriptions, but also customer reviews, technical specifications, and even common misspellings. The search results are returned in milliseconds, ranked by relevance and enriched with faceted navigation options.

While browsing through the search results, the customer adds a pair of premium wireless headphones to their cart. At this point, a Redis based cache is invoked. As a high-performance in-memory database, Redis cache is ideal for managing shopping cart sessions. It maintains the customer's cart state with sub-millisecond response times, crucial during high-traffic sales events when thousands of customers are simultaneously adding items to their carts.

The interaction becomes more complex when the customer decides to save several items to their wish list for later comparison. This operation involves MongoDB storing their wish list preferences while also updating recommendation algorithms. The system needs to maintain this information persistently while ensuring it can be quickly retrieved when the customer returns to the site later.

Finally, when the customer proceeds to checkout, the system transitions to PostgreSQL for order processing. This is where the strengths of a traditional relational database become crucial. The checkout process involves multiple related operations that must be executed as a single atomic transaction.

The order service creates the main order record, capturing essential details like shipping address and payment information. Simultaneously, it must verify inventory availability across multiple warehouses. The payment service processes the credit card transaction, while the inventory service adjusts stock levels. All these operations must succeed together, or none should proceed a perfect scenario for PostgreSQL's ACID compliance.

Behind the scenes, our time series database records various metrics about this entire shopping session. It captures data points about system performance, user behavior patterns, and business metrics. This information helps us understand peak shopping times, popular product combinations, and potential performance bottlenecks. For instance, we might notice that certain product categories see increased activity during specific time slots, allowing us to optimize our caching strategies accordingly.

The success of this multi-model approach relies heavily on careful orchestration. Each database type serves its specific purpose while contributing to the overall customer experience. When the customer returns to check their order status the next day, they will interact with this entire ecosystem again PostgreSQL providing order details, MongoDB serving up related product recommendations, Redis managing their session state, and Elasticsearch powering their ability to search through their order history.

This real-world example demonstrates why no single database type can efficiently handle all our platform's requirements. The combination of PostgreSQL's transactional integrity, MongoDB's flexibility with unstructured data, Redis's high-speed caching, Elasticsearch's search capabilities, and time series databases' temporal data management creates a robust foundation for our e-commerce platform.

In the next section, we will explore how we partition and shard data across these various database systems to maintain performance and scalability as our platform grows. We will see how these decisions impact real customer experiences and system reliability during high-traffic events like Black Friday sales.

In practice, our e-commerce platform employs multiple database types working together. Let us examine how different databases handle a single customer journey, as follows:

- **Product browse phase**:
    - MongoDB serves product details and catalog navigation
    - Redis caches frequently accessed products
    - Elasticsearch powers product search and filtering

- **Shopping cart**:
    - Redis maintains the temporary cart state
    - MongoDB tracks saved items and wish lists
    - PostgreSQL records cart conversion metrics

- **Order placement**:
    - PostgreSQL handles the core order transaction
    - MongoDB stores extended order details
    - Time series database records order metrics
    - Redis invalidates relevant caches

This multi-model approach allows each part of the system to use the most appropriate database for its specific requirements while maintaining overall system consistency and performance.

In the next section, we will explore how we partition and shard our data across these various database systems to achieve scalability while maintaining manageability.

Data partitioning and sharding

As our e-commerce platform grew from serving thousands to millions of customers, the volume of data expanded exponentially. What started as a single database instance for product listings and orders soon became insufficient.

Let us explore how we evolved our data partitioning strategy to handle this growth while maintaining performance and reliability.

Evolution of data storage needs

Consider our product catalog system's journey. Initially, storing a few thousand products in a single database worked well. Each product record contained basic information like name, description, price, and inventory level. However, as we expanded to support multiple sellers, international markets, and rich product content, our data requirements grew dramatically.

A single product record now encompasses the following:

```
{
    "product_id": "WH-MB-001",
    "base_info": {
        "name": "Premium Wireless Headphones",
        "brand": "AudioTech",
        "description": "High-fidelity audio with noise cancellation",
        "launch_date": "2024-01-15"
    },
    "localized_info": {
        "en_US": {
            "name": "Premium Wireless Headphones",
            "description": "Experience crystal-clear audio...",
            "currency": "USD",
            "price": 299.99
        },
        "es_MX": {
            "name": "Auriculares Inalámbricos Premium",
            "description": "Experimente audio cristalino...",
            "currency": "MXN",
            "price": 5999.99
        }
    },
```

```
    "inventory": {
        "NA_warehouse_1": 150,
        "NA_warehouse_2": 85,
        "MX_warehouse_1": 75
    },
    "rich_content": {
        "images": ["img_001.jpg", "img_002.jpg", "img_003.jpg"],
        "videos": ["product_demo.mp4"],
        "technical_specs": {
            "battery_life": "30 hours",
            "connectivity": "Bluetooth 5.0",
            "weight": "250g"
        }
    }
}
```

With millions of such products, each with multiple variants, managing this data in a single database became increasingly challenging. This led us to implement a sophisticated partitioning strategy.

Horizontal partitioning

Horizontal partitioning in our example, we can implement horizontal partitioning (sharding) based on product categories and geographical regions. This approach aligns with how customers would typically interact with the platform. Following is how the sharding strategy could evolve:

Analyze access patterns. The data can show if customers typically browse within specific categories, someone shopping for electronics rarely jumps to browsing furniture in the same session. Customers predominantly shop within their geographical region. This insight can also help to design a two-dimensional sharding approach.

Before implementing the sharding strategy, we need to address the challenge of future scalability and rebalancing. In consistent hashing, instead of mapping data directly to physical shards, we introduce virtual nodes multiple hash points for each physical shard on the hash ring. For example, if we have 3 physical shards, each shard might be represented by 100-200 virtual nodes distributed across the hash ring.

This approach offers several advantages, as follows:

- Better distribution of data across shards as virtual nodes reduces the variance in the hash space

- When adding or removing physical shards, only a fraction of keys needs to be remapped
- The number of virtual nodes per physical shard can be adjusted based on the shard's capacity
- Gradual redistribution of data is possible by moving virtual nodes one at a time

Consider the following enhanced database sharding function:

```
public class ProductShardingStrategy {
    private static final int VIRTUAL_NODES_PER_SHARD = 200;
    private final TreeMap<Long, String> hashRing = new TreeMap<>();

    public ProductShardingStrategy(List<String> physicalShards) {
        initializeHashRing(physicalShards);
    }

    private void initializeHashRing(List<String> physicalShards) {
        for (String shard : physicalShards) {
            addShardToRing(shard);
        }
    }

    private void addShardToRing(String shardId) {
        for (int i = 0; i < VIRTUAL_NODES_PER_SHARD; i++) {
            // Create virtual node keys by appending index to shard ID
            String virtualNode = shardId + "-" + i;
            long hash = HashFunction.hash(virtualNode);
            hashRing.put(hash, shardId);
        }
    }

    public String determineShardKey(Product product) {
        // Primary shard by region
        String region = product.getPrimaryRegion();
        // Secondary shard by category
        String category = product.getMainCategory();

        // Calculate hash for the product
```

```java
        long hash = calculateProductHash(region, category);

        // Find the appropriate shard using consistent hashing
        return findShardForHash(hash);
    }

    private long calculateProductHash(String region, String category) {
        // Combine region and category to generate final hash
        return HashFunction.combine(
            HashFunction.hash(region),
            HashFunction.hash(category)
        );
    }

    private String findShardForHash(long hash) {
        // Find the first virtual node with hash >= given hash
        Map.Entry<Long, String> entry = hashRing.ceilingEntry(hash);
        if (entry == null) {
            // Wrap around to first virtual node if at end of ring
            entry = hashRing.firstEntry();
        }
        return entry.getValue();
    }

    // Method to handle adding new physical shards
    public void addPhysicalShard(String newShardId) {
        addShardToRing(newShardId);
        // Only keys that hash to the virtual nodes of the new shard
        // will be automatically redistributed
    }

    // Method to handle removing physical shards
    public void removePhysicalShard(String shardId) {
        // Remove all virtual nodes for this shard
        hashRing.entrySet().removeIf(entry ->
            entry.getValue().equals(shardId));
```

```
        // Keys will be automatically redistributed to remaining shards
    }
}
```

This enhanced sharding strategy provides several benefits, as follows:

- When a customer from North America browses electronics, most queries hit a single shard, reducing cross-shard operations

- During regional sales events, the load naturally distributes across different shards

- If the electronics category experiences high traffic, we can scale by adding more shards

- Virtual nodes in the consistent hash ring ensure more even distribution of data

- Adding or removing shards requires redistributing only a fraction of the data

- The system can handle shard additions and removals with minimal disruption to existing data mappings

Vertical partitioning

While horizontal partitioning helps manage data volume, we can implement vertical partitioning to separate different aspects of our product data.

For instance, we can separate product reviews into their own database, as follows:

```
-- Core product information remains in the main product table
CREATE TABLE products (
    product_id UUID PRIMARY KEY,
    name VARCHAR(255),
    base_price DECIMAL,
    category_id UUID,
    -- Other essential fields
);


-- Reviews live in a separate database
CREATE TABLE product_reviews (
    review_id UUID PRIMARY KEY,
    product_id UUID,
    customer_id UUID,
    rating INTEGER,
    review_text TEXT,
```

```
    review_date TIMESTAMP,
    helpful_votes INTEGER,
    -- Additional review metadata
);
```

This separation serves multiple purposes. Review data has different access patterns and scaling requirements compared to core product data. During high-traffic periods, a surge in product views would not necessarily correlate with increased review writes. This separation allows us to scale and maintain each component independently.

Managing cross-partition queries

While our partitioning strategy optimizes for common access patterns, we still need to handle queries that span multiple partitions. For example, when a customer searches for **wireless headphones** across all categories, or when generating reports that aggregate data across regions.

We implemented a query routing system that intelligently handles cross-partition queries, as follows:

```
public class QueryRouter {
    public SearchResult executeSearch(SearchCriteria criteria) {
        if (isLocalizedSearch(criteria)) {
            // Query single shard for region-specific searches
            return executeLocalizedSearch(criteria);
        } else {
            // For global searches, fan out to multiple shards
            return executeDistributedSearch(criteria);
        }
    }

    private SearchResult executeDistributedSearch(SearchCriteria criteria)
{
        // Parallelize queries across relevant shards
        List<Future<PartialResult>> futureResults =
            relevantShards.stream()
                .map(shard -> executorService.submit(
                    () -> queryShard(shard, criteria)))
                .collect(Collectors.toList());

        // Gather and merge results
```

```
        return mergeResults(futureResults);
    }
}
```

This system balances the need for comprehensive search capabilities with performance considerations. Most customer searches are localized to their region and preferred categories, making them highly efficient. For broader searches, the system parallelizes queries across shards and aggregates results.

Rebalancing shards

As the platform continues to grow, we need to occasionally rebalance data across shards or add new shards. A consistent hashing approach minimizes the amount of data that needs to move during these operations. When adding a new shard, only a portion of the data from existing shards needs to be redistributed, rather than requiring a complete reshuffling of all data.

For example, if an expansion into new geographical markets is needed, we can add new shards for those regions.

The process has the following steps:

1. Create new physical database instances for the new region
2. Update the sharding map to include the new shards
3. Gradually migrate relevant data to the new shards
4. Update routing rules to direct traffic from the new region

This process happens without downtime, ensuring continuous availability of our platform while we scale our infrastructure.

In the next section, we will explore how we maintain data consistency across these partitions and handle the inevitable challenges of distributed data storage.

Data consistency and transactions

In our e-commerce platform example, maintaining data consistency while handling millions of concurrent operations presents complex challenges.

Let us explore how we can manage these challenges through the lens of the order processing system.

Understanding consistency requirements

Consider what happens during our platform's Black Friday sale. At exactly 8:00 AM, thousands of customers attempt to purchase a limited-edition gaming console. Our system must handle not just the high volume of requests, but also ensure that we don't oversell our inventory or create inconsistent order states.

Let us examine a typical order transaction, as follows:

```java
public class OrderProcessor {
    private final IdempotencyStore idempotencyStore;  // Store for tracking transaction states

    public OrderRecord processOrder(Order order, String idempotencyKey) {
        // First check if this order was already processed
        OrderRecord existingOrder = idempotencyStore.getProcessedOrder(idempotencyKey);
        if (existingOrder != null) {
            return existingOrder;  // Return the result of previous execution
        }

        TransactionContext ctx = transactionManager.begin();
        String transactionId = ctx.getTransactionId();

        try {
            // Record transaction attempt
            idempotencyStore.recordTransactionAttempt(idempotencyKey, transactionId);

            // Phase 1: Prepare - Reserve resources and validate
            TransactionState preparationState = prepare(order, ctx);

            // Record preparation state
            idempotencyStore.recordPreparationState(idempotencyKey, preparationState);

            if (!preparationState.isSuccessful()) {
                ctx.rollback();
                return OrderRecord.failure(preparationState.getError());
            }

            // Phase 2: Commit - Create order and finalize
```

```
        OrderRecord record = commit(order, preparationState, ctx);


        // Record successful completion
        idempotencyStore.recordSuccessfulCompletion(idempotencyKey,
record);


        return record;


    } catch (NetworkException e) {
        // Handle network failures during transaction
        TransactionState recoveryState =
recoverTransaction(idempotencyKey);
        if (recoveryState.isCompleted()) {
            return recoveryState.getOrderRecord();
        }
        ctx.rollback();
        throw new TransactionRetryableException("Network failure during
transaction", e);


    } catch (Exception e) {
        ctx.rollback();
        idempotencyStore.recordFailure(idempotencyKey, e);
        throw e;
    }
}


private TransactionState prepare(Order order, TransactionContext ctx) {
    TransactionState state = new TransactionState();

    // Check inventory availability
    InventoryStatus inventoryStatus = inventoryService.checkAndReserve(
        order.getItems(),
        ctx.getTransactionId()
    );
    state.setInventoryStatus(inventoryStatus);

    if (!inventoryStatus.isAvailable()) {
```

```
            return state.withError(new InsufficientInventoryException());
        }

        // Process payment
        PaymentResult payment = paymentService.processPayment(
            order.getPaymentDetails(),
            order.getTotalAmount(),
            ctx.getTransactionId()
        );
        state.setPaymentResult(payment);

        if (!payment.isSuccessful()) {
            return state.withError(new PaymentFailedException());
        }

        return state.asSuccessful();
    }

    private OrderRecord commit(Order order, TransactionState state,
TransactionContext ctx) {
        // Create order record with all preparation data
        OrderRecord record = orderRepository.createOrder(
            order,
            state.getInventoryStatus().getReservationId(),
            state.getPaymentResult().getTransactionId(),
            ctx.getTransactionId()
        );

        ctx.commit();
        return record;
    }

    private TransactionState recoverTransaction(String idempotencyKey) {
        TransactionState state = idempotencyStore.
getTransactionState(idempotencyKey);

        if (state == null) {
```

```
                return TransactionState.unknown();
        }


        // If preparation was successful but commit failed
        if (state.isPreparationComplete() && !state.isCommitComplete()) {
            // Retry commit phase
            try {
                TransactionContext recoveryCtx = transactionManager.
resume(state.getTransactionId());
                OrderRecord record = commit(state.getOrder(), state,
recoveryCtx);
                idempotencyStore.recordSuccessfulCompletion(idempotencyKey,
record);
                return TransactionState.completed(record);
            } catch (Exception e) {
                // Log recovery attempt failure
                return state;
            }
        }

        return state;
    }
}


class TransactionState {
    private String transactionId;
    private Order order;
    private InventoryStatus inventoryStatus;
    private PaymentResult paymentResult;
    private boolean preparationComplete;
    private boolean commitComplete;
    private OrderRecord orderRecord;
    private Exception error;

    // Getters, setters, and helper methods
}
```

```
interface IdempotencyStore {
    OrderRecord getProcessedOrder(String idempotencyKey);
    void recordTransactionAttempt(String idempotencyKey, String
transactionId);
    void recordPreparationState(String idempotencyKey, TransactionState
state);
    void recordSuccessfulCompletion(String idempotencyKey, OrderRecord
record);
    void recordFailure(String idempotencyKey, Exception e);
    TransactionState getTransactionState(String idempotencyKey);
}
```

This implementation ensures that the following:

- Transactions are not duplicated even if retried
- Network failures between prepare and commit can be recovered
- System state remains consistent even during failures
- Failed transactions can be safely retried
- Transaction state is tracked throughout the process

This seemingly straightforward process becomes complex in a distributed environment. Each step involves different services, potentially running on different machines, each with its own database. We must ensure that all these operations either complete successfully together or fail completely, there cannot be a situation where we charge a customer's credit card but fail to create the order record.

Implementing distributed transactions

To handle these complex scenarios, we implement a two-phase commit protocol.

Following is how it works in practice:

```
public class DistributedTransactionManager {
    public TransactionContext begin() {
        String txId = generateTransactionId();

        // Phase 1: Prepare
        Map<String, ServiceStatus> serviceStatuses = new HashMap<>();
        for (DistributedService service : participatingServices) {
            try {
                boolean prepared = service.prepare(txId);
                serviceStatuses.put(service.getName(),
```

```
                new ServiceStatus(prepared));
        } catch (Exception e) {
            // If any service fails to prepare, abort the transaction
            rollback(txId, serviceStatuses);
            throw new TransactionPreparationException(e);
        }
    }


    // Phase 2: Commit
    boolean success = true;
    for (DistributedService service : participatingServices) {
        try {
            service.commit(txId);
        } catch (Exception e) {
            success = false;
            // Log the failure for manual recovery if needed
            logFailure(txId, service.getName(), e);
        }
    }


    if (!success) {
        // Initiate recovery process for partial commit
        initiateRecoveryProcess(txId, serviceStatuses);
        throw new TransactionCommitException();
    }


    return new TransactionContext(txId);
    }
}
```

This implementation guards against partial failures. For example, if the payment service successfully charges the customer's card but the inventory service fails to update, we need to ensure the payment is reversed. During high-traffic periods, this becomes especially critical as the probability of partial failures increases.

Handling eventually consistent data

Not all operations in our system require strong consistency. Consider our product review system. When a customer posts a new review, it is not critical that all users see it immediately. This allows us to use eventual consistency for better performance, as follows:

```java
public class ReviewService {
    public void submitReview(ProductReview review) {
        // Write to primary storage
        reviewRepository.save(review);

        // Asynchronously update search index and analytics
        eventPublisher.publish(new ReviewSubmittedEvent(review));

        // Update product rating asynchronously
        asyncTaskExecutor.execute(() ->
            updateProductAggregates(review.getProductId())
        );
    }

    private void updateProductAggregates(String productId) {
        try {
            // Recalculate product rating
            List<ProductReview> reviews =
                reviewRepository.findByProductId(productId);

            double averageRating = calculateAverageRating(reviews);

            // Update product rating in cache and database
            productService.updateRating(productId, averageRating);
        } catch (Exception e) {
            // Queue for retry in case of failure
            retryQueue.add(new RatingUpdateTask(productId));
        }
    }
}
```

This approach means that for a brief period, different users might see slightly different average ratings for a product. However, this trade-off allows our system to handle thousands of review submissions per minute without impacting critical shopping functionality.

Managing data consistency across regions

Our platform operates across multiple geographical regions, each with its own set of databases. Some data, like product catalogs, needs to be replicated across regions, while other data, like customer orders, primarily lives in the customer's home region.

Following is how we manage catalog updates across regions:

```java
public class GlobalProductManager {
    public void updateProduct(Product product) {
        // Update in primary region
        ProductUpdateResult primaryUpdate =
            primaryRegionManager.updateProduct(product);

        if (!primaryUpdate.isSuccessful()) {
            throw new ProductUpdateException("Primary update failed");
        }

        // Propagate to other regions asynchronously
        for (RegionManager region : secondaryRegions) {
            replicationQueue.submit(new ReplicationTask(
                product,
                primaryUpdate.getVersion(),
                region.getRegionId()
            ));
        }

        // Monitor replication progress
        replicationMonitor.track(
            primaryUpdate.getVersion(),
            secondaryRegions.size()
        );
    }

    @Scheduled(fixedRate = 5000)
```

```
public void checkReplicationHealth() {
    // Monitor replication lag and health
    Map<String, ReplicationStatus> status =
        replicationMonitor.getReplicationStatus();

    for (Map.Entry<String, ReplicationStatus> entry :
        status.entrySet()) {
        if (entry.getValue().getLagSeconds() >
            acceptableReplicationLag) {
            alertingService.sendAlert(
                new ReplicationLagAlert(entry.getKey())
            );
        }
    }
}
}
```

This system ensures that product updates eventually propagate to all regions while monitoring the health of the replication process. During normal operations, replication lag might be just a few seconds. However, during network issues or regional outages, the lag might increase, and our system needs to handle these scenarios gracefully.

In the next section, we will explore how we protect our data through backup and disaster recovery strategies, ensuring that we can recover from both small-scale failures and major disasters.

Data protection and disaster recovery

In our e-commerce platform, data protection is not just about preventing loss, it is about maintaining business continuity and customer trust. Consider what happens during our platform's busiest day, Black Friday. Our systems process millions of orders, each representing a customer's purchase and personal information. A single hour of data loss could mean thousands of missing orders, frustrated customers, and significant revenue impact.

Evolution of our backup

Any large distributed system initially starts small. When the ecommerce platform is first launched, a simple daily backup would seem sufficient. Backing up our entire database each night during low-traffic hours could be feasible. However, as the business grows, this approach could reveal several critical limitations. Let us take a fictitious scenario, during one memorable holiday season, a database corruption issue occurred at 4 PM. Our only options were to roll back to the previous night's backup, losing nearly a day's worth of orders or spend hours attempting to reconstruct the corrupted data.

This incident led to a complete redesign of our backup strategy. Today, our system operates on multiple layers of protection, each serving a specific purpose in our data protection strategy.

Consider our order processing system. When a customer places an order for a popular gaming console during a flash sale, several data protection mechanisms activate simultaneously:

First, the order details are written to our primary database. Immediately, this write is replicated to a standby database in the same region. Within milliseconds, the transaction is also logged to our write-ahead logging system. Within seconds, this data begins replicating to our disaster recovery region on the opposite coast. Finally, our continuous backup system captures these changes as part of its ongoing backup process.

This layered approach means that if our primary database fails, we have multiple recovery options depending on the nature and severity of the failure. For a simple hardware issue, we can fail over to our standby database with minimal disruption. For more severe problems, we can restore from our continuous backup system to any point in time.

Real-time data protection in action

Let us take another fictitious example to walk through a situation to examine how this system handled a real incident during last year's holiday season. At 2:15 PM Eastern Time, we detected unusual behavior in our primary database cluster handling order processing. The monitoring system noticed increasing error rates and degrading performance.

Following is how our protection systems responded:

- The real-time monitoring system detected the issue within seconds, triggering our incident response protocol.

- Our operations team received immediate alerts about the degrading database performance.

- The system automatically began routing new orders to our standby database while maintaining transaction consistency.

- Background processes started verifying data integrity across our primary and standby systems.

- Our cross-region replication system continued ensuring that all transactions were safely copied to our disaster recovery site.

This real incident demonstrated the effectiveness of our layered protection approach. Despite the primary database issues, we maintained system availability with zero data loss. The entire incident, from detection to complete resolution, occurred without any customer-visible disruption.

Geographic distribution and disaster recovery

Let us see how we can make the platform's disaster recovery strategy extend beyond simple backups. We can maintain multiple active regions, each capable of handling the platform's full operational load. This approach can prove to be invaluable during an outage.

Consider the **Amazon Web Services** (**AWS**) us-east-1 outage in December 2021, which affected major e-commerce platforms and online retailers during the peak holiday shopping season. The outage lasted for about seven hours and caused widespread disruptions. Companies that relied solely on the us-east-1 region experienced complete service interruptions, with estimated losses in the millions of dollars per hour.

Major retailers reported the following:

- Shopping carts becoming inaccessible
- Payment processing failures
- Inventory systems going offline
- Product images and catalogs becoming unavailable
- Customer service systems being unreachable

This incident demonstrates why multi-region redundancy is essential. Let us examine how a properly implemented multi-region strategy would handle such a situation:

During this incident, let us assume hypothetically our ecommerce platform's entire US east region experienced connectivity issues. Our system detected the degrading performance and automatically began rerouting traffic to our US West region.

This failover process involved the following:

- Activating our global traffic manager to reroute customer requests
- Promoting the US West databases to primary status
- Adjusting our content delivery network to serve from West region caches
- Switching our payment processing systems to West region endpoints

The entire process completed within minutes, and while some customers experienced slightly higher latency, our platform remained fully operational. This stands in stark contrast to single-region deployments that suffered complete outages during the AWS incident. Once the US East region stabilized, we carefully orchestrated the rebalancing of traffic between regions.

The cost of implementing multi-region redundancy, while significant, is often justified by preventing revenue losses during such outages. For instance, during the 2021 AWS outage, systems with multi-region failover capabilities reported minimal disruption to their holiday season sales, while others faced complete inability to process orders during the peak shopping period.

Point-in-time recovery capabilities

Perhaps the most sophisticated aspect of our data protection strategy is our point-in-time recovery system. This capability proved critical during a recent pricing engine malfunction. For approximately 45 minutes, our system applied incorrect discounts to certain products.

We need the following:

- Identify the exact time the pricing engine began malfunctioning
- Restore the correct pricing data without losing subsequent valid orders
- Maintain consistency across our entire platform

Our point-in-time recovery system allowed us to restore just the affected pricing data to the correct state while preserving all other transactions. This surgical precision in data recovery represents a significant advancement from the traditional **restore everything** approach.

Testing and validation

The true test of any disaster recovery system lies not in its design but in its proven effectiveness. We maintain a rigorous testing schedule that includes the following:

- **Monthly recovery tests**: We regularly perform controlled failover exercises, simulating various failure scenarios. These tests involve actual production data (in an isolated environment) and help us validate our **recovery time objectives (RTO)** and **recovery point objectives (RPO)**.

- **Chaos engineering**: Our platform includes controlled fault injection, regularly testing our system's resilience by simulating various types of failures. For instance, we might terminate database instances, degrade network performance, or introduce latency to verify our protection mechanisms work as designed.

These tests revealed various hidden issues. For example, we discovered that certain backup verification processes were not accounting for specific types of product variant data, leading us to enhance our verification protocols.

In the next section, we will explore how we balance these robust data protection mechanisms with increasingly complex data privacy requirements and governance considerations.

Modern storage solutions

In today's rapidly evolving technological landscape, modern storage solutions have become increasingly sophisticated to meet the diverse needs of distributed systems.

Different storage technologies serve a specific purpose, the key is knowing which to use when. Let us explore these solutions through our ecommerce platform case study, complete with real-world comparisons.

Cloud storage services

Our ecommerce platform handles millions of product images, customer documents, and transaction records daily. Traditional on-premises storage would struggle with this scale and demand for high availability. Cloud storage services provide a robust solution to these challenges.

Consider our product catalog service, which must serve high-resolution images and detailed product specifications to customers worldwide. Cloud object storage services like Amazon S3 or Google Cloud Storage are ideal for this use case. These services store product images and marketing materials, providing several key advantages. First, they offer automatic replication across multiple geographic regions, ensuring that customers can quickly access product images regardless of their location. Second, they integrate seamlessly with **content delivery networks** (**CDNs**), allowing for efficient global content distribution.

For example, when a vendor uploads new product images to our platform, the system automatically stores them in cloud object storage. The storage service creates multiple variants of each image optimized for different devices and screen sizes. These images are then automatically distributed to edge locations worldwide through the CDN. This approach ensures fast access times for customers while minimizing the operational overhead of managing a complex storage infrastructure.

Distributed file systems

While cloud storage excels at serving static content, our platform also needs sophisticated file management capabilities for operational data. Distributed file systems provide this functionality while maintaining high availability and consistency.

For instance, our order processing system needs to manage various documents like invoices, shipping labels, and customs declarations. A distributed file system allows these documents to be accessed and modified by multiple services simultaneously while maintaining consistency. When an order is placed, the system generates an invoice PDF, stores it in the distributed file system, and makes it immediately available to both the customer service team and the fulfillment center.

Modern distributed file systems like *GlusterFS* or *Amazon EFS* provide features like automatic replication, snapshots for point-in-time recovery, and elastic scaling. These capabilities are crucial for maintaining business continuity and managing growing data volumes effectively.

Container storage

As our ecommerce platform adopts containerization for improved scalability and deployment flexibility, storage for containerized applications becomes a critical consideration. Container storage must balance the ephemeral nature of containers with the need for persistent data storage.

Consider our shopping cart service, which runs in containers for scalability. While the containers themselves are ephemeral, the cart data must persist across container restarts and scaling events. Container storage solutions like *Kubernetes Persistent Volumes* provide this capability, allowing the shopping cart service to maintain state while benefiting from containerization's flexibility.

Modern container storage solutions also offer features like storage classes, which allow different types of storage to be provisioned based on application requirements. For example, our high-performance price calculation service might use premium storage with guaranteed IOPS, while less critical services use standard storage options.

Serverless storage options

The adoption of serverless computing in our platform introduces unique storage challenges. Serverless functions need quick access to data, but traditional storage approaches might introduce too much latency.

For example, our product recommendation service uses serverless functions to generate personalized recommendations. These functions need rapid access to user preference data and product information. Serverless-optimized storage solutions like *Amazon Aurora Serverless* or *DynamoDB* provide the necessary performance characteristics while maintaining cost efficiency through automatic scaling.

Edge storage solutions

With the growing importance of edge computing, our platform needs to manage data effectively at the edge. Edge storage solutions help reduce latency and bandwidth usage while maintaining data consistency.

Consider our inventory management system. When a customer checks product availability at a specific store, the request is handled by an edge location close to them. Edge storage solutions allow us to maintain a local cache of inventory data, updated periodically from the central system. This approach provides fast response times while managing the eventual consistency of inventory data.

Hybrid storage architectures

Many enterprises require a combination of storage solutions to meet various business requirements. Our platform employs a hybrid storage architecture that combines the benefits of different storage approaches.

For instance, our customer data management system might store sensitive personal information in on-premises databases for compliance reasons, while keeping fewer sensitive data in cloud storage. Product catalog data might be distributed across edge locations for performance, while maintaining a central source of truth in the cloud.

The hybrid approach allows us to optimize for different requirements, as follows:

- Regulatory compliance for customer data
- Performance for frequently accessed product information
- Cost efficiency for historical transaction records
- Global availability for marketing content

This hybrid model requires sophisticated data synchronization and consistency management, but provides the flexibility needed to meet diverse business requirements while maintaining system reliability and performance.

The following table provides the summary:

Storage type	Primary usage	Technologies	Strengths	Trade-off
Cloud object storage	Static assets	S3, Cloud Storage	Infinite scale	Higher latency
Distributed file systems	Shared operational files	EFS, GlusterFS	Strong consistency	Complex management
Container storage	Stateful containers	Kubernetes PVs	Ephemeral persistence	Storage class tuning
Serverless storage	Event-driven workloads	DynamoDB, Aurora Serverless	Auto-scaling	Cost of large storage
Edge storage	Low-latency access	Redis Edge, LocalDB	Sub-50ms responses	Consistency delays
Hybrid architecture	Compliance/ performance	AWS Storage Gateway	Flexibility	Sync complexity

Table 9.1: Mixing solutions

The table above shows how we mix solutions based on the following:
- Access patterns (random vs. sequential)
- Consistency needs (strong vs. eventual)
- Scale requirements (predictable vs. spiky)

Always test your storage choices with real-world failure scenarios, a solution that works during peak sales might crumble under network partitions!

Modern storage solutions continue to evolve, with new technologies emerging to address specific challenges in distributed systems. The key to success lies in choosing the right combination of storage solutions based on careful analysis of business requirements, performance needs, and operational constraints.

Conclusion

Data storage in distributed systems represents a complex interplay of various strategies, technologies, and trade-offs. Through our examination of an ecommerce platform, we've seen how different storage solutions serve distinct needs within the same system. From handling millions of product images in cloud storage to managing critical transaction data in relational databases, each storage solution plays a vital role in the overall architecture.

The key lesson is that no single storage solution can effectively address all requirements in a modern distributed system. Success lies in carefully choosing and combining different storage approaches based on specific use cases, access patterns, and business requirements. Whether it's using object storage for product images, distributed file systems for operational documents, or specialized databases for different data types, each choice must be made with careful consideration of factors like consistency requirements, performance needs, and operational constraints. As distributed systems continue to evolve, storage strategies must adapt to new challenges and opportunities. The emergence of edge computing, serverless architectures, and increasingly stringent data privacy requirements will continue to shape how we approach data storage. Organizations must remain flexible and ready to embrace new storage technologies while maintaining the reliability and performance their applications require.

In the next chapter, we will look at observability and operational readiness. As systems grow bigger, they have to mature in various dimensions. One part of that evolution is creating a feedback system which measure the system's various sub systems. Once we know how the system is doing only then can we create ways to react to those situations.

Join our book's Discord space

Join the book's Discord Workspace for Latest updates, Offers, Tech happenings around the world, New Release and Sessions with the Authors:

https://discord.bpbonline.com

CHAPTER 10

Observability and Operational Readiness

Introduction

In today's digital landscape, where microseconds can mean the difference between a completed purchase and an abandoned cart, understanding system behavior is not just an operational necessity, it is a business imperative. Take a typical ecommerce platform at any given moment, thousands of customers might be browsing products, adding items to their carts, or completing purchases. Each of these actions generates a cascade of events across multiple services. A single checkout process involves the coordination of inventory management, payment processing, shipping calculations, and customer notification services. In this chapter, we will try to find ways to ensure the above-mentioned components work together seamlessly. We will try to explore ways to detect and resolve issues before they impact customers. This is where observability comes into play.

Observability is fundamentally different from traditional monitoring. While monitoring tells us whether a system is working, observability helps us understand why it might not be working. Consider the difference between knowing that a checkout service is slow (monitoring) and understanding that it is slow because a recent database index change has caused query performance to degrade under specific conditions (observability).

Let us examine a scenario in an ecommerce platform. When customers experience occasional payment failures, traditional monitoring might show that all services are up and basic health checks are passing. However, with proper observability in place, engineers can trace the customer's journey through the system and discover that under specific conditions. When inventory checks coincide with a promotional price update, a race condition might cause the payment service to receive outdated price information, leading to transaction failures.

Structure

The chapter covers the following topics:

- Pillars of observability
- Operational readiness
- Observability platforms
- Cloud provider solutions
- Future trends in observability

Objectives

By the end of this chapter, readers will have a comprehensive understanding of observability and operational readiness in modern distributed systems. Through practical examples centered around an ecommerce platform, readers will learn how to implement effective observability strategies, understand the three pillars of observability (logs, metrics, and traces), and develop robust operational practices. The book bridges the gap between theoretical knowledge and practical implementation, helping readers grasp complex concepts through real-world scenarios. Whether you are an engineer, architect, or technical leader, you will learn how to design and maintain reliable distributed systems, implement effective monitoring strategies, and build resilient operations teams. By the end of this book, you will have the knowledge and tools needed to implement comprehensive observability solutions and ensure your distributed systems operate reliably at scale.

Pillars of observability

Modern observability rests on three fundamental pillars, that is, logs, metrics, and traces. Each plays a crucial role in understanding system behavior, but their true power emerges when they work together to provide a complete picture of system health and performance.

Logs

Logs are the most basic and essential form of observability data. They provide a detailed record of events occurring within the system. However, in a distributed system, logging requires careful thought and planning. It is not enough to simply write messages to a file, organizations need structured, searchable, and contextually rich log data that can help understand system behavior across service boundaries.

In an ecommerce platform, consider how logging might be handled for the order processing flow. When a customer places an order, multiple services are involved as follows:

- The order service initiates the process and generates an order ID
- The inventory service checks and reserves stock
- The payment service processes the payment
- The shipping service calculates delivery options
- The notification service sends confirmation emails

Each service generates its own logs but without proper correlation these separate log streams tell only part of the story. This is where structured logging and correlation IDs become crucial. Every log entry related to a specific order should contain the following:

- The order ID
- The customer ID
- The service name
- The operation being performed
- The outcome (success/failure)
- Any relevant business context (order value, items, shipping method)

By including this structured information in the logs, teams can later reconstruct the entire order flow and understand exactly what happened at each step. For instance, if a customer reports an issue with their order, support teams can search for their order ID and see the complete sequence of events across all services.

Advanced logging techniques

When building distributed systems like an ecommerce platform, basic logging often falls short. Organizations need sophisticated techniques to track requests as they flow through multiple services and maintain contextual information throughout the entire transaction lifecycle.

Mapped Diagnostic Context

Mapped Diagnostic Context (MDC) is a powerful mechanism for enriching log entries with contextual information that persists across multiple service calls. Think of MDC as a thread-local map that carries important contextual data throughout a request's lifecycle. In an ecommerce platform, this becomes crucial for understanding customer journeys and troubleshooting issues.

Consider a customer placing an order, as soon as they initiate the checkout process, key contextual information can be established and tracked across all services, as follows:

```
[2024-02-15   10:15:32]   [INFO]   [OrderService]   [Transaction:T123456]
[CustomerID:C789] [SessionID:S456]
```

```
Starting checkout process for cart total: $156.89
```

```
[2024-02-15  10:15:32]  [INFO]  [InventoryService]  [Transaction:T123456]
[CustomerID:C789] [SessionID:S456]
Checking inventory for SKU: PROD-123, Quantity: 2
```

```
[2024-02-15  10:15:33]  [INFO]  [PaymentService]  [Transaction:T123456]
[CustomerID:C789] [SessionID:S456]
Initiating payment processing for amount: $156.89
```

Without MDC, debugging issues across service boundaries becomes a complex puzzle trying to correlate different log entries. With MDC, engineers can easily trace the entire transaction flow by searching for a single transaction ID.

Context propagation in distributed systems

In a distributed system, maintaining context across service boundaries requires careful consideration.

Following is how it can be implemented in an ecommerce platform:

- **Request initiation**: When a customer starts the checkout process, the `OrderService` creates a transaction context containing the following:
  - Transaction ID
  - Customer ID
  - Session ID
  - Request timestamp
  - Origin (web/mobile app)

- **Inter-service communication**: As the request flows to other services, context propagation occurs through, as follows:
  - HTTP headers for synchronous REST calls
  - Message metadata for asynchronous events
  - Database transaction context for data operations

- **Async processing**: For background jobs and event processing, context preservation requires, as follows:
  - Event messages carrying the original transaction context
  - Background jobs maintaining correlation with the original request
  - Retry mechanisms preserving the original context

This consistent context helps teams understand complex scenarios. For example, if a customer reports that their order confirmation email arrived late, the trace will be as follows:

```
10:15:32.120 - Order Service receives order submission
10:15:32.350 - Payment Service initiates transaction
10:15:32.355 - Notification Service queues confirmation email
10:15:32.890 - Notification Service sends email
10:15:33.100 - Payment Service receives bank approval
```

Such traces might reveal that the notification service triggered too early in the process, leading engineers to modify the event sequencing to ensure confirmation emails are only sent after payment confirmation.

Metrics

The second crucial pillar of observability is metrics collection and analysis. Unlike logs, which provide detailed information about specific events, metrics offer quantifiable measurements of system behavior over time. These measurements help teams understand trends, identify patterns, and make data-driven decisions about system optimization and capacity planning.

Understanding business metrics

In an e-commerce platform, business metrics can provide direct insight into operational health. Consider the checkout process: thousands of customers move through various stages of purchasing daily from adding items to their cart to completing payment. By tracking conversion rates at each step, teams can gain valuable insights into customer behavior and potential system issues.

For example, during flash sale events, metrics might reveal that while overall traffic increases by 300%, the checkout completion rate drops from 70% to 45%. Further investigation might show that customers experience payment processing delays during peak periods. Such metrics can help identify not just the existence of a problem, but its precise scope and impact on the business.

Figure 10.1 illustrates this visually:

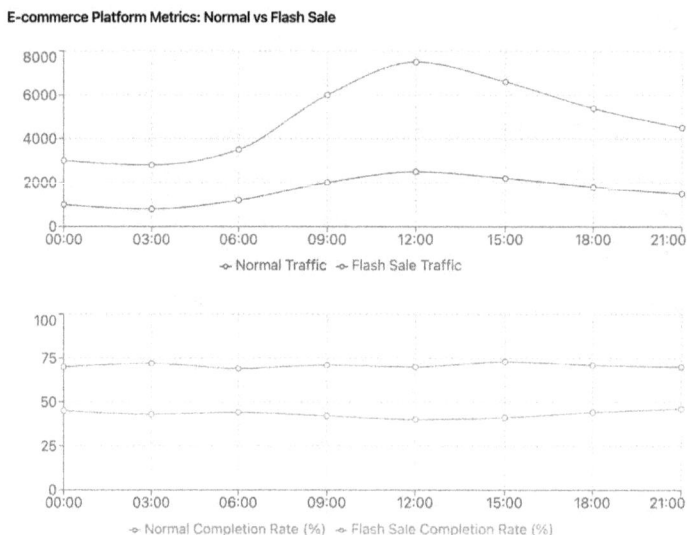

E-commerce Platform Metrics: Normal vs Flash Sale

Figure 10.1: *Illustration of overall traffic spikes (top) and corresponding completion rate (bottom)*

This visualization helps identify several insights, as follows:

- Inverse relationship between traffic volume and completion rates during flash sales

- Consistency of normal operations versus the strain during peak events

- Specific times when the system experiences the most stress, which can help in capacity planning

These insights in turn can help teams plan infrastructure for their scaling needs, identify optimal times for the flash sales, set realistic performance targets and justify infrastructure investments.

Infrastructure metrics

Infrastructure metrics reveal how system resources perform under load. In a product catalog service handling millions of requests daily, teams typically track the following:

- CPU utilization
- Memory usage
- Network statistics (packet loss, no of hops, DNS resolution time, round trip time)
- Disk I/O
- Cache hit rates

These raw numbers become meaningful when correlated with business events. For instance, a spike in CPU usage during a promotional event might indicate the need for improved caching strategies or automatic scaling configurations.

Application performance metrics

Application metrics bridge the gap between infrastructure and business metrics, helping teams understand how software behaves in production.

For an order processing service, key metrics include the following:

- Request latency
- Error rates
- Throughput
- Queue depths
- Transaction success rates

These metrics can help identify subtle performance issues. For example, metrics might reveal that orders from European customers take 40% longer to process during evening hours in the US. Analysis might show correlation with increased latency in the tax calculation service during European peak hours, leading to implementation of regional caching for tax rates.

Response time analysis

Response time analysis is critical for understanding user experience. In an ecommerce platform, the checkout process involves several operations, as follows:

- Payment validation
- Inventory check
- Order creation
- Confirmation email dispatch

Detailed metrics might reveal that while most steps complete quickly, inventory checks occasionally take up to two seconds during peak hours. This insight helps teams prioritize optimization efforts where they would have the most impact.

Cache performance monitoring

Cache performance significantly impacts both system efficiency and user experience. A product catalog service might rely heavily on caching to handle millions of requests daily. Key metrics to monitor include the following:

- Cache hit rates
- Eviction rates
- Cache size
- Cache latency
- Memory usage

Consider the following scenario:

Metrics show that product image cache hit rates drop dramatically every morning at 4 AM EST. Investigation reveals that daily product catalog updates invalidate the entire cache, causing slow page loads for early morning shoppers. The solution might involve implementing a more granular cache invalidation strategy to maintain a steady 95% hit rate throughout the day.

Service level objectives

Metrics form the foundation of **service level objectives** (**SLO**). For a checkout service, organizations might maintain SLO of 99.95% availability and require that 99% of transactions complete within three seconds. These numbers should not be arbitrary, they should be based on careful analysis of metrics and their correlation with business outcomes.

When SLO metrics trend towards their thresholds, teams can take proactive action. For instance, if payment processing time starts trending upward and approaching the three-second thresholds, metrics might reveal that the slowdown correlates with increased traffic from mobile devices. This insight could lead to optimization of the payment processing workflow specifically for mobile users.

Tracing

Distributed tracing provides the crucial ability to follow a single customer interaction as it flows through various services. While logs tell us what happened and metrics tell us how well it happened, traces show exactly how a request traverses the distributed system.

Understanding request flow

Consider a typical scenario in an ecommerce platform, that is, a customer placing an order during a flash sale. What appears to the customer as a single **Place Order** action triggers a complex sequence of interactions across multiple services.

Following is how tracing helps understand this flow:

When a customer clicks on **Place Order** for a limited-edition item, the tracing system begins tracking the request's journey. The trace might show that their order touches seven different services, as follows:

- Order service
- Inventory service
- Pricing service
- Payment service
- Fraud detection service

- Shipping service
- Notification service

Each interaction is recorded with timing information and contextual data.

A trace might reveal an interesting pattern as follows:

Some orders take five seconds longer than others to complete. Analysis of trace data could show that these delayed orders share a common characteristic, that is, they are being routed through a particular instance of the fraud detection service experiencing higher latency due to a degraded database connection. Without distributed tracing, such subtle correlations would be nearly impossible to detect.

Trace correlation and context propagation

One of the most challenging aspects of distributed tracing is maintaining context as requests move between services. Context propagation can be implemented through the following:

- Trace headers for synchronous REST calls
- Message metadata for asynchronous events
- Database transaction context for data operations

Consider the following scenario:

A customer reports that their order confirmation email arrived before their payment was processed. Trace analysis might reveal the following:

```
10:15:32.120 - Order Service receives order submission
10:15:32.350 - Payment Service initiates transaction
10:15:32.355 - Notification Service queues confirmation email
10:15:32.890 - Notification Service sends email
10:15:33.100 - Payment Service receives bank approval
```

The trace reveals incorrect event sequencing, indicating a need to modify the notification service timing logic.

Root cause analysis using traces

When issues occur in a distributed system, finding the root cause can be challenging. Traces make this process more manageable.

Consider the following scenario:

During a promotional period, customers report intermittent failures when applying discount codes. Initial investigation of logs and metrics might show no obvious issues, all services appear to be functioning normally. However, examination of traces from failed transactions could reveal a pattern:

Requests taking more than 100ms to validate inventory consistently fail when reaching the pricing service. Further investigation might reveal an overly aggressive circuit breaker configuration, timing out requests that take longer than expected to check inventory. The solution might involve adjusting the circuit breaker timeout threshold to accommodate occasional slower inventory checks during high-traffic periods.

Sampling strategies in production

While comprehensive tracing provides invaluable insights, tracing every request in a high-volume production environment would be prohibitively expensive. An effective sampling strategy will be as follows:

- **Normal operations**: 5% of all requests
- **Anomaly detection**: Increased sampling (up to 25%) for affected request types
- **Critical workflows (checkout)**: 10% base sampling rate
- **Holiday season**: Temporary increase to 15% for important customer interactions

Performance analysis through traces

Traces provide unique insights into performance optimization opportunities. For example, trace data might reveal that a product detail page makes three separate calls to the inventory service, as follows:

- Stock level check
- Warehouse location lookup
- Shipping estimate calculation

By consolidating these into a single API call, page load time could be reduced significantly.

Operational readiness

Operational readiness in modern distributed systems goes far beyond having the right monitoring tools in place. It encompasses the entire approach to running production systems reliably, safely, and efficiently. While monitoring tells us what is happening in our systems, operational readiness ensures we are prepared to handle whatever situations arise, whether they are planned changes or unexpected incidents.

Release management and deployment readiness

The journey of a new feature or system change from development to production is fraught with potential risks, particularly in distributed systems where components are interconnected in complex ways. Consider the introduction of a new payment gateway in an ecommerce platform. While it might seem like a straightforward integration on the surface, its implications ripple throughout the entire system.

A well-prepared organization approaches such changes with a comprehensive release management strategy. This begins with a thorough impact analysis that considers not just the technical changes but their business implications as well. For a payment gateway integration, this means understanding how the change affects the entire purchase flow, from the moment a customer enters their payment information to when they receive their order confirmation.

The deployment strategy itself should be built around the principle of risk minimization. Rather than releasing changes to all users simultaneously, organizations often employ sophisticated deployment patterns. A common approach is to begin with internal testing, followed by a small percentage of real users, often called a canary deployment, gradually increasing the deployment scope as confidence builds. This approach allows teams to catch potential issues early when their impact is limited.

For instance, a payment gateway deployment might follow this progression:

First, the new gateway processes test transactions in a production environment, allowing teams to verify integration points and monitoring systems. Next, perhaps 5% of real transactions from a specific geographic region route through the new gateway. This limited exposure provides real-world validation while containing risk. As performance metrics and error rates prove satisfactory, the traffic percentage gradually increases, with careful monitoring at each stage.

Deployment readiness extends beyond the technical implementation. Teams need to prepare comprehensive rollback procedures, establish enhanced monitoring specific to the new functionality, and ensure support teams are properly staffed and trained. Documentation needs to be updated, and customer service teams need to be briefed on potential issues and their resolutions.

Building and maintaining runbooks

Runbooks serve as the operational foundation of any production system but their effectiveness lies in how they are created and maintained. Rather than dry and procedural documents, effective runbooks tell a story of how to handle various operational scenarios. They should be living documents that evolve based on real-world experience and lessons learned.

Take the example of database failover procedures. A good runbook does not just list steps to execute; it provides context for decisions and helps operators understand the implications of their actions. It might explain why checking replication lag is crucial before initiating failover, or how to interpret various error scenarios they might encounter.

The most valuable runbooks often emerge from actual incidents. When a team handles a production issue, the experience should be captured and transformed into operational guidance. This will include the following:

- Initial incident assessment guidelines that help teams quickly understand the scope and severity of problems
- Decision frameworks that help operators make confident choices under pressure
- Clear, tested procedures that have proven effective in real situations
- Validation steps that confirm the success of operations
- Recovery procedures that ensure systems return to their normal state

These documents should acknowledge the complexity of distributed systems while providing clear guidance. For example, a database failover runbook might explain how the process affects different services differently, perhaps the product catalog service can handle a brief interruption, while the checkout service requires special handling to prevent lost transactions.

Critical metrics and monitoring implementation

The transition from development to production requires a shift in thinking about what matters most. While development environments focus on functionality, production systems demand a deeper understanding of performance, reliability, and business impact. This understanding comes from carefully chosen metrics that tell the story of system health and business success.

Consider how different metrics interrelate in an ecommerce platform. Technical metrics like response times and error rates directly impact business metrics like conversion rates and average order value. A sophisticated monitoring implementation connects these dots, helping teams understand how technical performance affects business outcomes.

For instance, during a flash sale event, teams might monitor not just server response times, but how those times correlate with cart abandonment rates. This correlation helps establish concrete performance targets perhaps discovering that when page load times exceed three seconds, cart abandonment rates increase significantly.

Observability platforms

Understanding and selecting the right observability tools is crucial for maintaining visibility into distributed systems. Let us explore how different platforms serve various observability needs, using the ecommerce platform as a context for understanding their capabilities.

Prometheus

Prometheus has emerged as the de facto standard for metrics collection in distributed systems, particularly in cloud-native environments. At its core, Prometheus employs a pull-based architecture where it scrapes metrics from configured targets at regular intervals.

This approach provides reliable metrics collection even in highly dynamic environments where services come and go frequently.

Prometheus excels at collecting and storing time-series data from various components of the system. Its multi-dimensional data model allows us to label metrics in ways that make sense for the business context, we can tag metrics by service name, environment, region, or any other relevant dimension. This flexibility is particularly valuable when we need to analyze performance patterns across different aspects of the platform.

The real power of Prometheus lies in PromQL, its query language. Unlike traditional monitoring systems that provide basic aggregation capabilities, PromQL allows for sophisticated analysis of metrics data. This becomes invaluable when we need to understand complex patterns in the system's behavior, such as correlating increased latency with specific customer segments or geographic regions.

Prometheus's architecture is designed for reliability and scalability. It maintains a local time-series database, which means it continues collecting metrics even if other parts of the monitoring system fail. This local storage also enables fast query performance, which is crucial when investigating ongoing incidents.

However, Prometheus does have its limitations. Its pull-based model means that ephemeral metrics might be missed if they occur between scrape intervals. The local storage, while excellent for recent data, isn't designed for long-term metrics retention. Organizations typically address these limitations by complementing Prometheus with other tools for long-term storage and analysis.

Elastic Stack

The Elastic Stack, comprising **Elasticsearch, Logstash, and Kibana** (**ELK**), provides a comprehensive solution for log management and analysis in distributed systems. Unlike metrics which give us quantitative measures of system behavior, logs provide the narrative, the detailed story of what is happening within the system.

Elasticsearch's strength lies in its powerful full-text search capabilities combined with its ability to handle structured and unstructured data at scale. Its distributed nature aligns well with modern system architectures, allowing it to scale horizontally as log volumes grow. The schema-less nature of Elasticsearch is particularly valuable in evolving systems where log formats might change as new features are added or services are modified.

Logstash serves as a powerful data processing pipeline. It can ingest data from multiple sources, transform it into a consistent format, and enrich it with additional context before indexing in Elasticsearch. This capability is crucial in distributed systems where logs come from various sources in different formats.

Kibana completes the stack by providing visualization and analysis capabilities. Its strength lies in making complex log data accessible and understandable, enabling both technical and non-technical users to gain insights from log data. The ability to create custom dashboards that combine different types of visualizations helps bridge the gap between technical metrics and business insights.

Datadog

Datadog represents a shift in how we think about observability platforms, offering a unified approach to monitoring distributed systems. Unlike specialized tools that focus on specific aspects of observability, Datadog provides a comprehensive view across infrastructure, applications, and user experience. This unified approach becomes increasingly valuable as systems grow more complex and the boundaries between different layers of the technology stack blur.

At its foundation, Datadog's architecture is built for scale and flexibility. The platform ingests data from multiple sources simultaneously infrastructure metrics, application traces, logs, and user experience data and correlates this information automatically. This correlation capability is particularly valuable in distributed systems where a single user interaction might touch dozens of services and infrastructure components.

One of Datadog's key strengths lies in its automated service discovery and mapping. In dynamic environments where services are constantly being deployed, updated, and scaled, maintaining an accurate view of system topology is challenging. Datadog automatically discovers services and their dependencies, creating and updating service maps that reflect the current state of the system.

The platform's approach to data retention and aggregation is sophisticated, automatically balancing granularity with storage efficiency. Recent data is preserved at full fidelity for detailed analysis, while historical data is intelligently aggregated to maintain long-term trends without overwhelming storage resources.

New Relic

New Relic has evolved from an application performance monitoring tool into a comprehensive observability platform, but its strength in application performance monitoring remains a distinguishing feature. The platform's approach to understanding application behavior goes beyond simple metrics collection, providing deep insights into how code execution affects user experience.

What sets New Relic apart is its focus on connecting technical performance metrics to business outcomes. The platform's architecture is designed to maintain context across different types of telemetry data. This contextual awareness enables organizations to understand not just that performance degraded, but how that degradation impacts business metrics.

New Relic's approach to distributed tracing deserves special mention, rather than treating traces as isolated technical artifacts, the platform correlates trace data with other telemetry data to provide a complete picture of system behavior. This correlation helps organizations understand the full impact of performance issues across their distributed system.

The platform's data modeling is particularly sophisticated, enabling complex analysis without requiring deep expertise in query languages or data structures. This democratization of observability data makes it accessible to a broader range of stakeholders within an organization.

Jaeger

Jaeger represents a specialized approach to distributed tracing, focusing exclusively on providing deep visibility into request flows across distributed systems. Originally developed by *Uber* and now a *Cloud Native Computing Foundation* graduated project, Jaeger's architecture is specifically designed for large-scale distributed trace collection and analysis.

What distinguishes Jaeger is its approach to trace sampling and storage rather than attempting to collect every trace, which would be prohibitively expensive in large-scale systems, Jaeger implements sophisticated sampling strategies. These strategies can be dynamically adjusted based on current system behavior and specific analysis needs.

Jaeger's architecture is built around the OpenTelemetry standard, making it highly interoperable with other observability tools and platforms. This standardization is particularly important in distributed systems where different components might be instrumented with different tools.

The platform's approach to trace visualization and analysis is also noteworthy. Rather than simply displaying timing data, Jaeger provides tools for understanding causal relationships between services and identifying patterns in system behavior. This capability is crucial for understanding complex interactions in distributed systems.

Cloud provider solutions

The landscape of observability has been significantly influenced by cloud providers' native monitoring solutions. Unlike third-party tools that need to adapt to different cloud environments, native solutions like AWS CloudWatch, Google Cloud Operations (formerly Stackdriver), and Azure Monitor are deeply integrated with their respective platforms.

Let us explore how these native solutions contribute to the observability strategy.

Understanding cloud-native observability

Cloud provider observability solutions offer a unique advantage, that is, deep integration with the platform's infrastructure and services. This integration provides visibility that external tools cannot easily replicate. Imagine trying to understand the behavior of a

Lambda function or the internal workings of a managed Kubernetes, cluster cloud-native tools have access to metrics and insights that are not exposed to external monitoring systems.

Consider how this manifest in practice. When an application spans multiple cloud services, that is, compute, storage, messaging, and databases, cloud provider tools can automatically correlate events and metrics across these services. This native understanding of service relationships provides context that would be difficult or impossible to reconstruct from external monitoring.

Power of platform integration

Cloud providers' observability solutions shine in their ability to understand platform-specific behaviors and patterns. Take auto-scaling events, for instance. While external tools can observe the results of scaling actions, native tools understand the decision-making process behind these actions. They can show us not just that scaling occurred but we have to know why it occurred, including the specific metrics and thresholds that triggered the scaling decision.

This integration extends to cost monitoring as well. Cloud-native observability tools can directly correlate system behavior with its cost implications. When a service-experiences increased load, these tools can show both the performance impact and the associated cost increase, enabling better capacity planning and cost optimization decisions.

Beyond basic monitoring

Modern cloud provider observability solutions have evolved far beyond simple resource monitoring. They now offer sophisticated capabilities, as follows:

- **Automated anomaly detection**: Using machine learning models trained on vast amounts of operational data, these systems can identify unusual patterns that might indicate emerging issues.

- **Predictive analytics**: By analyzing historical patterns, cloud-native tools can predict future resource needs and potential performance issues before they impact users.

- **Security integration**: Native observability tools integrate deeply with the cloud provider's security services, providing visibility into security-related events and their impact on system behavior.

Zipkin

Zipkin, originally developed by *Twitter*, brings a different philosophy to distributed tracing. While Jaeger focuses on enterprise-scale deployments, Zipkin's strength lies in its simplicity and lightweight approach to tracing distributed systems. This simplicity makes it particularly appealing for organizations starting their observability journey or those preferring a more focused tool over comprehensive platform.

At its core, Zipkin's architecture reflects its roots in Twitter's microservices environment. The platform thinks about distributed traces as a collection of spans, logical units of work that together form a complete request path through the system. This model is particularly intuitive for developers new to distributed tracing, making it easier to understand how requests flow through their services.

What sets Zipkin apart is its approach to trace collection and storage rather than implementing complex sampling strategies upfront, Zipkin provides simple, configurable sampling rates that can be adjusted based on traffic volumes. This straightforward approach makes it easier for teams to start with distributed tracing and gradually refine their sampling strategies as they better understand their needs.

Zipkin's visualization approach deserves special mention. Instead of attempting to provide comprehensive system analytics, it focuses on making trace data easily understandable. Its UI is designed to answer specific questions about request flow: Where did the request spend most of its time? Which service dependencies were involved? What caused the latency in this particular request? This focused approach helps teams quickly identify and resolve performance bottlenecks.

Another strength of Zipkin lies in its extensive language support and integration capabilities. The platform provides libraries for most popular programming languages and frameworks, making it relatively straightforward to add tracing to existing applications. This broad support means organizations can gradually roll out tracing across their services without needing to modify their technology stack significantly.

Integration with the broader observability ecosystem is also a key consideration in Zipkin's design. The platform supports the OpenTelemetry standard, allowing organizations to use Zipkin alongside other observability tools. This interoperability ensures that investing in Zipkin does not lock organizations into a particular vendor or tool chain.

However, what truly distinguishes Zipkin is its community-driven development model. As an open-source project, its feature set and development priorities are shaped by real-world use cases from its user community. This has led to practical features that address common challenges in distributed tracing, rather than trying to be a comprehensive observability platform.

Multi-cloud challenge

However, the strength of native integration becomes a challenge in multi-cloud environments. Each cloud provider's observability solution is optimized for its own platform, leading to potential fragmentation in observability data and practices. Organizations running multi-cloud architectures often need to either maintain multiple observability systems or implement additional tools to provide a unified view.

This challenge has led to interesting architectural patterns. Some organizations use cloud-native tools for deep platform-specific insights while maintaining a separate, unified observability layer for cross-cloud visibility. Others leverage emerging standards like OpenTelemetry to create consistency across different cloud environments.

Evolution of cloud observability

Cloud provider observability solutions continue to evolve rapidly. The trend is moving toward more integrated, intelligent platforms that can not only collect and display data but also provide actionable insights and automated responses. We are seeing the emergence of AIOps capabilities, where machine learning is applied to observability data to identify patterns and predict potential issues.

The future of cloud-native observability likely lies in the convergence of monitoring, logging, and tracing capabilities with artificial intelligence and machine learning. This convergence promises to transform observability from a reactive tool into a proactive system that can predict and prevent issues before they impact users.

Future trends in observability

As distributed systems continue to grow in complexity, the field of observability is evolving rapidly to meet new challenges.

Let us explore the emerging trends that are shaping the future of how we understand and monitor the systems.

Rise of AI-enhanced observability

Artificial intelligence and machine learning are transforming how we approach system observability. Traditional rule-based monitoring, while still valuable, is giving way to more sophisticated approaches that can handle the complexity of modern distributed systems.

Consider how anomaly detection is evolving. In traditional systems, we might set static thresholds for metrics like response time or error rates. In a complex distributed system, what constitutes normal behavior can vary significantly based on numerous factors. AI-powered observability systems can learn these patterns and identify subtle anomalies that traditional approaches would miss.

For instance, an AI system might notice that while overall system load is within normal ranges, the pattern of service interactions has changed in a way that historically preceded system failures. This predictive capability allows teams to address potential issues before they impact users.

Observability as code

The concept of **as code** has revolutionized infrastructure and deployment practices, and observability is following suit, rather than treating monitoring and observability as an afterthought, organizations are beginning to define their observability requirements alongside their application code.

This shift means that observability configurations: what to monitor, how to alert, and what constitutes healthy behavior are version controlled, tested, and deployed alongside the application itself. When a new service is deployed, its observability requirements are automatically implemented, ensuring consistent monitoring across the system.

Context aware observability

The future of observability lies in understanding context. Modern systems are moving beyond simple metric collection toward understanding the business context of system behavior. This trend is particularly evident in how observability systems are beginning to correlate technical metrics with business outcomes.

Consider a scenario where an observability system does not just tell you that a service is experiencing increased latency but also understands and communicates the business impact, such a system can predict how many orders are at risk for a commerce platform or which customer segments are affected. These systems can predict what revenue impact to expect if the trend continues.

OpenTelemetry and standardization

The observability landscape is moving toward standardization through initiatives like OpenTelemetry. This standardization is crucial for the future of observability, as it allows organizations to instrument their applications once and use that instrumentation with multiple observability platforms.

This trend is particularly important as systems become more distributed and complex. Standardized instrumentation means that organizations can change or upgrade their observability tools without requiring massive re-instrumentation efforts.

Conclusion

Observability and operational readiness in distributed systems represent more than just technical implementations. They embody a philosophy of proactive system management and deep understanding. Throughout this book, we explored how modern distributed systems require a sophisticated approach to monitoring, troubleshooting, and maintenance, using an ecommerce platform to illustrate these concepts in practical terms.

The journey from basic monitoring to comprehensive observability reveals the evolution of our industry's approach to managing complex systems. We have seen how logs, metrics, and traces work together to provide a complete picture of system behavior, and how modern observability platforms enable teams to derive actionable insights from vast amounts of telemetry data.

The key takeaway is that observability is not just about collecting data, it is about understanding systems deeply enough to make informed decisions, predict potential issues, and maintain reliable operations at scale. As distributed systems continue to grow in complexity, the principles and practices discussed in this book become increasingly crucial for organizations aiming to deliver reliable, performant services to their users.

Remember, the journey to operational excellence is continuous. The tools and practices will evolve, but the fundamental principles of understanding system behavior, preparing for failures, and maintaining operational readiness will remain essential for building and operating successful distributed systems.

In the next chapter, we will look at distributed caching and how distributed systems could leverage low latency temporary data storage for ensuring customers/users see a much better user experience and intuitive systems.

Join our book's Discord space

Join the book's Discord Workspace for Latest updates, Offers, Tech happenings around the world, New Release and Sessions with the Authors:

https://discord.bpbonline.com

CHAPTER 11
Distributed Caching

Introduction

In the fast-paced world of modern e-commerce, every millisecond matters. Imagine you are shopping on your favorite online store during a flash sale. Along with millions of other shoppers, you are browsing products, adding items to your cart, and racing to checkout. Behind the scenes, a complex distributed system is working tirelessly to ensure your experience remains smooth and responsive. At the heart of this system lies one of the most crucial yet often misunderstood components, that is, distributed caching.

Just as a well-organized store keeps its most popular items within easy reach rather than in a distant warehouse, distributed caching brings frequently accessed data closer to where it is needed. In this chapter we will look at how distributed systems are built, what they can help solve and what are their challenges.

Structure

The chapter covers the following topics:
- Understanding distributed caching
- Caching strategies in distributed systems
- Building caching hierarchy
- Cache eviction

- Maintaining cache consistency
- Common pitfalls and solutions
- Monitoring and optimization
- Real-world applications

Objectives

By the end of this chapter, readers will be equipped with both theoretical knowledge and practical insights into distributed caching systems. Using a large-scale e-commerce platform as our running example, we will explore how different caching strategies can be implemented to solve real-world performance and scalability challenges. You will learn to identify when and where to implement caching in your distributed architecture, understand the trade-offs between different caching strategies, and recognize common pitfalls that can turn your caching solution from a performance boost into a system bottleneck.

By the end of this chapter, you will be able to design caching hierarchies that balance speed with consistency, implement appropriate eviction policies, and monitor cache performance effectively. Whether you are building a new distributed system or optimizing an existing one, the principles and patterns discussed here will help you make informed decisions about your caching strategy. While we explore how different caching strategies can solve real-world performance and scalability challenges we will also navigate their inherent trade-offs.

Understanding distributed caching

A distributed cache is a system that stores data across multiple computers or servers, allowing for faster access to data. A distributed cache pools the RAM of multiple computers into a single data store. The data is stored in RAM, which is faster than a hard drive. Each cache key is assigned to a specific shard, or partition. If a node fails, the cache system can retrieve the data from another node.

Figure 11.1 illustrates a distributed cache-based architecture:

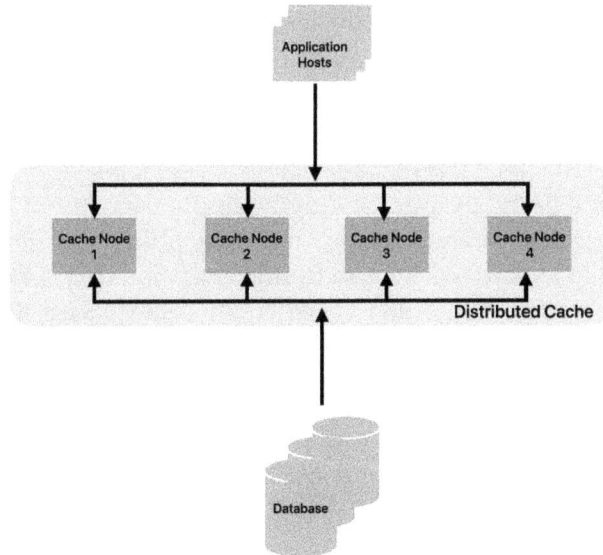

Figure 11.1: Illustration of a distributed cache-based system

Now, let us try to understand from a business use case. Consider a bustling e-commerce platform during a major sale event. Every second, thousands of customers are browsing products, checking prices, and making purchases. Each of these actions requires data, that is, product details, inventory levels, user preferences, shopping cart contents. Without caching, each request would need to traverse the network to reach a database, retrieve the information, and return it to the user.

Evolution of caching systems

The journey of caching systems mirrors the evolution of distributed computing itself. Early applications used simple in-memory caches within single servers. As applications grew and distributed architectures became prevalent, new challenges emerged, as follows:

```
Single Server Era:
Application -> Local Cache -> Database


Modern Distributed Era:
User Request -> Load Balancer -> Application Servers -> Distributed Cache
Layer -> Database Cluster
```

Let us examine how a modern e-commerce platform utilizes caching at different levels, as follows:

- **Browser cache**: Product images and static content
- **CDN cache**: Static assets and frequently accessed pages
- **Application cache (L1)**: Session data and application-specific information

- **Distributed cache (L2)**: Product details, inventory levels, user profiles
- **Database cache**: Frequently accessed query results

Core concepts of a cache

The core concepts of a cache include: storing a temporary copy of frequently accessed data from a slower source to enable faster retrieval, utilizing a limited storage space, employing a key-based lookup mechanism to efficiently find data, implementing eviction policies to manage when to remove old data when the cache fills up, and maintaining data consistency with the original source through strategies like write-through or write-back; essentially, a cache prioritizes speed by sacrificing some capacity to avoid repeated access to slower storage layers.

Caching strategies in distributed systems

Let us explore how different caching strategies apply to our e-commerce platform. Imagine you are building a product catalog service that needs to handle millions of requests per day while maintaining sub-second response times.

Read-through caching

In read-through caching, the cache acts as an intelligent intermediary between your application and the database. When the application requests data, it only needs to talk to the cache, as follows:

```
# Without read-through caching
def get_product(product_id):
    product = cache.get(product_id)
    if not product:
        product = database.get(product_id)
        cache.set(product_id, product)
    return product


# With read-through caching
def get_product(product_id):
    return cache_client.get(product_id)  # Cache handles DB interaction if
needed
```

Write through caching

Write-through cache is a caching strategy that simultaneously writes data to the cache and the main memory. This ensures that the cache and main memory are always consistent. In this mechanism, the application updates the primary database, the data is then immediately written to the cache.

In our e-commerce platform, price updates are critical operations that must be handled reliably. Write-through caching ensures that no customer sees an outdated price by updating both the cache and the database simultaneously.

Refer to the following code:

```
class PricingService:
    def update_price(self, product_id, new_price):
        # Update database first
        success = database.update_price(product_id, new_price)
        if success:
            # Then update cache
            cache.set(f"price:{product_id}", new_price)
            # Notify other services
            event_bus.publish("price_updated", {
                "product_id": product_id,
                "new_price": new_price
            })
        return success
```

While this approach ensures consistency, it comes with a performance cost. Every write operation must wait for the database to confirm the update before proceeding to then update the cache thus increasing latency. For our pricing service, this trade-off makes sense. we will rather have slightly slower price updates than risk showing incorrect prices to customers.

Write behind caching

In this system, data is written to the cache first and asynchronously updated to primary storage via a persistent, disk-backed queue. This improves write performance through batched updates while maintaining crash resilience, if the system fails before committing to the database, the queue retains pending writes. However, temporary inconsistency remains possible until the queue is fully processed.

Now, consider our product review system. When customers submit reviews, we can afford eventual consistency in favor of better performance. Write-behind caching allows us to acknowledge the review submission quickly while deferring the database update.

Refer to the following code:

```
class ReviewService:
    def __init__(self):
        # Persistent queue (e.g., Kafka, disk-based Redis Streams)
        self.write_queue = PersistentQueue("review_writes")  # <-- Explicit
```

```
durability
        self.retry_queue = PersistentQueue("review_retries") # <--
Persistent retries

    def submit_review(self, product_id, review_data):
        review_id = generate_unique_id()

        # Atomic cache+queue operation
        with transaction:  # <-- Ensures both operations succeed
            cache.set(f"review:{review_id}", review_data)
            self.write_queue.push({
                "review_id": review_id,
                "product_id": product_id,
                "data": review_data
            })

        return review_id  # Immediate acknowledgment

    def process_write_queue(self):
        # On service restart, first process existing queue items
        self._recover_unprocessed_items()  # <-- Crash recovery mechanism

        while True:
            batch = self.write_queue.get_batch(size=100)
            for review in batch:
                try:
                    database.save_review(review)
                    metrics.increment("review_write_success")
                except DatabaseError as e:
                    # Exponential backoff with max 3 retries
                    self.retry_with_backoff(review, max_retries=3)  # <--
Resilient retries

    def _recover_unprocessed_items(self):
        """Move unconsumed queue items back to processing"""
        for msg in self.write_queue.get_unacknowledged():
            self.write_queue.repush(msg)
        metrics.counter("queue_recovery_count").inc()
```

Building caching hierarchy

In distributed systems, data access patterns often follow a multi-tiered approach where different types of caches serve different purposes. Understanding these layers and their interactions is crucial for building efficient distributed systems.

Local caches

Local caches provide the fastest possible access to data by storing it directly in the application's memory space. Consider a product catalog service in a distributed e-commerce system, as follows:

```python
class LocalCacheManager:
    def __init__(self):
        self.l1_cache = LRUCache(max_size=10000)  # Local cache
        self.l2_cache = DistributedCache()        # Remote shared cache

    def get_data(self, key):
        # Fast path: check local cache
        data = self.l1_cache.get(key)
        if data:
            metrics.increment("l1_cache_hit")
            return data

        # Slower path: check distributed cache
        data = self.l2_cache.get(key)
        if data:
            metrics.increment("l2_cache_hit")
            # Populate local cache for future requests
            self.l1_cache.set(key, data)
            return data

        # Slowest path: fetch from source
        metrics.increment("cache_miss")
        return None
```

The advantages of local caching are as follows:

- Minimal latency (microseconds vs. milliseconds)
- Reduced network traffic
- Lower operational costs
- Improved application resilience

However, local caches introduce complexity around data consistency and resource utilization.

Distributed caches

Distributed caches serve as a coordination layer between application instances, providing a consistent view of cached data across the system. They help solve several key challenges, as follows:

- **Data consistency**: Ensuring all application instances see the same data
- **Resource efficiency**: Sharing cache capacity across instances
- **Failure resilience**: Maintaining availability despite instance failures

Figure 11.2 Illustrates the data flow through a multi-level cache system:

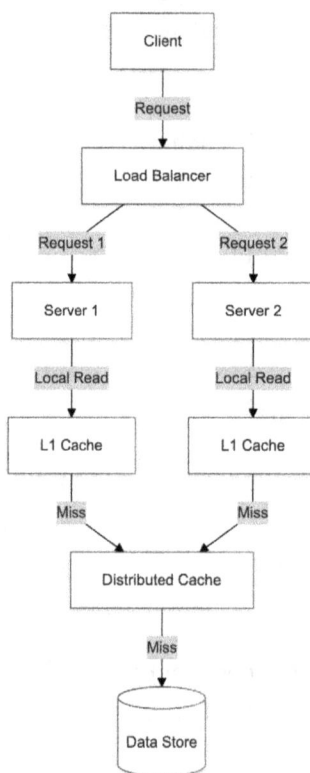

Figure 11.2: Data flow through a multi-level cache system

Cache coherency protocols

In a distributed environment, maintaining cache coherency requires careful coordination, as follows:

```
class CoherentCacheManager:
    def update_data(self, key, value):
        # Update shared cache first
        self.l2_cache.set(key, value)

        # Broadcast invalidation to all instances
        self.broadcast_invalidation(key, time.now())

        # Update local cache
        self.l1_cache.set(key, value)

    def handle_invalidation(self, message):
        key = message["key"]
        timestamp = message["timestamp"]

        if self.l1_cache.get_timestamp(key) < timestamp:
            self.l1_cache.invalidate(key)
            metrics.increment("cache_invalidation")
```

Multi-level caching strategy

Multi-level caching refers to a caching design that incorporates more than one level of cache between the application and the primary data store. Each level serves a specific purpose and may have different characteristics in terms of speed, size, and proximity to the application.

Multi-level caching can be imagined as a pyramid of storage layers, each offering different trade-offs between speed, capacity, and cost. At the top of the pyramid sits the fastest but most expensive cache, while each subsequent layer provides greater capacity at lower cost but with increased latency.

Figure 11.3 illustrates this caching strategy:

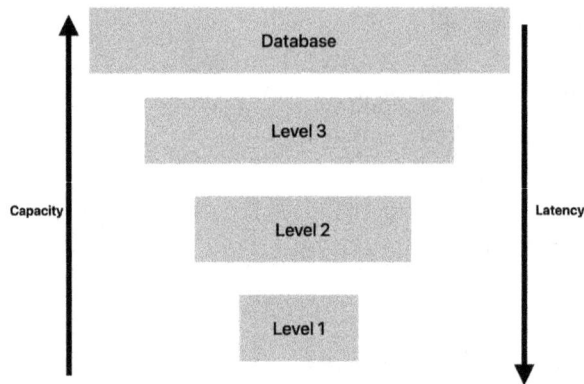

Figure 11.3: Illustration of multi cache strategy

The most common multi-level caching architecture is a two-tier design consisting of the following:

- **Level 1 (L1) cache**: An in-memory cache located closest to the application, typically on the same server. L1 caches are extremely fast but limited in size.

- **Level 2 (L2) cache**: A distributed cache running on dedicated servers, accessed over the network. L2 caches have higher capacity than L1 but slower access times.

Requests first check the L1 cache. If the data is not found (a **cache miss**), the L2 cache is checked next before finally querying the primary data store as a last resort. This hierarchy allows the faster but smaller L1 cache to handle most requests while the capacious L2 cache serves a higher aggregate throughput.

Multi-level caching provides several key benefits, as follows:

- **Improved performance**: Requests are served from the fastest available cache, minimizing latency thus improving performance.

- **Reduced backend load**: Most requests are handled by the caches, reducing traffic to backend services.

- **Graceful degradation**: If an L1 cache fails, the L2 can still serve data, avoiding a total cache outage.

However, multi-level caching also introduces complexities, as follows:

- **Increased architectural complexity**: Additional caching tiers add moving parts and potential failure points.

- **Data consistency challenges**: Changes must be propagated through multiple cache levels to avoid stale data.

- **Higher infrastructure costs**: Running multiple caching layers consumes more computing resources.

Common architectures for multi-level cache

Multi-level caching architectures can be implemented in various configurations, as follows:

- **On-Server L1 with distributed L2**: L1 caches reside on each application server, with a shared distributed L2 cache. This is the most common two-tier setup.

- **On-Server L1 and L2 with distributed L3**: The L2 cache also resides on application servers, with an L3 distributed cache. This provides the benefits of L2 without the network overhead.

- **Multiple distributed cache tiers**: For very high scale deployments, architectures may employ two or more distributed cache layers, often with different technologies optimized for specific access patterns.

Ultimately, the ideal multi-level caching architecture depends on the specific performance requirements, data access patterns, and scale of the application. A well-designed multi-level cache provides an optimal balance between low latency, high throughput, and acceptable consistency.

Cache eviction

Cache eviction is the process of removing data from a cache to free up space for new data when the cache reaches its capacity limit, essentially deciding which stored data to delete based on specific policies to maintain optimal performance and resource utilization within the cache.

Understanding eviction policies

A cache eviction policy is an algorithm that decides which data to remove from a cache when it's full. The goal of these policies is to keep the most relevant data in the cache and reduce cache misses.

Let us explore the main approaches.

Least recently used

Removes the item that has not been used the most recently. **Least recently used (LRU)** is useful when items are used frequently for a while, then usage drops. This policy works particularly well for systems with temporal locality where recently accessed data is likely to be accessed again soon. For instance, in a content delivery system, articles that were just published or shared on social media are more likely to be requested again in the near future.

Following is an example use case:

Social media trends: Recently shared articles get heavy traffic then relevance decreases.

Strengths:

- Automatically adapts to shifting popularity
- Low computational overhead

Weakness:

- Might evict sporadically used but critical data

Least frequently used

Removes the item that is been used the least frequently. **Least frequently used (LFU)** is useful for data with varying access patterns. LFU shines in scenarios with clear frequency patterns. However, it can be slow to adapt to changing patterns. Just as a once-popular textbook might become less relevant after the semester ends, cached data can become stale despite its historical popularity.

Following is an example use case:

Product catalog: certain items get consistent views, for example, bestsellers.

Strengths:

- Preserves frequently used data
- Handles eternally popular content

Weakness:

- Slow to adapt to new trends (e.g., seasonal items)

Time-based eviction

Removes items after a set amount of time. A **time-to-live (TTL)** configuration ensures data does not go stale after a while. The more recent data is prioritized over older data.

Consider a weather forecasting service: caching tomorrow's forecast for a week makes little sense, the data has a natural lifetime after which it becomes not just stale but meaningless. Time-based eviction handles such scenarios well.

Following is an example use case:

Weather forecast: Past data is not relevant and becomes meaningless.

Strengths:

- Guaranteed data freshness
- Simple to implement

Weakness:

- Might evict still relevant data prematurely

Table 11.1 is a summary:

Policy	Best for	Avoid when	Key metric to watch	Implementation complexity
LRU	Bursty traffic patterns	Long-term reference data	Cache hit rate	Low
LFU	Stable popularity hierarchies	Rapidly changing trends	Frequency distribution	Medium (count tracking)
TTL	Time-sensitive information	Indefinitely useful data	Expiration accuracy	Low

Table 11.1: Caching policy considerations

Maintaining cache consistency

Picture a newsroom managing breaking news across multiple locations. Each location has its own news board (cache), but they all need to stay synchronized with the central news desk (source of truth). This scenario mirrors the challenge of maintaining cache consistency in distributed systems.

Consistency patterns

Consistency patterns in a distributed caching world refers to the various gradation of the data being consistent across all nodes. Depending on the use case one may be preferred over the above.

Strong consistency

In our newsroom analogy, strong consistency would mean that no location can display a story until all news boards have been updated and acknowledged. This ensures everyone sees the same information but significantly slows down breaking news dissemination, like delaying a critical alert until all regional editors confirm receipt.

In distributed caching, strong consistency requires all cache instances to be updated/ invalidated before confirming a write. While crucial for financial transactions or inventory systems, this synchronization creates unavoidable trade-offs, as follows:

- **Increased write latency**: Operations wait for all nodes to confirm (e.g., 100ms becomes 300ms with 3 global nodes)

- **Reduced throughput**: Concurrent updates create coordination overhead

- **Failure sensitivity**: One unavailable node can block all writes
- **Real-world impact**: A stock trading platform using strong consistency might achieve 99.999% accuracy but process only 1,200 trades/sec versus 15,000/sec with eventual consistency.

Eventual consistency

Now imagine a different approach where each location updates its news board as quickly as possible, knowing that any discrepancies will be resolved shortly. This is eventual consistency, prioritizing availability and performance while accepting temporary inconsistencies.

This pattern works well in scenarios where temporary inconsistencies would not cause significant problems. Social media feeds, product reviews, or content recommendations can all tolerate brief periods where different users see slightly different versions of the data.

Race conditions

Consider two journalists simultaneously updating the same story on different news boards. Making sure the latest version of the story prevails is important. This is the essence of race conditions in distributed caching.

To handle such scenarios, systems often employ versioning or timestamps. Think of it as each version of a story having a timestamp, with the most recent version taking precedence. However, even this approach requires careful consideration: Let us see what happens if the timestamps are nearly simultaneous. Sometimes, network delays can make it unclear which update truly came first. Addressing race conditions involves synchronizing access to shared resources, using techniques like locks or atomic operations.

Common pitfalls and solutions

In distributed caching, as in many complex systems, the devil lies in the details.

Let us explore common challenges through real-world scenarios.

Cache penetration

Imagine a store where customers keep asking for a product that has never been in stock. Each request forces staff to check the stockroom unnecessarily. This is analogous to cache penetration, where requests for non-existent data repeatedly bypass the cache and hit the database.

Consider a product catalog where users might request items using invalid IDs, either by mistake or maliciously. Each request for a non-existent product ID causes the system for the following:

- Check the cache (miss)
- Query the database (miss)
- Return null
- Repeat for the next request

The solution is to store negative results. Just as a store might put up a **Not Available** sign for frequently requested but unavailable items, we can cache null results with a shorter TTL. This prevents repeated database lookups for non-existent data.

Cache avalanche

Imagine a shopping mall at midnight on Black Friday. If all stores opened their doors simultaneously, the sudden rush could overwhelm the mall's infrastructure. Cache avalanche presents a similar challenge when many cache entries expire simultaneously.

This commonly occurs when the following happens:

- A large number of cache entries are set with the same TTL
- A cache server fails
- Cache clearing operations affect too many entries

Following are the ways to prevent avalanche scenarios:

- Add random jitter to TTL values
- Use rolling cache updates
- Implement circuit breakers for database protection

Thundering herd or stadium gate problem

Consider a stadium with thousands of fans waiting for the gates to open. When they do, everyone rushes in at once, creating chaos. In caching, this occurs when many requests for the same uncached data arrive simultaneously.

Following is a real-world example:

During a major sporting event, thousands of users might request the same score update simultaneously after a cache miss. Without protection, all these requests could hit the database concurrently.

The solution involves request coalescing, as follows:

- The first request triggers the data fetch
- Subsequent requests wait for the first to complete
- All requests receive the same cached result

Monitoring and optimization

Monitoring and optimization for distributed caching means actively tracking key performance metrics of a distributed cache system, like cache hit rate, latency, throughput, and memory usage, to identify bottlenecks and make adjustments to the cache configuration and eviction policies, ensuring it operates efficiently and scales effectively to meet application demands; essentially, it is about fine-tuning a distributed cache to maximize its performance and reliability by continuously analyzing its behavior across multiple nodes.

Cache monitoring

Cache monitoring is the process of actively tracking and collecting data on the performance and health of a distributed cache system, including metrics like cache hit ratio, latency, throughput, memory usage, data consistency, and error rates across all cache nodes, allowing administrators to identify potential issues and optimize the cache's efficiency and scalability.

Following are the essential metrics to look for:

- **Cache hit ratio**: This is the percentage of requests successfully served from the cache. A high ratio indicates effective caching. It should typically be above 80% for frequently accessed data.

- **Latency**: This is the time taken to retrieve data from the cache. Measurements must be separately tracked for cache hits versus misses. This helps identify performance bottlenecks and find what should or should not be cached.

- **Memory usage**: This is the amount of memory consumed by the cache on each node. It is important to track both capacity and fragmentation of the cached data and set alerts for approaching limits and trigger eviction policies.

- **Eviction rates**: This is the rate at which cache entries are being marked as invalid. A high rate might indicate insufficient cache size. A change in the pattern can also signal underlying issues.

Real-world applications

Consider the fictional global ecommerce platform, with millions of concurrent users and diverse caching requirements across its components. This case study explores how a multi-level distributed caching architecture can be designed to optimize performance while maintaining consistency where necessary.

Now, let us look at three of its core components, as follows:

- **Product catalog**: This is the landing page for users to browse various products available across sellers on the ecommerce platform. Its characteristics are as follows:
    o Extremely read-heavy with millions of concurrent users
    o There is minimal updates per product
    o Needs to be optimized for fast reads and high scalability
    o Eventual consistency is acceptable

- **User reviews**: This is where users can look at reviews from other users who bought a specific item. The characteristics are as follows:
    o More frequent updates as new reviews are added
    o We need to balance fast reads with timely updates
    o Some staleness in reviews is tolerable

- **Shopping cart**: Shopping carts can be specific to a single user and is impacted by inventory, current offers and shipping systems. The characteristics are as follows:
    o It has a mix of static product data and dynamic inventory
    o Will need strong consistency critical to avoid overselling
    o Real-time inventory updates will be required

Incorporating multi-level cache

Let us look at how multi-level caching architecture could help components by first revisiting each cache level, as follows:

- **Level 1 (L1) cache**:
    o In-memory cache on each application server
    o Fastest access but limited capacity
    o Ideal for small, frequently accessed data

- **Level 2 (L2) cache**:
    o Distributed cache (Redis, Memcached, etc.)
    o More capacity than L1, very fast reads
    o Sits between app servers and databases

- **Database**:
    o Source of truth for all data
    o Final fallback when data not in caches

Product catalog caching strategy

Optimize for high read traffic while balancing consistency needs. Our e-commerce platform uses a tiered approach to handle millions of daily product views and infrequent updates.

This strategy prioritizes the following:

- Speed for high-demand items (L1 cache)
- Scalability for long-tail products (L2 cache)
- Tolerable staleness (up to 5 minutes) for non-critical metadata

The implementation breaks down as follows:

- Store product metadata in both L1 and L2 caches
  - **L1**: frequently accessed products
  - **L2**: much larger set of products
- On cache miss, query from DB and write to L2, then L1
- Write-through caching
  - All updates go to DB first
  - Then invalidate L1 and L2
- Eventual consistency acceptable due to infrequent updates

User review caching strategy

Optimize for write-heavy workloads while managing trust and freshness. Unlike product data, user-generated reviews prioritize the following:

- Low-latency submissions (users hate waiting for review confirmation)
- Tolerance for 15-30s consistency delays (instant visibility isn't critical)
- Aggressive anti-abuse checks (requiring frequent invalidations)

The following strategy balances these needs with:

- Smaller dataset, store only in L2 cache (avoids memory bloat from volatile UGC)
- Write-back caching
  - Writes go to L2 cache queue, then DB
  - Faster writes, slight delay in consistency
- More frequent cache invalidation than products

Shopping cart caching strategy

Balance real-time accuracy with performance for high-concurrency scenarios. Unlike static product data, cart interactions demand, as follows:

- Instant access to product details (descriptions, images)
- Strong consistency for inventory checks (to prevent overselling)
- Graceful degradation during flash sales (avoiding database meltdowns)

This dual approach ensures the following:

- Static product data cached in L1/L2 (fast reads for non-volatile info)
- Real-time inventory requires strong consistency
- Changes must immediately invalidate L1/L2
- Aggregate inventory cached in L2
- Set to expire quickly, for example, every minute

Repopulate from DB

- Ensures freshness without constant invalidation storms

Cache hierarchy evolution

During the platform's growth, the caching strategy evolved from a simple two-layer system to a sophisticated hierarchy. Each layer served a specific purpose, as follows:

- **Edge caching or content delivery network**:
  - This can handle 80% of read traffic for static content and be close to dense concentration of users in a sub-region
  - This can reduce cross-continental latency from seconds to milliseconds
  - This will work when required and when consistency guarantees are not required. For example, for the Product Catalog.

- **Application caches**:
  - Maintained session data and user preferences
  - Protected backend services during traffic spikes
  - Implemented circuit breakers to prevent cascade failures

Designing an effective distributed caching architecture requires careful analysis of each subsystem's access patterns and consistency needs. By combining local and distributed caches, and employing targeted cache invalidation strategies, we can optimize performance while ensuring data consistency where necessary. This case study illustrates how a multi-level caching approach can be applied to address the diverse requirements of a large-scale ecommerce platform.

Future considerations in distributed caching

As we look ahead, several trends are shaping the future of distributed caching.

Following are the trends:

- **Machine learning integration**: Modern caching systems are becoming smarter about the following:

  o Predictive cache warming

  o Adaptive TTL adjustment

  o Intelligent resource allocation

  o Pattern-based prefetching

- **Edge computing impact**: The rise of edge computing is changing caching strategies, as follows:

  o More sophisticated edge caching capabilities

  o Increased need for partial data caching

  o Complex consistency requirements across edges

  o Dynamic resource allocation between edges

- **Real-time processing demands**: As systems become more real-time, following takes place:

  o Cache coherency becomes more challenging

  o Update propagation speed becomes critical

  o Need for smarter invalidation strategies

  o Balance between freshness and performance

Finding balance when caching

Distributed caching is fundamentally about balance like a skilled conductor leading an orchestra, you must harmonize multiple competing concerns, as follows:

- **Performance versus consistency**:

  o When to sacrifice consistency for speed

  o How to maintain data integrity without compromising user experience

  o Where to place caches in your architecture

- **Resource management**:

  o Balancing memory usage across cache layers

  o Managing network bandwidth efficiently

  o Optimizing cost versus performance

- **Complexity versus maintainability**:
    - o   Keeping the system simple enough to debug
    - o   Building in adequate monitoring and observability
    - o   Planning for future scale while managing current needs

Best practices

When designing a distributed caching system, it is important to follow best practices to ensure your system is efficient, resilient, and scalable.

Start simple and iterate

One of the most important principles in distributed system design is to start with simplicity. Begin by implementing a basic caching strategy that meets your core requirements. This might mean using a single level of caching or caching only your most critical data at first.

The key is to get a working system up and running and then iterate and add complexity as needed based on real-world usage patterns. Avoid the temptation to build an overly complex caching system right from the start. You can always add more sophisticated strategies like multi-level caching, different caching layers for different data types, or more advanced invalidation techniques later on, once you have a clearer picture of your system's needs.

As you build your caching system, be sure to install your code and monitor everything from the beginning. Collect metrics on cache hit/miss rates, latency, throughput, and error rates. This monitoring data will be invaluable in guiding your iterations and identifying areas for optimization.

> **Note: An e-commerce team once implemented three caching layers (local, Redis, CDN) pre-launch just in case.**

When a pricing error occurred, they spent 14 hours identifying which layer served stale data. More layers ≠ better performance, they create:

- Cascading failure risks
- Debugging dependency chains
- Versioning nightmares

The key is to get a working system up and running first, then add complexity only when metrics demand it. Monitor these signals before adding layers:

- Cache hit ratio < 60%
- 95th percentile latency > 200ms
- Database CPU > 70% sustained

Note: Every new caching layer should solve a documented problem, not anticipate hypothetical ones. You can always add sophistication later, but over-engineered caching is harder to remove than to implement.

Design for failure

In any distributed system, failures are inevitable. Network outages, server crashes, and software bugs can all lead to parts of your system becoming unavailable. Your caching system must be designed to handle these failures gracefully.

One key aspect of this is planning for cache misses. There will be times when requested data is not found in the cache, either because it has not been cached yet or because the cache is unavailable. Your application code needs to be prepared to handle these misses by falling back to loading data from the primary data store.

In addition to graceful fallback mechanisms, you should also use techniques like circuit breakers to prevent cascading failures. If a particular cache server is experiencing high error rates or latency, a circuit breaker can automatically route requests away from that server to healthy nodes. This helps isolate failures and prevents them from bringing down the entire system.

Know your data

To design an effective caching strategy, you need to have a deep understanding of your data and how it is used. Analyze your application's data access patterns to identify which pieces of data are read frequently and which are written too often.

Data that is read often but rarely updated is a prime candidate for caching, as you can serve many requests from the cache without worrying too much about stale data. On the other hand, data that is updated frequently may be better suited to a write-through or write-behind caching strategy to ensure consistency.

You also need to consider the consistency requirements for different types of data. Some data may be fine with eventual consistency, meaning it is okay if the cache serves slightly stale data for a short period of time. Other data may require strong consistency, where you always need to serve the most up-to-date version.

Finally, plan for the entire lifecycle of your cached data. Determine how long data should be cached before being evicted and have a strategy for invalidating or updating cached data when the primary data store is updated.

Monitor and adapt

Designing a caching system is not a one-time task. To ensure your caching continues to meet your application's needs, you need to continuously monitor its performance and adapt your strategies based on actual usage patterns.

Track key metrics like cache hit ratio, latency, and throughput on an ongoing basis. Set up alerts to notify you if these metrics deviate significantly from expected ranges. Regularly review this data to identify opportunities for optimization.

You may find that certain types of data are being evicted from the cache too quickly and could benefit from a longer TTL. Or you might discover that some cached data is rarely being accessed and is just taking up valuable cache space. Adjust your caching strategies based on these real-world insights.

Finally, always be planned for growth and change. As your application scales and evolves, your caching system will need to adapt. Make sure your caching architecture can accommodate rising demand by adding cache servers or shifting to a distributed caching solution. Stay proactive about capacity planning to avoid performance bottlenecks.

Conclusion

Distributed caching is not just about improving performance, it is about building systems that scale gracefully, fail gracefully, and adapt to changing requirements. As you implement caching in your own systems, remember that the goal is not to cache everything, but to cache the right things in the right way at the right time.

Success in distributed caching comes not from following a rigid set of rules, but from understanding the principles and applying them thoughtfully to your specific context. The patterns and practices discussed in this chapter provide a foundation, but the art lies in how you adapt and apply them to solve real-world challenges.

In the next chapter, we will explore factors to consider when choosing the right infrastructure platforms and technologies.

Join our book's Discord space

Join the book's Discord Workspace for Latest updates, Offers, Tech happenings around the world, New Release and Sessions with the Authors:

https://discord.bpbonline.com

CHAPTER 12
Choosing Platform and Technologies

Introduction

The selection of platforms and technologies for distributed systems represents one of the most consequential decisions in modern software architecture. These decisions create long-lasting implications that extend far beyond the initial implementation phase, influencing everything from system performance to team productivity and operational costs.

In the context of a large-scale distributed systems platform, these decisions become particularly critical due to the diverse set of technical requirements. Consider a typical e-commerce system processing millions of daily transactions, it must simultaneously handle high-volume read operations for product browsing, maintain consistency for inventory updates, process financial transactions with strict ACID guarantees, and manage real-time user sessions. Each of these operations presents unique technical challenges that influence platform selection. As in previous chapters, we will continue to follow the ecommerce platform components to help understand various tradeoffs and considerations when making a choice among available options.

Structure

The chapter covers the following topics:

- Evaluating application runtime platforms
- Data storage technology selection
- Message brokers and event processing
- Serverless systems in distributed architecture
- Fully serverless platforms

Objectives

By the end of this chapter, readers will have a comprehensive framework for selecting platforms and technologies in distributed systems, with a specific focus on e-commerce applications. We explore how early architectural decisions create lasting implications for system scalability, performance, and maintainability. The chapter examines the critical considerations in choosing application runtime platforms, data storage technologies, message brokers, and deployment infrastructures. Through the lens of a large-scale e-commerce platform, we demonstrate how different technological choices impact various aspects of the system, from handling high-volume product browsing to maintaining consistency in inventory updates and processing financial transactions. Understanding these trade-offs is crucial for architects and developers in making informed decisions that align with both immediate requirements and long-term scalability goals.

Impact of early architecture decisions

Early architectural decisions create technological inertia that becomes increasingly difficult to overcome as systems scale. For instance, the choice between a synchronous request-response model versus an event-driven architecture for order processing fundamentally shapes how the system evolves. A synchronous architecture might offer simplicity in initial development but could introduce scalability challenges as order volume grows. Conversely, an event-driven approach might better handle scale but introduces complexity in maintaining transaction boundaries and ensuring exactly-once processing guarantees.

Technical debt implications

The concept of technical debt takes on new dimensions in distributed systems. Beyond the usual considerations of code quality and documentation, distributed systems accumulate **architectural debt** through suboptimal platform choices.

Following is the explanation:

- **Performance limitations**: A database choice that adequately serves thousands of daily users might become a bottleneck for millions of users, requiring complex sharding or caching strategies.

- **Operational complexity**: As system scale increases, operational challenges often emerge from initial platform choices. For instance, a monolithic application server might require increasingly complex deployment procedures and downtime windows that become untenable at scale.

- **Integration overhead**: The choice of communication protocols and data formats can create lasting integration challenges, particularly when systems need to evolve to support new business requirements.

Hidden costs of framework lock-in

Framework selection introduces subtle but significant lock-in effects that extend beyond the immediate technical stack. Consider an e-commerce platform built on a specific web framework, as follows:

- **Ecosystem dependencies**: Modern frameworks often come with their own ecosystems of libraries and tools. While these accelerate initial development, they can create deep dependencies that make future transitions costly.

- **Team expertise**: As teams develop expertise in specific frameworks, the organizational cost of switching technologies increases. This creates a form of human capital lock-in that must be considered in platform selection.

- **Architectural patterns**: Frameworks often encourage specific architectural patterns that may not align with long-term scalability requirements. For example, an ORM that works well for simple CRUD operations might become a performance bottleneck when handling complex product catalog queries at scale.

Evaluating application runtime platforms

The selection of application runtime platforms represents a fundamental architectural decision that influences nearly every aspect of system development and operation. In the context of distributed systems, this decision becomes particularly nuanced due to varying workload characteristics across different services.

Runtime performance characteristics

Generally, developers choose the platform that they are most comfortable in writing their code in. While that is an important criterion for long term maintainability of the application, it is worthwhile to look at different runtime platforms that exhibit distinct performance characteristics that can become critical at scale as is listed as follows:

- **JVM ecosystem**:
  - o Advantages in long-running processes with complex business logic
  - o Sophisticated garbage collection suitable for large in-memory datasets
  - o Higher memory footprint but predictable performance under load
  - o Particularly effective for services handling complex product catalog operations

- **Node.js**:
  - o Excels in I/O-intensive operations common in web APIs
  - o Lower memory footprint per instance
  - o Event-driven architecture suitable for real-time features
  - o Effective for services handling user sessions and shopping cart operations

- **Go**:
  - o Consistent performance with low latency
  - o Efficient resource utilization
  - o Built-in concurrency support
  - o Well-suited for high-throughput services like inventory management

Memory management

Memory management significantly impacts system behavior under load. A write-heavy system may work well with runtimes which have more aggressive garbage collection policies, as this helps prevent memory fragmentation and ensures consistent performance during peak write operations. For example, in a system processing millions of transactions per second, frequent garbage collection cycles can prevent the accumulation of dead objects that could otherwise lead to memory pressure and degraded performance.

Product catalog has a large product dataset that requires careful consideration of memory usage patterns.

Let us look at aspects of various runtimes, as follows:

- JVM's generational garbage collection can efficiently handle large, long-lived objects

- Go's simpler memory model might require more explicit memory management but offers more predictable performance

- Node.js's single-threaded model necessitates careful handling of large datasets

For the product catalog service, which processes a large, write-heavy dataset requiring stable memory behavior under load, the JVM (Java/OpenJDK) emerges as the most fitting choice. Its generational garbage collection mechanism is optimized for managing long-lived objects (common in large catalogs) while mitigating memory fragmentation during sustained write operations. This ensures consistent throughput and minimizes performance degradation during peak loads, critical for high-transaction systems.

While Go's predictable memory model offers advantages for low-latency use cases, its requirement for more manual tuning may introduce complexity for large, evolving datasets. Node.js, though agile for I/O-heavy tasks, struggles with memory-intensive operations due to its single-threaded design, making it less ideal for catalog-scale workloads.

However, if the team prioritizes low-latency responsiveness over raw throughput and has expertise in explicit memory optimization, Go could still be a contender. Rigorous load testing and profiling under realistic conditions simulating catalog updates and queries will ultimately validate the runtime choice, ensuring alignment with scalability, maintenance, and performance goals.

Framework maturity and ecosystem support

The evaluation of framework maturity extends beyond mere version numbers or release dates. In distributed e-commerce systems, framework selection must consider the entire development and operational lifecycle.

Following are the ecosystem maturity indicators:

- **Library coverage for essential functions**: The availability of well-maintained libraries for crucial e-commerce operations such as payment processing, session management, and data validation significantly impacts development velocity. For instance, mature frameworks typically offer robust solutions for rate limiting, which becomes critical when protecting inventory checking APIs from abuse or managing concurrent cart updates.

- **Community support and knowledge base**: Active communities contribute to problem resolution and knowledge sharing. Consider how Spring's extensive community has developed patterns for handling distributed transactions in order processing, or how the Node.js ecosystem has evolved solutions for managing real-time inventory updates across multiple services.

- **Enterprise adoption and production proven cases**: Frameworks with significant enterprise adoption often develop better patterns for handling edge cases in production environments. This becomes particularly relevant when dealing with scenarios like partial failures in distributed transactions or managing session state across multiple instances.

Performance characteristics under load

This is a crucial consideration when evaluating application runtime platforms for your distributed e-commerce system. The way a framework behaves under heavy traffic can make the difference between a profitable day and costly outages. Let us dive deeper into two key aspects that influence this: request processing models and load handling patterns.

First, let us consider request processing models. These determine how the framework handles incoming client requests. Broadly, there are two approaches, as follows:

- **Synchronous processing**: This is the traditional request-response model where the client sends a request, the server processes it and sends back a response. The client waits for the response before proceeding. While straightforward to understand and implement, this model can lead to resource exhaustion under high load. If the server receives more requests than it can process, pending requests start accumulating, consuming memory and eventually causing the system to become unresponsive.

- **Asynchronous processing**: In this model, the server acknowledges the request immediately and processes it later. This frees up the server to handle more incoming requests. Asynchronous processing is more complex to implement as you need to handle eventual consistency and choreograph responses, but it allows for much better resource utilization under load. This model is essential for any long-running operations in your e-commerce system, such as order processing or inventory updates.

Next, let us look at how different frameworks handle load. This is determined by their concurrency and resource management models, as follows:

- **Thread-based model (Java)**: Frameworks like Spring that run on the JVM use a thread pool to handle concurrency. Each request is assigned to a thread from the pool. This allows for fine-grained control over resource usage and works well for CPU-intensive tasks. However, the downside is the higher memory overhead per request as each thread has its own stack. Additionally, under heavy load, the cost of context switching between threads can become significant.

- **Event loop model (Node.js)**: Node.js and frameworks like Express take a different approach. They use a single thread that processes events in a loop. When a request comes in, it is processed asynchronously without blocking the main thread. This model is highly efficient for I/O bound tasks as the single thread can juggle multiple requests without the overhead of thread context switches. However, the downside is that CPU-intensive tasks can starve the event loop, making the process unresponsive.

So, how do these concepts apply to our e-commerce system? Let us consider a Product Search service. This is typically a read-heavy operation where speed is paramount. Every millisecond of latency directly impacts user experience and conversion rates. For this service, an event loop model like Node.js with its fast I/O processing is a good fit.

On the other hand, consider an order processing service. Here, each order might trigger multiple steps, that is, inventory checks, payment processing, shipping updates. Many of these are long-running, CPU-intensive tasks. Using a thread-based model like Java's can provide the necessary control and isolation to ensure each order is processed reliably without starving other parts of the system.

Performance underload hinges on selecting runtimes whose concurrency models and resource management align with the specific demands of each service.

Table 12.1 is a summary of framework strengths and ideal use cases:

Language/Runtime	Strengths	Ideal for
Java/JVM	Thread-based concurrency, CPU-intensive tasks, strong typing, high throughput	Transaction processing, inventory management, services requiring complex business logic
Node.js	Event-loop model, non-blocking I/O, real-time responsiveness	Product search, cart updates, lightweight APIs, real-time notifications
Go	Goroutines (lightweight threads), low-latency, balanced CPU/I/O	Concurrent order processing, payment gateways, middleware services

Table 12.1: Language/Runtime strengths comparison

Understanding a framework's performance characteristics under load is key to building a responsive, resilient e-commerce system. It is not a one-size-fits-all choice, different services in your architecture might have different optimal solutions. The key is to match the framework's strengths to the service's requirements. By making informed choices that optimize for your specific load patterns, you can ensure your system remains performant and reliable even under the heaviest of traffic.

Development team considerations

The impact of framework choice on development team productivity warrants careful consideration, as follows:

- **Initial development speed versus long-term maintainability**: While some frameworks offer rapid initial development through convention over configuration, others might require more upfront learning but provide better long-term maintainability. For instance, TypeScript with Node.js might require more initial setup but can prevent numerous runtime errors in complex e-commerce business logic.

- **Team expertise and training requirements**: The availability of developers with relevant expertise affects both development velocity and operational capabilities. Consider how this impacts different services.

Refer to *Table 12.2*:

Service type	Primary concerns	Framework implications
Cart service	Real-time updates	Event-driven frameworks
Product search	Complex queries	Strong ORM support
Order processing	Transaction consistency	Mature transaction handling

Table 12.2: Expertise required for developing services for distributed systems

Migration and evolution capabilities

Framework selection must consider future evolution paths, as follows:

- **Incremental migration support**:
  - Ability to run multiple versions simultaneously during migration
  - Support for gradual service migration
  - Compatibility with existing systems and protocols

Following is an example of migration scenario:

Consider a product catalog service migration with the following phases:

- **Phase 1**: Introduce new framework alongside existing service
- **Phase 2**: Gradually shift read traffic to new service
- **Phase 3**: Migrate write operations
- **Phase 4**: Decommission old service

Following are the key migration considerations:

- Data consistency during transition
- Performance monitoring and comparison
- Rollback capabilities
- Team training and knowledge transfer

Data storage technology selection

The selection of data storage technologies in distributed e-commerce systems requires careful consideration of data characteristics, access patterns, and consistency requirements. Modern architectures often employ polyglot persistence, where different storage technologies serve specific use cases within the same system.

ACID versus BASE

At a grossly generalized level, there are two broad storage design choices **Atomic, Consistent, Isolated, Durable (ACID)** and **Basically Available, Soft state, Eventually**

consistent (BASE) Let us consider what we could use for each of the different components in the ecommerce platform.

Table 12.3 shows the transaction criticality matrix:

Operation type	Consistency needs	Typical choice
Payment processing	Strong ACID	RDBMS
Product views	Eventually	Document Store
Inventory updates	Strong ACID1	RDBMS/CQRS
Shopping cart	Session	In-Memory/Doc

Table 12.3: Comparison of consistency requirements across components

Following are the critical considerations:

- Business impact of inconsistency
- Recovery mechanisms
- Read versus write scalability requirements

Emphasizing read replicas for relational databases

For high read volumes in ACID-compliant services, for example, payment history or inventory checks, read replicas are critical. They allow the following:

- **Reduced load on the primary database**: Offload read traffic, for example, customers checking order status.

- **Improved latency**: Serve read requests from geographically distributed replicas.

- **Disaster recovery**: Promote a replica to primary during outages.

Following is an example:

In inventory management, replicas can handle real-time stock availability queries, while the primary database focuses on ACID-compliant stock deductions.

Different parts of an e-commerce platform have very distinct data storage requirements. Let us explore two key domains, that is, product catalog and shopping cart and see how their unique characteristics influence our storage choices.

Product catalogue storage

The product catalog is the heart of any e-commerce system. It is a read-heavy domain where customers browse, filter, and search for products. The key requirements here are fast querying, efficient filtering, and the ability to handle high concurrent traffic.

In terms of data characteristics, product catalogs are typically semi-structured and hierarchical. Each product might have dozens of attributes, categories, tags, and relationships to other products. This semi-structured nature makes relational databases less ideal. They can struggle with the complex join queries needed for product filtering and search.

Instead, a common approach is to use a document-oriented database like MongoDB or Elasticsearch. These databases excel at storing semi-structured data and provide built-in support for rich querying and full-text search. They allow you to store each product as a self-contained document, making it efficient to retrieve all the necessary product details in a single query.

However, the product catalog is not just a storage problem. It is also a data modeling and querying challenge. You need to structure your product data in a way that efficiently supports your most common access patterns. This is where techniques like denormalization and indexing come into play.

For example, if your e-commerce site heavily relies on faceted navigation (drilling down by attributes like brand, price, color), you might choose to de-normalize product attributes into a flattened structure optimized for faceted search. Or if full-text search is a key requirement, you would setup inverted indexes on product names and descriptions.

Another aspect to consider is caching. While databases like Elasticsearch can handle high read throughput, caching frequently accessed products in a distributed cache like Redis can significantly reduce load on your primary database and improve response times.

Shopping cart storage

The shopping cart domain has a very different set of requirements compared to the product catalog. The focus is on per-user data that is frequently modified as users add, remove, or change items in their cart.

The key requirements for shopping cart storage are as follows:

- High read and write throughput to handle numerous cart updates
- Low latency to ensure snappy user experience
- Scalability to handle traffic spikes during peak shopping periods
- Durability to prevent data loss

Relational databases can work for shopping carts but can face challenges in scaling to high throughput workloads. They can also introduce latency due to the need for disk-based persistence.

An increasingly popular approach for shopping cart storage is to use an in-memory datastore like Redis. Redis is a key-value store that keeps all data in memory, providing extremely fast read and write operations. It can handle hundreds of thousands of operations per second with sub-millisecond latency, making it ideal for the high-throughput, low-latency requirements of shopping carts.

In-memory datastores like Redis typically sacrifice durability for performance. If the Redis node crashes, you could lose data. However, for shopping cart data, this is often an acceptable tradeoff. Carts are transient by nature and losing a few carts is less catastrophic than, say, losing order data. Moreover, Redis does provide options for persistence if needed, such as snapshotting data to disk periodically or using append-only file persistence.

Another aspect to consider for shopping carts is session management. Shopping carts are tied to user sessions and need to be available across all servers in your cluster. This is where Redis' distributed capabilities come into play. You can use Redis as a centralized session store, allowing any server in your cluster to access a user's cart data.

So, a typical storage architecture for the shopping cart domain involve the following:

- Redis as the primary in-memory data store for cart data
- Redis' persistence options (e.g., snapshotting) for basic durability if needed
- Redis' pub/sub or streams for real-time updates (e.g., stock notifications)
- Integration with session management to tie carts to user sessions

In summary, selecting storage solutions in an e-commerce system requires a deep understanding of each domain's data characteristics and access patterns. By aligning your database choices with these requirements, you can build a system that scales seamlessly, performs optimally, and provides a great user experience. The product catalog and shopping cart domains demonstrate how different parts of the same system can have very different storage needs. The key is to use the right tool for each job and to structure your data in a way that supports your most critical use cases.

Table 12.4 can be used as a general guideline for considerations:

Aspect	Requirement	Technology implication
Data lifetime	Temporary	In-memory store
Consistency	Session-level	Distributed caching (Redis)
Recovery	Reconstructable	Event sourcing backup

Table 12.4: Factors that impact storage choice based on the requirement for a component

Data access patterns analysis

Understanding how data is accessed is crucial for optimizing storage solutions. Different parts of our system will have very distinct data access patterns. Let us focus on two key areas: read-heavy operations like product listing and price checks, and write-heavy operations like inventory updates.

For read-heavy operations, consider the product listing page. This is one of the most frequently accessed parts of an e-commerce site. Customers view product listings far more often than they add items to their cart or make a purchase. The key requirement here is fast, consistent reads. We want to minimize latency and ensure that product information is always up to date.

To achieve this, we might employ a combination of caching and eventual consistency. Product data can be cached heavily, both at the application level and in a distributed cache like Redis. This reduces load on the primary database and provides sub-millisecond response times. However, caching introduces the challenge of data staleness. If a product's price or availability changes, we need to ensure the cache is updated. One approach is to use event-driven cache invalidation. When a product is updated, an event is emitted which triggers cache updates across the system.

On the other hand, inventory updates represent a write-heavy workload. Every time a product is sold, its inventory count needs to be decremented. In a high-volume system, this can lead to a high rate of concurrent writes to the same data. If not handled properly, this can result in lost updates or inconsistent data.

To handle this, we might use a combination of techniques. First, we can apply a pattern like event sourcing. Instead of updating the inventory count directly, we record each inventory change as a separate event. This allows us to decouple the write operation from the read operation and handle them asynchronously. We can process inventory change events in the background, updating the current inventory count in a separate read model.

Another technique is to use optimistic concurrency control. This involves versioning each inventory record and checking the version before applying an update. If the version has changed since we last read the record, we know another update has occurred concurrently and we can retry the operation.

Performance optimization strategies

When optimizing performance in a distributed system, we need to approach it from multiple angles. Like a car, our system needs regular tune-ups and upgrades in different areas to run at its best.

One key area is caching. Caching is like keeping frequently used tools in your tool belt instead of walking back to the toolbox each time. In our system, we can apply caching at different levels. At the application level, we can cache data that is frequently read but rarely changes, like product categories or user preferences. This way, we do not need to fetch this data from the database on each request, speeding up response times.

Moving down a level, we have distributed caching. This is like a shared tool cache for all the workers on the construction site. By using a distributed cache like Redis, we can store commonly accessed data in memory across our cluster. This is great for things like frequently viewed product details or shopping cart data.

Caching is just the start. We also need to think about how we structure and access our data. This is where techniques like indexing and query optimization come in. Indexing is like organizing your tools by type and size, it makes it faster to find what you need. In databases, indexes allow us to quickly locate data based on specific columns, speeding up read queries.

Another powerful technique is read or write splitting. This is like having dedicated tools for different jobs. We can route read operations to separate read replicas of our database, reducing load on the primary write database. This allows us to scale our read capacity independently of writes.

Sometimes, we need to rethink our data model entirely. Techniques like denormalization and materialized views can greatly speed up specific queries by recalculating and storing data in a format optimized for those queries. It is like creating a specialized tool for a specific, repeated task.

All these optimizations need to be balanced against factors like consistency and maintainability. Aggressive caching and denormalization can introduce data staleness and make updates more complex. It is a tradeoff we need to evaluate based on our specific workload and business requirements.

Message brokers and event processing

In distributed e-commerce systems, message brokers and event processing frameworks form the backbone of asynchronous communication and event-driven architectures. Their selection significantly impacts system scalability, reliability, and maintainability.

Message broker architecture patterns

Modern e-commerce systems typically handle diverse messaging patterns, each serving different business requirements. Consider an order processing flow: when a customer places an order, this single action triggers a cascade of events like inventory checks, payment processing, fulfillment notifications, and analytics updates. Each of these subsequent processes has distinct requirements for reliability, timing, and processing guarantees.

For high-stakes transactional messages, such as order processing and payment events, Apache Kafka emerges as a robust choice. Its log-based architecture provides crucial exactly-once delivery semantics and maintains message ordering within partitions. Kafka's persistence model, where messages are retained for configurable periods, enables event replay and system recovery critical features when processing financial transactions.

However, for real-time inventory updates and price changes requiring immediate fan-out to multiple consumers, RabbitMQ offers advantages through its sophisticated routing capabilities and immediate message delivery. Its exchange-based routing model efficiently handles complex message distribution patterns, making it particularly suitable for inventory synchronization across multiple services.

For teams prioritizing operational simplicity and serverless scalability, fully managed services like AWS SQS/SNS or Google Pub/Sub offer zero infrastructure management, automatic scaling, built-in redundancy, and pay-as-you-go pricing. The help decoupling microservices with help of AWS SQS (queues) for point-to-point messaging and SNS (pub/sub) for broadcasting; Google Pub/Sub unifies both patterns in one service. One big advantage that these offerings have is. native cloud integration, one can directly trigger serverless functions (e.g., AWS Lambda, Google Cloud Functions) or sync with data warehouses (BigQuery, Redshift). Use cases to consider are when a service has to send order confirmation emails (SNS) while decoupling payment processing from fulfillment using queues (SQS). Google Pub/Sub can help stream real-time analytics, for example, user clickstreams to BigQuery.

By aligning broker capabilities with business and technical requirements, distributed systems can achieve resilience, scalability, and cost efficiency.

Event flow orchestration

The orchestration of event flows in e-commerce requires careful consideration of message routing, transformation, and processing guarantees. Consider implementing this through Apache Camel, which provides sophisticated enterprise integration patterns while maintaining flexibility in underlying transport mechanisms.

Order processing implementation

A typical order processing flow will be as follows:

Order Created | Validate Inventory | Process Payment | Initiate Fulfillment | Notify Customer

Apache Camel can coordinate the flow while using different messaging patterns for each stage, as follows:

- **OrderCreated**: Kafka topic for durability
- **ValidateInventory**: Request-reply pattern through RabbitMQ
- **ProcessPayment**: Dedicated Kafka topic with exactly-once semantics
- **InitiateFulfillment**: Asynchronous RabbitMQ queue
- **NotifyCustomer**: Pub/sub topic in RabbitMQ

Back-pressure and flow control

Back-pressure management becomes critical as system scale increases. Consider an e-commerce platform during a flash sale, that is, surge in orders can overwhelm downstream processing systems if not properly managed.

Project Reactor or RxJava provide sophisticated tools for handling back-pressure at the application level. These frameworks implement the Reactive Streams specification, offering mechanisms, as follows:

- Buffer and drop strategies for handling overflow
- Time-based windowing for batch processing
- Dynamic throttling based on consumer capacity

Following is an example of implementation:

During high load periods, implement a tiered approach, as follows:

- Use Kafka's consumer groups for parallel processing
- Implement application-level rate limiting using Project Reactor
- Configure RabbitMQ prefetch counts to prevent consumer overflow

State management strategies

State management in event-driven e-commerce systems requires balancing consistency, availability, and partition tolerance. Event sourcing, implemented through tools like EventStoreDB, provides a robust foundation for maintaining system state.

Consider a shopping cart implementation, as follows:

- Store cart events in EventStoreDB
- Maintain a materialized view in Redis for fast reads
- Use Kafka Streams for real-time analytics

This approach provides the following:

- Complete audit capability for compliance requirements
- High-performance read access for active shopping sessions
- Real-time analytics for inventory management

Scalability implementation

Achieving scalable event processing requires careful consideration of partitioning and deployment strategies. Apache Kafka's partitioning model provides a foundation for horizontal scaling, while Kubernetes offers the infrastructure for dynamic scaling of processing components.

Following is a real-world implementation:

- Deploy Kafka on Kubernetes using Strimzi operator
- Implement horizontal pod autoscaling based on consumer lag
- Use Kafka Streams for stateful processing, particularly for inventory and pricing updates
- Leverage Kafka Connect for integration with external systems

Monitoring and observability

Effective monitoring of event-driven systems requires visibility across multiple dimensions. A comprehensive monitoring stack will include the following:

- **Metrics collection**:
  - Prometheus for systems metrics
  - Kafka Exporter for broker-specific metrics
  - Custom application metrics exposed through Micrometer

- **Visualization and analysis**:
  - Grafana for real-time dashboards
  - Jaeger for distributed tracing
  - Elasticsearch for log aggregation

- **Alert management**:
  - AlertManager for notification routing
  - PagerDuty for incident management
  - Custom alerting thresholds based on business impact

Following are the key performance indicators:

- Consumer lag (should remain under 1000 messages)
- End-to-end latency (target < 500ms for critical paths)
- Dead letter queue size (alert on non-zero values)
- Message throughput rates (baseline + deviation alerts)

The combination of these tools and practices creates a robust event processing infrastructure capable of handling the complex requirements of modern e-commerce systems. Regular review and adjustment of these components ensure the system remains responsive and reliable as business requirements evolve.

Serverless systems in distributed architecture

Distributed systems architecture has evolved over time with cloud computing make it accessible to developers and organization who may not have the infrastructure capacity to build an elaborate system from scratch. The general direction should be to leverage these cloud services. It is difficult to duplicate their scale and reliability as a journey. When duplicated, they may not offer the same level of cost advantage than those offered by these organizations due to their economies of scale. So, let us look at this as a journey to mature our systems and at a broad architecture level and then dive into individual components of such an architecture with each stop representing a significant shift in how we think about building applications. Let us look at how serverless is a new way to design in itself.

Let us start by going back to where systems evolved from. The journey begins with the monolithic architecture, where all application components, that is, user interface, business logic, data access are tightly coupled in a single unit. While simple to develop initially, monoliths become increasingly difficult to scale and maintain as the application grows.

The next stop is the N-tier architecture, which separates the presentation, application processing, and data management functions into separate tiers. This separation allows for more flexibility and scalability compared to monoliths, but still requires careful capacity planning and resource management.

The journey then takes us to microservices, where the application is decomposed into small, independently deployable services. Each service has its own lifecycle and can be scaled independently, providing a high degree of flexibility. However, managing a fleet of microservices brings its own set of challenges, such as service discovery, inter-service communication, and distributed data management.

Finally, we arrive at our destination: serverless architecture. In the serverless world, developers no longer have to think about servers at all. They simply write their code as functions, which are executed in ephemeral containers managed entirely by the cloud provider. Resources are automatically provisioned and scaled based on the incoming workload. This is a radically different way of building applications, and it fundamentally changes many aspects of how we design, develop, and operate distributed systems.

When considering serverless compute options, cold start has been a significant bottleneck, this issue though has been slowly fading away with innovative approaches (AWS Lambda SnapStart) where the initialized state is saved and drastically reduce the cold start issue. Concurrency is another issue area to consider, due to widespread abuse cloud providers have been forced to add limits on how much concurrency is available in an account. This problem reduces gradually with increased time with the cloud provider but will be an important consideration for someone to get started into the serverless compute adoption.

Core tenets of serverless

To truly appreciate the serverless paradigm, we need to understand its core principles. These are the fundamental characteristics that define a serverless system.

Event-driven execution

In the serverless world, compute resources are provisioned in response to events. These could be HTTP requests, database updates, file uploads, scheduled events, and more. When an event triggers a function, the cloud provider spins up an execution environment, runs the function, and then tears down the environment when the function completes. This event-driven model is a key enabler of the serverless promise of automatic scaling and pay-per-use pricing.

Ephemeral compute resources

Serverless functions are stateless and ephemeral. They do not maintain in-memory state between invocations, and the execution environment may be created or destroyed at any point. This has significant implications for application design. Any state that needs to persist between invocations must be stored in an external service, such as a database or a key-value store. This encourages a loosely coupled, stateless design that is inherently scalable.

Automatic scaling

One of the biggest selling points of serverless is its automatic scaling capabilities. As the workload increases, the cloud provider automatically spins up more function instances to handle the increased load. When the workload decreases, excess instances are torn down. Developers do not have to worry about capacity planning or resource provisioning the platform takes care of it automatically. This is a game-changer for applications with unpredictable or spiky workloads.

Pay-per-use pricing

In the serverless model, you only pay for the compute resources you actually consume. Billing is typically done at a very granular level, often measured in milliseconds of CPU time and gigabytes of memory used. This is a significant departure from the traditional model of paying for provisioned capacity, whether it is used or not. For applications with infrequent or bursty usage patterns, this can lead to significant cost savings.

Understanding serverless workloads

Not all applications are well-suited for serverless. To determine if serverless is a good fit, you need to understand the characteristics of your workload. Let us look at some common workload patterns and their suitability for serverless.

Request-driven workloads

These are workloads that are triggered by HTTP requests, typically serving web applications or APIs. Serverless is a great fit for these workloads, as each incoming request can trigger a function invocation. The platform can automatically scale the number of function instances based on the request volume. API Gateway, a managed service provided by AWS, is often used in conjunction with Lambda functions to create serverless APIs.

Event-driven workloads

Event-driven workloads are triggered by events, such as changes in a database, uploads to a storage bucket, or messages in a queue. Serverless is ideal for these workloads, as each event can trigger a function invocation. This enables the creation of highly scalable, loosely coupled architectures. AWS services like S3, DynamoDB, and Kinesis can serve as event sources for Lambda functions.

Stream processing workloads

These are workloads that process continuous streams of data in real-time. While serverless can handle stream processing, it is not always the best fit. Serverless functions are typically limited in execution time, for example, 15 minutes on AWS Lambda, so they are not suitable for processing infinite streams. However, for simple transformations or filtering of streaming data, serverless can still be a good choice. AWS Kinesis and DynamoDB Streams are often used as event sources for serverless stream processing.

Batch processing workloads

Batch processing workloads are characterized by the processing of large volumes of data at scheduled intervals. Serverless can be a good fit for certain batch processing tasks, particularly those that can be parallelized. Each batch job can trigger multiple function invocations, which can process the data in parallel. However, for very large batch jobs that require high-performance computing resources, traditional server-based or containerized architectures may be more suitable.

Long-running workloads

Serverless is generally not a good fit for long-running workloads, such as complex machine learning model training or large-scale data analysis. These workloads typically require dedicated, high-performance computing resources that can run for hours or even days. Serverless platforms typically have constraints on execution time and available memory, which make them unsuitable for these types of workloads.

Choosing the right compute pattern

Within the serverless landscape, there are different compute patterns to choose from. The two main patterns are **function as a service** (**FaaS**) and container-based serverless.

Function as a service

FaaS is the most fine-grained and event-driven compute pattern. In the FaaS model, developers write individual functions that are triggered by events. Each function typically performs a single, discrete task. FaaS platforms, like AWS Lambda, handle the execution environment, automatically scaling the number of function instances based on the incoming event rate.

FaaS functions are typically stateless and ephemeral. They do not maintain in-memory state between invocations, and the execution environment may be created or destroyed at any point. This means that any state that needs to persist between invocations must be stored in an external service, such as a database or a key-value store.

FaaS is well-suited for workloads that are highly event-driven and can be decomposed into small, independent tasks. However, it may not be the best fit for workloads that require long-running processes, stateful operations, or complex dependencies.

Container-based serverless

Container-based serverless platforms, like AWS Fargate or Google Cloud Run, provide a slightly higher level of abstraction compared to FaaS. Instead of individual functions, developers deploy entire containers, which can encapsulate more complex applications and dependencies.

While containers are typically more heavyweight than functions, container-based serverless platforms still provide the key benefits of serverless, such as automatic scaling and pay-per-use pricing. Containers are spun up in response to incoming requests and automatically scaled based on demand.

Container-based serverless can be a good fit for workloads that require more complex application environments, such as legacy applications that are being migrated to the cloud. However, it may not provide the same level of fine-grained scalability and event-driven capabilities as FaaS.

Serverless data management

Data management is one of the areas that is most impacted by the shift to serverless architectures. The ephemeral and stateless nature of serverless functions fundamentally changes how we store, access, and manage data.

Stateless data access patterns

In a serverless environment, compute resources are ephemeral, they may be created or destroyed at any point. This means that any state stored in memory will be lost when the function completes. Therefore, serverless functions must rely on external services for state management.

This has significant implications for data access patterns. Traditional patterns, like connection pooling and per-process caching, become less relevant in a serverless world. Instead, serverless architectures rely heavily on managed services for data storage and retrieval, such as Amazon S3 for file storage, DynamoDB for NoSQL data, and Aurora Serverless for relational data.

When designing data access for serverless, it is important to keep in mind the characteristics of serverless platforms. Functions should be designed to minimize startup time, which means avoiding heavy initialization routines like establishing database connections. Instead, connections should be established on-demand and released as soon as they are no longer needed.

Another key consideration is transaction management. Serverless functions are typically short-lived, so any transactions must be completed within the lifecycle of a single function invocation. This often requires the use of distributed transaction protocols, such as the Saga pattern, which breaks up a long-running transaction into a series of smaller, compensable transactions.

Choosing the right data store

The choice of data store is critical in a serverless architecture. Different workloads have different data requirements, and choosing the right data store can have a significant impact on performance, scalability, and cost.

For workloads that require strong consistency and ACID transactions, a serverless relational database like Aurora Serverless can be a good fit. Aurora Serverless provides the familiarity of a relational database while still offering the benefits of serverless, such as automatic scaling and pay-per-use pricing.

For workloads that are more read-heavy and can tolerate eventual consistency, a NoSQL database like DynamoDB can be a better choice. DynamoDB is designed for scale, offering single-digit millisecond performance at any scale. It's also fully managed, which means you do not have to worry about provisioning, patching, or managing servers.

For workloads that require full-text search or complex querying, a search engine like Amazon OpenSearch Service (successor to Amazon Elasticsearch Service) can be used. OpenSearch provides distributed, multi-tenant-capable full-text search engine with an HTTP web interface and schema-free JSON documents.

Event-driven data processing

Serverless architectures are inherently event-driven, and this extends to data processing as well. Many serverless workflows are triggered by data events, such as the creation of a new object in S3, an update to a DynamoDB table, or a message being added to a Kinesis stream.

This event-driven model enables the creation of highly scalable, loosely coupled data processing pipelines. Each stage in the pipeline can be implemented as a serverless function, which is triggered by the output of the previous stage. This allows for easy composition and chaining of data processing tasks.

There are several common patterns for event-driven data processing in serverless architectures, as follows:

- **Fan-out pattern**: In this pattern, an event is used to trigger multiple downstream functions in parallel. Each function performs a specific task, such as transforming the data, enriching it with additional information, or writing it to a data store. This pattern is useful for workloads that require high throughput and can be easily parallelized.

- **Aggregation pattern**: This pattern is the inverse of the fan-out pattern. Multiple upstream events are aggregated and processed by a single downstream function. This can be useful for workloads that require data to be collected and processed in batches, such as time-series data aggregation or batch reporting.

- **Event sourcing pattern**: In this pattern, all changes to application state are stored as a sequence of events. Each event represents a state change, and the current state can be reconstructed by replaying the events in sequence. This pattern provides a complete audit trail and enables advanced capabilities like time-travel debugging and retroactive analysis.

Serverless best practices

While serverless architectures offer many benefits, they also come with their own set of challenges and best practices. Here are some key considerations when designing and building serverless systems.

Function design

Serverless functions should be designed to be small, focused, and stateless. Each function should perform a single, well-defined task, and should be able to run to completion in a short amount of time (typically seconds to minutes). Functions should also be designed to be idempotent, meaning that they can be safely retried in case of failure without causing unintended side effects.

Event-driven architecture

Serverless systems are inherently event-driven, so it is important to design your architecture around events. This means using event sources like S3, DynamoDB, and Kinesis to trigger your functions, and using event-driven patterns like fan-out and event sourcing to process data.

Stateless design

Serverless functions are stateless, so any state that needs to persist between invocations must be stored externally. This means using services like S3, DynamoDB, or ElastiCache for state management, and designing your functions to be as stateless as possible.

Fully serverless platforms

Let us dive into building a fully serverless product catalog service using AWS services. We will create a system that allows you to manage and display product information, providing a scalable and cost-effective solution.

To start, let us outline the key components we will need, as follows:

- Product data storage
- API for managing and retrieving product data
- Front-end for displaying the product catalog

Now, let us map these components to AWS services and see how they fit together.

Product data storage with DynamoDB

For storing our product data, we will use Amazon DynamoDB. DynamoDB is a fully managed NoSQL database that provides fast and predictable performance with seamless scalability. It is a perfect fit for a serverless architecture.

We will create a DynamoDB table called **products** with the following attributes:

- **ProductID (Primary key)**: A unique identifier for each product.
- **Name**: The name of the product.
- **Description**: A description of the product.
- **Price**: The price of the product.
- **Category**: The category the product belongs to.

DynamoDB will automatically scale to handle any amount of data we need to store, and we only pay for the resources we actually use.

API with Lambda and API Gateway

To manage our product data, we need an API that can handle **Create, Read, Update, Delete (CRUD)** operations. We will use AWS Lambda and API Gateway to create a serverless API.

First, we will create Lambda functions for each API operation, as follows:

- **CreateProduct**: Adds a new product to the DynamoDB table.
- **GetProduct**: Retrieves a single product by its ProductID.
- **ListProducts**: Retrieves a list of all products, with optional filtering by category.
- **UpdateProduct**: Updates an existing product's details.
- **DeleteProduct**: Removes a product from the catalog.

Next, we will use API Gateway to create REST endpoints that trigger these Lambda functions. For example, we will create the following endpoints:

- **POST/products**: Creates a new product (triggers the CreateProduct Lambda).

- **GET/products/{ProductID}**: Retrieves a single product (triggers the GetProduct Lambda).

- **GET/products**: Retrieves a list of products (triggers the ListProducts Lambda).

- **PUT/products/{ProductID}**: Updates a product (triggers the UpdateProduct Lambda).

- **DELETE/products/{ProductID}**: Deletes a product (triggers the DeleteProduct Lambda).

API Gateway will handle all the details of routing requests to the appropriate Lambda function.

Front-end with S3 and CloudFront

For the front-end of our product catalog, we can use simple HTML, CSS, and JavaScript files. We'll host these files in an Amazon S3 bucket configured for static website hosting.

To ensure fast load times for users around the world, we will distribute our static content via Amazon CloudFront. CloudFront is a global **content delivery network** (**CDN**) that caches copies of our files at edge locations worldwide.

Handling authorization with Cognito

If we want to add user authentication and authorization to our product catalog (for example, to allow only admins to add or update products), we can use Amazon Cognito.

Cognito allows us to easily add user sign-up, sign-in, and access control to our web app. It can provide an OAuth 2.0 endpoint for our front-end to authenticate against, and it can generate temporary AWS credentials for authenticated users to directly access our API.

To secure our API, we can configure API Gateway to validate OAuth tokens from Cognito. We can use IAM policies to specify fine-grained permissions, controlling which actions authenticated users are allowed to perform.

Monitoring and logging with CloudWatch

To monitor our serverless product catalog, we can use Amazon CloudWatch. CloudWatch collects monitoring and operational data in the form of logs, metrics, and events, providing a unified view of AWS resources, applications, and services.

We can use CloudWatch to monitor the invocation counts, durations, and error rates of our Lambda functions. We can set up alarms to notify us if any of these metrics exceed expected thresholds.

CloudWatch also integrates with API Gateway, allowing us to track request counts, latency, and 4xx/5xx error rates for our API endpoints.

For our front-end, we can use CloudWatch Synthetics to create canary tests that regularly check the availability and performance of our website.

Infrastructure as code with CloudFormation

Managing a serverless application with many moving parts can become complex. To make our infrastructure manageable and reproducible, we can use AWS CloudFormation to define it as code.

With CloudFormation, we can write templates that describe all the AWS resources our application needs (Lambda functions, DynamoDB tables, API Gateway endpoints, etc.) and any configuration required. CloudFormation then takes care of provisioning and configuring those resources for us.

Using CloudFormation has several benefits, as follows:

- Infrastructure becomes version controlled, just like our application code.
- We can easily replicate our infrastructure in multiple environments (dev, test, prod).
- We can automate our infrastructure deployment as part of our CI/CD pipeline.

By leveraging AWS services like DynamoDB, Lambda, API Gateway, S3, CloudFront, Cognito, CloudWatch, and CloudFormation, we can build a fully serverless product catalog that is scalable, cost-effective, and easy to manage.

This is just a high-level overview. In a real-world application, we would need to consider many additional details, such as data validation, error handling, caching strategies, and more.

But the basic pattern remains the same: by composing serverless services, we can create powerful applications that are resilient, scalable, and require less operational overhead than traditional server-based architectures.

This architecture allows us to focus on our application code, while AWS handles the undifferentiated heavy lifting of provisioning, scaling, and managing infrastructure.

Serverless systems, such as AWS Lambda or Google Cloud Functions, offer compelling advantages writing scalable and highly available systems, including automatic scaling, reduced operational overhead, and a pay-per-execution pricing model that aligns costs with actual usage. These traits make serverless ideal for sporadic or unpredictable workloads, such as handling flash sales, processing seasonal order spikes, or running event-driven background tasks (e.g., sending confirmation emails or updating user recommendations). However, the cost-effectiveness of serverless solutions is highly context-dependent. While they excel in minimizing expenses at low-to-moderate traffic volumes, where idle infrastructure costs are eliminated they can quickly become prohibitively expensive for sustained high-load scenarios. For example, a product catalog API experiencing consistent heavy traffic might incur higher costs through thousands of daily Lambda invocations compared to provisioning a fixed-cost container cluster. Additionally, hidden expenses such as cold-start latency, data transfer fees, and egress charges can erode savings, particularly for data-intensive operations like image processing or real-time analytics. To mitigate these risks, teams must implement rigorous usage monitoring, adopt architectural optimizations (e.g., request batching), and evaluate hybrid approaches that combine serverless for bursty workloads with reserved instances for stable, high-volume services. Ultimately, serverless adoption requires a nuanced cost-benefit analysis tailored to the specific load patterns and growth trajectory of the business.

As the serverless ecosystem continues to evolve, with new services and capabilities being added regularly, the possibilities for what we can build with serverless architectures are constantly expanding. It is an exciting space to watch and to be a part of.

Conclusion

The selection of platforms and technologies in distributed systems represents a complex decision matrix where trade-offs must be carefully evaluated against business requirements, scalability needs, and operational constraints. Throughout this chapter, we examined how these choices manifest in real-world e-commerce scenarios, from handling millions of product queries to ensuring consistent order processing and managing real-time inventory updates.

The evolution toward serverless architectures and cloud-native solutions has expanded the available options while introducing new considerations around state management, data consistency, and operational complexity. We have seen how modern e-commerce platforms benefit from polyglot persistence strategies, employing different storage solutions for various data access patterns, and how message brokers enable robust event-driven architectures for handling complex business workflows.

The key takeaway is that successful platform selection requires a holistic understanding of both technical capabilities and business context. It is not just about choosing the most advanced or popular technologies, but about finding the right balance between innovation and reliability, between development velocity and operational stability. As systems continue to evolve, the ability to make informed technological choices becomes increasingly crucial for building resilient, scalable, and maintainable distributed systems.

In the next chapter, we will look at deployment strategies for distributed systems.

CHAPTER 13

Deployment Strategies and Production Readiness

Introduction

Modern software deployment has evolved far beyond the traditional practice of updating applications during scheduled maintenance windows. Today's systems demand sophisticated deployment strategies that minimize risk while maximizing system availability. This chapter explores contemporary deployment approaches, examining how organizations can safely and efficiently deliver changes to production environments while serving traffic at scale. These systems ensure that while systems do not break, they also do not break the user functionality. We will look at different approaches of deployment and continuous testing as new iterations of the software are deployed into production.

Structure

The chapter covers the following topics:

- Foundations of modern deployment
- Feature flags
- Progressive deployment patterns
- Testing and monitoring strategy
- Safety mechanisms
- Container based deployment

Objectives

By the end of this chapter, readers will have a comprehensive understanding of modern deployment strategies and the essential elements of production readiness in distributed systems. It explores the evolution from traditional deployment methods to sophisticated progressive delivery approaches, emphasizing the critical balance between rapid deployment and system stability. The chapter delves into key concepts including feature flags, blue-green deployments, canary releases, and container orchestration, presenting them not just as technical solutions but as strategic tools for managing risk and ensuring system reliability. Readers will gain insights into implementing robust testing frameworks, monitoring strategies, and automated safety mechanisms that form the foundation of reliable production systems. The chapter focuses on practical applications while addressing the complexities and challenges organizations face when implementing these strategies, providing a roadmap for building resilient deployment pipelines that can scale with growing system demands.

Foundations of modern deployment

The landscape of software deployment has transformed dramatically over the past decade. Where organizations once relied on lengthy maintenance windows and complete system shutdowns, modern deployment strategies enable continuous service delivery with minimal disruption. Consider an online retailer's checkout service, even a few minutes of downtime can result in substantial revenue loss and damaged customer trust. This reality has driven the evolution of deployment practices.

Understanding modern deployment challenges

Today's deployment challenges extend beyond simple code updates. Systems must handle the following:

- **Complex dependencies**: Modern applications often comprise dozens or hundreds of interconnected services. A payment processing service, for instance, might depend on fraud detection, inventory management, and customer profile services. Each dependency introduces potential deployment complications.

- **State management**: Stateful applications present unique challenges during deployment. Consider a shopping cart service maintaining session state during updates requires careful orchestration to prevent data loss or inconsistency.

- **Scale considerations**: Large-scale systems may process thousands of transactions per second. Deployment strategies must account for this load, ensuring seamless transitions without degrading performance.

Rise of progressive deployment

Progressive deployment emerged as a response to these challenges, introducing methodologies that reduce risk through incremental change. This approach breaks down deployments into manageable stages, each with its own validation criteria.

Key principles of progressive deployment

Following are the key principles of progressive deployment:

- **Gradual rollout**: Instead of updating all instances simultaneously, changes are introduced incrementally. For example, a new recommendation algorithm might initially process only 5% of requests, allowing teams to assess its performance before wider deployment.

- **Controlled exposure**: Modern deployment strategies employ sophisticated control mechanisms. When deploying a new search service implementation, teams can route traffic based on various criteria:

  Refer to the following:

  o Geographic regions
  o User segments
  o Request patterns
  o System load

- **Automated verification**: Each deployment stage incorporates automated checks that validate system behavior. These might include the following:

  o Performance metrics
  o Error rates
  o Business KPIs
  o Integration health

- **Rapid rollback capability**: Despite careful planning, issues can emerge. Modern deployment systems must support quick rollback mechanisms. For instance, if a new pricing calculation service shows unexpected behavior, the system should automatically revert to the previous version based on predefined criteria.

Understanding modern deployment challenges

Today's deployment challenges extend beyond simple code updates. Systems must handle the following:

- **Complex dependencies**: Modern applications often comprise dozens or hundreds of interconnected services. A payment processing service, for instance, might depend on fraud detection, inventory management, and customer profile services. Each dependency introduces potential deployment complications.

- **State management**: Stateful applications present unique challenges during deployment. Consider a shopping cart service maintaining session state during updates, which requires careful orchestration to prevent data loss or inconsistency. For example, deploying a new cart service version to all regions simultaneously could disrupt active user sessions if state-handling logic changes. Progressive deployment mitigates this by limiting the rollout to a single region first.

- **Scale considerations**: Large-scale systems may process thousands of transactions per second. Deployment strategies must account for this load, ensuring seamless transitions without degrading performance.

Rise of progressive deployment

Progressive deployment emerged as a response to these challenges, introducing methodologies that reduce risk through incremental change. This approach breaks down deployments into manageable stages, each with its own validation criteria. Unlike older all-or-nothing methods, for example, updating every server at once, progressive deployment prioritizes safety over speed.

Key principles of progressive deployment

Following are the key principles of progressive deployment:

- **Gradual rollout**: Instead of updating all instances simultaneously, changes are introduced incrementally. Following are the examples:
  - A new recommendation algorithm might initially process only 5% of requests, allowing teams to assess its performance before wider deployment.
  - For stateful services like shopping carts, a regional rollout ensures session data integrity. Example: Deploy the updated cart service to users in Europe only first. Monitor for session state errors or crashes, then expand to other regions once stability is confirmed.

- **Controlled exposure**: Modern deployment strategies employ sophisticated control mechanisms. When deploying a new search service implementation, teams can route traffic based on criteria as follows:
  - Geographic regions, for example, test in a low-traffic region before global rollout.
  - User segments, for example, internal employees first, then premium customers.

- o Request patterns, for example, route only GET requests to the new service initially.

- o System load, for example, limit deployment to off-peak hours.

- **Automated verification**: Each deployment stage incorporates automated checks that validate system behavior. These include the following:

  - o Performance metrics, for example, 95th percentile latency below 500ms.

  - o Error rates, for example, API errors < 0.5%.

  - o Business KPIs, for example, no drop in add-to-cart rates.

  - o Integration of health, for example, downstream inventory service responds within 2s.

- **Rapid rollback capability**: Despite careful planning, issues can emerge. Modern systems support quick rollbacks using the following:

  - o **Feature toggles**: Instantly disable the new cart service in Europe if session errors spike.

  - o **Traffic shifting**: Redirect users back to the stable version via load balancer rules.

  - o **Versioned state storage**: Ensure old and new service versions can coexist during rollouts by versioning session data (e.g., cart data schema v1 vs. v2).

Partial rollouts matter for stateful services

The shopping cart example highlights how progressive deployment differs from legacy approaches, as follows:

- **Traditional method**: Deploy the new cart service globally. If state handling has a bug, all active sessions risk corruption.

- **Progressive method**:
  - o Deploy to Europe first.
  - o Monitor session state health, for example, cart abandonment rates, error logs.
  - o If stable, proceed to North America and APAC.
  - o If unstable, roll back Europe only, minimizing user impact.

This approach isolates risk to a subset of users, ensuring business continuity even during failures.

Risk management in modern deployment

Effective risk management in deployment requires a multi-faceted approach, as follows:

- **Monitoring and observability**: Modern systems require comprehensive monitoring that extends beyond basic health checks. Consider the following key aspects:

- o   Service behavior patterns
- o   Performance metrics across different time scales
- o   Error rates and patterns
- o   Business metric impact

- **Infrastructure considerations**: Deployment strategies must account for infrastructure capabilities, as follows:
  - o   Load balancer configuration
  - o   Network capacity
  - o   Database connection management
  - o   Cache coherence

- **Evolution of deployment tooling**: Modern deployment relies heavily on sophisticated tooling that enables the following:
  - o   Automated deployment pipelines
  - o   Traffic management
  - o   State synchronization
  - o   Health monitoring
  - o   Rollback automation

These tools have evolved from simple script-based deployments to complex orchestration systems that manage the entire deployment lifecycle.

For example, when deploying a significant database schema change the following:

- **Traditional approach**:
  - o   Schedule maintenance window
  - o   Stop application
  - o   Update schema
  - o   Verify changes
  - o   Restart application

- **Modern approach**:
  - o   Deploy new schema alongside existing
  - o   Gradually migrate data in background
  - o   Route traffic incrementally to new schema
  - o   Verify at each stage
  - o   Remove old schema when safe

This evolution enables organizations to deploy changes with significantly reduced risk and minimal service interruption.

Feature flags

Feature flags represent a fundamental shift in how we think about software deployment and release management. While deployment traditionally meant pushing code changes directly to production, feature flags introduce a layer of sophistication that separates the deployment of code from its activation. This separation creates unprecedented control over how and when features become available to users.

Feature flag architecture

At its core, feature flag architecture is built on the principle of conditional execution. Modern feature flag systems, however, have evolved far beyond simple Boolean switches. Today's architectures represent complex decision-making systems that can process multiple inputs and conditions to determine whether and how a feature should be enabled.

The foundation of a modern feature flag system rests on three primary pillars: the management layer, the evaluation engine, and the integration layer. The management layer serves as the control center, where teams configure and maintain flag states. This centralized approach ensures consistency across the system and provides a single source of truth for feature states. More importantly, it maintains a comprehensive audit trail of all changes, crucial for debugging and compliance requirements.

The evaluation engine represents the system's brain, processing complex rules and conditions in real-time. Unlike simple on-off switches, modern evaluation engines can process multiple parameters simultaneously. They consider user attributes, system conditions, time-based rules, and even complex business logic to make activation decisions. This sophistication allows for highly targeted feature rollouts, essential in today's diverse user landscapes.

Strategic implementation patterns

The true power of feature flags emerges through their strategic implementation patterns. Gradual rollouts represent one of the most powerful patterns, allowing organizations to introduce changes incrementally rather than all at once. This approach begins by exposing new features to a small percentage of users, gradually increasing exposure as confidence grows. The beauty of this pattern lies in its risk management capabilities, any issues that arise affect only a small subset of users, containing potential negative impact.

Targeted releases take this concept further by introducing sophisticated user segmentation. Rather than releasing features based purely on percentages, organizations can target specific user segments based on various attributes. This might include geographic location, user preferences, usage patterns, or any combination of attributes. This granular control allows organizations to test features with specific user groups before broader rollout, gathering valuable feedback and ensuring feature readiness.

Technical debt and management

While feature flags offer powerful capabilities, they also introduce complexity that must be carefully managed to prevent technical debt accumulation. The challenge lies not in implementing feature flags but in managing them throughout their lifecycle. Every feature flag added to the system represents a decision point that must be maintained, documented, and eventually removed.

Proper feature flag management requires a comprehensive strategy that begins even before a flag is implemented. Each flag should have a clearly defined purpose and, more importantly, an exit strategy. Organizations must establish clear criteria for when and how flags will be removed. This includes defining success metrics, establishing monitoring requirements, and planning for eventual code cleanup.

Documentation plays a crucial role in managing feature flag complexity. Beyond basic implementation details, documentation should capture the business context, expected lifetime, and dependencies of each flag. This information becomes invaluable as systems grow and team members change, ensuring that future maintainers understand not just how a flag works, but why it exists and when it can be removed.

Impact analysis and organizational considerations

The introduction of feature flags fundamentally changes how organizations approach software development and deployment. While the technical implementation might seem straightforward, the organizational impact can be significant. Teams must adapt their development processes to account for feature flag states during testing. Quality assurance processes need to consider multiple feature combinations, significantly increasing the testing matrix.

Performance considerations become increasingly important as feature flag systems scale. Each flag evaluation represents a decision point that must be processed quickly to maintain system responsiveness. Organizations must carefully balance the granularity of control with performance requirements, often implementing sophisticated caching strategies to minimize evaluation overhead.

Monitoring and observability take on new dimensions with feature flags. Teams need visibility not just into whether features are working, but how they are being accessed, by whom, and with what impact on system performance and business metrics. This requires sophisticated monitoring systems that can correlate feature flag states with system behavior and business outcomes.

The success of a feature flag system ultimately depends on establishing clear governance processes. This includes defining who can create flags, who can modify them, and how changes are approved and implemented. These processes must balance the need for control with the ability to move quickly, especially in emergency situations where rapid feature toggles might be necessary.

Progressive deployment patterns

The evolution of software deployment has led to sophisticated patterns that prioritize safety, reliability, and user experience. Two prominent patterns have emerged as industry standards: blue-green deployment and canary releases. These patterns, while distinct in their approaches, share a common goal: minimizing risk while maximizing deployment efficiency.

Blue-green deployment

Blue-Green deployment represents an elegant solution to the challenge of updating production systems with zero downtime. The pattern's strength lies in its simplicity: maintaining two identical production environments, running different versions of the application. At any given time, only one environment serves production traffic, while the other stands ready for the next deployment.

Consider the sequence of events in a blue-green deployment. The process begins with two identical environments like Blue, currently serving production traffic, and green, standing idle. When a new version requires deployment, it first goes to the green environment. This staging ground allows for comprehensive testing under production-like conditions, without affecting real users. The identical nature of these environments is crucial, they must mirror each other in terms of configuration, capacity, and connectivity.

The critical moment in blue-green deployment comes during the traffic switch. Load balancers redirect user traffic from blue to green in a single, atomic operation. This instant transition eliminates the complexity of managing multiple active versions simultaneously. If issues arise after the switch, returning to the previous version is equally straightforward, simply redirect traffic back to blue. This rollback capability provides a safety net that traditional deployment methods cannot match.

However, blue-green deployment introduces its own set of challenges. Database schema changes require particular attention, as both environments must maintain compatibility during the transition period. State management becomes crucial with user sessions, cached data, and in-flight transactions must all be considered in the deployment strategy. Organizations must also account for the cost of maintaining two full production environments, though cloud infrastructure has made this more feasible.

Canary releases

While blue-green deployment offers clean transitions, canary releases provide a more granular approach to risk management. Named after the historical practice of using canaries to detect dangerous conditions in coal mines, this pattern involves gradually exposing new versions to increasing portions of user traffic.

The canary process begins by deploying the new version alongside the existing one. Initially, only a small percentage of traffic, perhaps 1% or 5%, routes to the new version. This limited exposure provides real production testing while minimizing potential impact. Monitoring systems play a crucial role here, carefully tracking performance metrics, error rates, and user behavior patterns.

As confidence grows, traffic allocation to the new version increases incrementally. Each increase represents a decision point, backed by data from the monitoring systems. This gradual approach allows organizations to detect issues early, before they affect a significant portion of users. The pattern particularly shines in detecting performance degradation, unusual error patterns, or unexpected user behavior that might not surface in test environments.

The sophistication of modern canary deployments extends beyond simple traffic percentages. Advanced implementations might consider user segments, geographic regions, or other attributes when routing traffic. This targeted approach allows organizations to test new versions with specific user groups before broader rollout, gathering valuable feedback while managing risk.

Table 13.1 illustrates considerations to keep in mind when choosing one pattern over the other:

Aspect	Blue-green deployment	Canary releases
Downtime	Zero downtime	Zero downtime
Rollback speed	Instant (traffic shift)	Gradual (traffic re-routing)
Infrastructure cost	High (2x environments)	Low (no full duplication)
Risk exposure	All users at once	Controlled subset of users/traffic
Complexity	Moderate (state/database sync)	High (monitoring, version coexistence)
Typical use cases	Mission-critical systems, for example, payments Large monolithic applications	User-facing features Microservices with variable traffic

Table 13.1: Considerations when choosing deployment strategies

Implementation considerations

Both patterns require careful consideration of infrastructure and operational requirements. Load balancers must support sophisticated traffic management capabilities. Monitoring systems need to provide granular visibility into system behavior across versions. Organizations must develop clear criteria for success and rollback decisions.

Database management deserves special attention in both patterns. Changes must maintain backward compatibility during the deployment period. This often means implementing schema changes in multiple steps, ensuring both old and new versions can operate simultaneously. Organizations might need to maintain multiple database versions or implement sophisticated migration strategies.

State management presents another crucial consideration. User sessions, cache data, and in-flight transactions must transition smoothly between versions. This might require implementing session replication, shared caching layers, or other state management strategies. The complexity increases in distributed systems, where state might exist across multiple services.

Infrastructure automation plays a vital role in both patterns. The ability to provision, configure, and validate environments automatically becomes crucial for maintaining deployment efficiency. IaC practices ensure environment consistency and enable rapid recovery in failure scenarios.

Risk management and monitoring

Successful implementation of either pattern requires sophisticated monitoring and alerting systems. These systems must provide real-time visibility into application behavior, performance metrics, and business KPIs. More importantly, they must be able to detect subtle anomalies that might indicate potential issues.

The monitoring strategy should encompass multiple layers, as follows:

- Application performance and behavior
- Infrastructure health and capacity
- Users experience metrics
- Business impact indicators

Automated rollback triggers become crucial safety mechanisms. These systems must balance sensitivity with reliability, avoiding false positives while catching real issues quickly. Organizations need to define clear thresholds and decision criteria for automated rollbacks.

Testing and monitoring strategy

In the realm of modern deployment, testing and monitoring form an intricate web of safety mechanisms that ensure system reliability and performance. While traditional testing focused primarily on pre-deployment verification, today's systems require continuous validation throughout the deployment lifecycle. This comprehensive approach bridges the gap between controlled testing environments and the unpredictability of production systems.

Synthetic monitoring

Synthetic monitoring represents a proactive approach to system validation, continuously executing artificial transactions that mirror real user behavior. Unlike passive monitoring that waits for actual user interactions, synthetic monitoring provides consistent, predictable validation of critical system paths. This approach becomes particularly valuable during deployment phases, where early detection of issues can prevent widespread impact.

The sophistication of modern synthetic monitoring extends far beyond simple endpoint checks. Advanced systems simulate complex user journeys, replicating multi-step processes that users perform in production. For instance, a synthetic transaction might simulate the entire user journey from authentication through complex business processes, validating not just individual components but the intricate interactions between them.

The true power of synthetic monitoring emerges in its ability to maintain consistent baseline measurements. These baseline metrics become crucial during deployments, providing immediate feedback on system behavior changes. When a new version deploys, synthetic monitoring can quickly identify performance degradation or functional issues by comparing current behavior against established baselines.

Following is an example:

After deploying a cart service update, synthetic monitoring detects that 10% of simulated checkouts fail due to mismatched product SKUs. The team halts the rollout, fixes the bug, and retests using the same synthetic workflow preventing a site-wide outage.

In this hypothetical case, the ecommerce company may have identified a single broken payment flow that could cost thousands in lost sales per hour. Synthetic monitoring acts as a 24/7 safety net. By simulating critical paths continuously, teams gain confidence in deployments and ensure seamless user experiences.

Integration testing in production

The complexity of modern distributed systems has transformed how we approach integration testing. Traditional pre-deployment integration tests, while valuable, cannot fully replicate the complexity of production environments. This reality has led to the emergence of production integration testing, carefully controlled validation of system interactions in the actual production environment.

Production integration testing requires sophisticated isolation mechanisms to prevent test activities from affecting real users. This might involve creating separate test paths through the system, using synthetic user accounts, or implementing special test modes in production services. The goal is to validate real production interactions without risking impact to actual users.

The scope of integration testing must extend beyond functional validation to include performance and scalability aspects. Systems need to verify not just that services can communicate, but that they maintain expected performance characteristics under various load conditions. This becomes particularly crucial during deployments, where new versions might introduce subtle performance implications that only surface under production conditions.

Cross-stage verification

Modern deployment processes implement multiple verification stages, each focusing on different aspects of system behavior. This staged approach provides increasing confidence as deployment progresses, while maintaining the ability to catch issues early in the process.

The first stage typically focuses on basic health checks, that is, verifying that all components start correctly and can handle basic requests. These checks provide rapid feedback on fundamental issues that might prevent successful deployment. The speed of these checks becomes crucial, as they often gate the progression to subsequent stages.

As deployment progresses, verification expands to include more sophisticated validation. Performance testing becomes more comprehensive, examining system behavior under various load conditions. Integration testing broadens to cover more complex scenarios. Business metric validation begins, ensuring that the system not only functions technically but delivers expected business outcomes.

The final stages of verification often involve gradual exposure to real user traffic, carefully monitored for any deviations from expected behavior. This phase requires particularly sophisticated monitoring, as it must detect subtle issues that might affect user experience or business outcomes. The monitoring systems must balance sensitivity with accuracy, avoiding false alarms while catching real issues quickly.

Data-driven validation

Modern testing and monitoring strategies increasingly rely on data-driven approaches to validation rather than relying solely on predefined thresh marks, systems analyze historical patterns to establish dynamic baselines. This approach recognizes that **normal** system behavior varies by time of day, day of week, and other factors.

Statistical analysis plays a crucial role in this approach. Systems must distinguish between normal variations and potential issues, often using advanced anomaly detection algorithms. These systems learn from historical patterns, continuously refining their understanding of normal behavior while adapting to changing conditions.

Machine learning techniques have begun to enhance these capabilities, enabling more sophisticated pattern recognition and predictive analytics. These systems can often identify potential issues before they become significant problems, enabling proactive intervention rather than reactive response.

Observability and debugging

The complexity of modern systems demands sophisticated observability capabilities. Traditional logging and metrics, while still important, must be supplemented with more advanced observability tools. Distributed tracing becomes crucial in understanding request flows through complex service architectures. Detailed performance profiling helps identify bottlenecks and optimization opportunities.

Deployment processes must ensure these observability capabilities remain effective across version changes. This includes maintaining consistent correlation identifiers, preserving logging context, and ensuring trace continuity across service boundaries. The ability to debug issues effectively becomes particularly crucial during deployment phases, where rapid problem identification and resolution can prevent widespread impact.

Safety mechanisms

In the complex landscape of modern deployment, safety mechanisms serve as the critical infrastructure that prevents minor issues from escalating into major incidents. These mechanisms represent more than simple checks; they form a comprehensive safety net that protects system integrity throughout the deployment process.

Automated deployment safeguards

The foundation of deployment safety lies in automated safeguards that continuously evaluate system health and performance. These safeguards operate at multiple levels, creating layers of protection that together ensure safe and reliable deployments. Unlike manual interventions, automated safeguards can react instantly to emerging issues, often preventing problems before they impact users.

Modern safeguard systems employ sophisticated decision matrices that consider multiple factors simultaneously. These systems move beyond simple binary health checks to evaluate complex interactions between different system components. For instance, when evaluating the health of a newly deployed service, the system considers not just the service's direct metrics (e.g., latency, error rates) but also its impact on dependent services, overall system performance, and business outcomes. In complex microservices architectures, this nuanced evaluation often leads to partial rollbacks or targeted hotfixes rather than full environment reversions. For example, if a faulty recommendation service degrades checkout conversion rates, the system might roll back *only that component* while preserving updates to unrelated services like inventory management. Similarly, a configuration error in a payment gateway could trigger a hotfix deployment to that specific microservice, minimizing downtime for unaffected workflows. This granular approach ensures system stability while preserving deployment velocity in distributed environments.

The timing of these evaluations becomes crucial in deployment scenarios. Early detection systems monitor initial deployment stages, looking for immediate issues that might warrant immediate rollback. As deployment progresses, the scope of evaluation broadens to include more subtle indicators of potential problems. This graduated approach balances the need for quick problem detection with the reality that some issues only become apparent over time.

Health assessment systems

Modern health assessment extends far beyond simple uptime monitoring. These systems implement sophisticated health models that consider multiple dimensions of system behavior. Performance metrics, error rates, and resource utilization form the basic layer of health assessment. However, modern systems also consider higher-level indicators such as user experience metrics, business transaction success rates, and even customer satisfaction indicators.

The sophistication of health assessment systems lies in their ability to understand context. What constitutes **healthy** behavior often varies by time of day, day of week, or other environmental factors. Modern systems maintain dynamic baselines that adapt to these variations, enabling more accurate detection of genuine issues while reducing false alarms.

These systems must also account for the transitional nature of deployments. During deployment phases, some variation from normal patterns is expected. The challenge lies in distinguishing between acceptable deployment-related variations and genuine problems that require intervention. This often involves implementing specialized evaluation rules during deployment windows, with gradually tightening thresholds as the deployment stabilizes.

Rollback automation

Automated rollback represents the ultimate safety net in modern deployment systems. These systems must balance two competing requirements: the need to react quickly to serious issues while avoiding unnecessary rollbacks due to temporary anomalies. This balance requires sophisticated decision algorithms that consider multiple factors before initiating a rollback.

The rollback process itself requires careful orchestration. Modern systems implement phased rollbacks that minimize disruption while ensuring system stability. The first phase might involve stopping the progression of the deployment and preventing new traffic from reaching the updated components. Subsequent phases gradually redirect traffic back to the previous version while ensuring no data loss or transaction interruption.

State management becomes particularly crucial during rollback operations. The system must maintain data consistency across version changes, handling in-flight transactions and ensuring no loss of critical information. This often requires implementing sophisticated state tracking mechanisms and carefully managed transition procedures.

Recovery procedures

While rollback capabilities provide immediate incident response, comprehensive recovery procedures ensure long-term system stability. These procedures extend beyond simple version reversion to include data reconciliation, state verification, and system rebalancing.

Recovery systems must account for the distributed nature of modern applications. When rolling back changes, the system must consider the impact on dependent services and ensure proper synchronization across the entire service ecosystem. This might involve implementing compensating transactions or state reconciliation procedures to maintain system consistency.

The sophistication of modern recovery systems lies in their ability to handle partial failures. Not all issues require complete system rollback; sometimes, targeted recovery of specific components or transactions provides a more appropriate response. These systems must implement fine-grained recovery capabilities while maintaining overall system consistency.

Learning and adaptation

Modern safety mechanisms implement learning systems that continuously improve their effectiveness. These systems analyze incident patterns, identifying common failure modes and refining detection algorithms accordingly. This learning extends to understanding the effectiveness of different recovery strategies, enabling more targeted responses to future incidents.

Adaptation capability becomes particularly valuable in evolving system architectures. As systems grow and change, safety mechanisms must adapt to new patterns of behavior and potential failure modes. This often involves implementing machine learning algorithms that can identify new patterns and adjust safety thresholds accordingly.

Container based deployment

The emergence of container orchestration platforms, particularly Kubernetes, has revolutionized deployment strategies in modern distributed systems. This transformation extends beyond simple containerization, encompassing sophisticated orchestration patterns that enhance deployment reliability, scalability, and manageability.

Orchestrated deployment strategies

Modern container orchestration platforms like Kubernetes and AWS **Elastic Container Service (ECS)** introduce deployment patterns that automatically manage the complexities of container lifecycle management. Unlike traditional deployment approaches, these tools handle intricate details such as container scheduling, networking, and state management through declarative configurations. For example, Kubernetes' Deployment objects automate rolling updates and rollbacks, while AWS ECS coordinates service discovery and load balancing via integration with **Application Load Balancers (ALBs)**.

The sophistication of orchestrated deployments lies in their ability to manage complex scenarios seamlessly. Kubernetes rolling updates, for instance, incrementally replace old container pods with new ones while maintaining service availability. The orchestration system carefully coordinates this process, draining connections from old containers, spinning up new ones, and verifying health checks to ensure uninterrupted service delivery. Similarly, AWS ECS uses blue-green deployments with CodeDeploy to shift traffic between task sets gradually, minimizing risk during transitions.

For stateful applications like databases, orchestration tools provide specialized patterns. Kubernetes StatefulSets preserve persistent storage and network identities during updates, while Amazon ECS volume mounts enable seamless state management for tasks. This automation fundamentally changes deployment planning, allowing teams to focus on business logic rather than infrastructure mechanics.

Advanced deployment strategies in container environments introduce sophisticated traffic management capabilities. These systems can automatically adjust routing rules, gradually shifting traffic between old and new versions while monitoring system health. This capability enables sophisticated deployment patterns without requiring complex external tooling.

Stateful set management

Stateful applications present unique challenges in containerized environments. Modern orchestration platforms address these challenges through specialized controllers that understand and manage application state. These controllers ensure proper ordering during deployment operations, maintaining data consistency and service availability.

The complexity of stateful deployments requires careful consideration of data persistence and state synchronization. Modern systems implement sophisticated volume management capabilities that ensure data availability across container instances. These systems must handle scenarios such as container rescheduling, node failures, and scaling operations while maintaining data integrity.

State management in containerized environments extends beyond simple data persistence. Modern systems must handle distributed state, managing aspects such as session information, caching layers, and temporary storage. This often requires implementing sophisticated state synchronization mechanisms that ensure consistency across the distributed system.

Configuration management

Configuration management takes on new dimensions in containerized deployments. Modern systems implement sophisticated configuration management patterns that separate configuration from container images, enabling dynamic configuration updates without requiring container rebuilds.

The sophistication of configuration management extends to secrets handling sensitive information such as credentials and encryption keys. Modern systems implement secure storage and distribution mechanisms that ensure sensitive information remains protected while remaining accessible to authorized services.

Version management becomes particularly crucial in containerized environments. Systems must track not just application versions but also configuration versions, ensuring proper synchronization between application components and their configurations. This often requires implementing sophisticated version control mechanisms that maintain configuration history and enable rapid rollback when needed.

Resource management and scaling

Container orchestration platforms introduce sophisticated resource management capabilities that automatically handle scaling and resource allocation. These systems continuously monitor resource utilization, automatically adjusting resource allocation based on actual usage patterns and defined policies.

The complexity of resource management extends beyond simple CPU and memory allocation. Modern systems must consider network resources, storage capacity, and other infrastructure components. This requires implementing sophisticated scheduling algorithms that optimize resource utilization while maintaining system performance and reliability.

Scaling operations in containerized environments require careful coordination between multiple system components. When scaling services, systems must consider not just container instances but also associated resources such as persistent volumes, network configurations, and load balancer settings. This coordination ensures smooth scaling operations without service disruption.

Operational considerations

Running containerized deployments at scale requires sophisticated monitoring and observability solutions. These systems must provide visibility into container health, resource utilization, and application performance. More importantly, they must correlate this information across the distributed system, enabling quick problem identification and resolution.

Security considerations take on additional importance in containerized environments. Systems must implement robust security policies that control container execution, network access, and resource usage. This often involves implementing multiple security layers, from container image scanning to runtime security monitoring.

Disaster recovery planning becomes more complex in containerized environments. Systems must account for not just application recovery but also container orchestration recovery. This requires implementing sophisticated backup and recovery procedures that ensure system resilience in various failure scenarios.

Future considerations

As container technologies continue to evolve, deployment strategies must adapt to new capabilities and requirements. Emerging trends such as service mesh integration, serverless container execution, and edge computing introduce new considerations for deployment planning and execution.

The future of containerized deployments likely involves increased automation and intelligence. ML algorithms may optimize deployment patterns based on historical performance data. Automated systems may predict potential issues before they occur, enabling proactive intervention rather than reactive response.

Conclusion

The landscape of software deployment has evolved significantly, driven by the increasing complexity of distributed systems and the demanding requirements of modern applications. Throughout this chapter, we have explored how organizations can leverage sophisticated deployment strategies to minimize risk while maximizing system reliability and user satisfaction. The integration of feature flags, progressive deployment patterns, and automated safety mechanisms represents not just technical advancement but a fundamental shift in how we approach software delivery.

The success of modern deployment strategies relies heavily on the careful orchestration of multiple components, from comprehensive testing frameworks to sophisticated monitoring systems and automated rollback mechanisms. As systems continue to grow in complexity, the importance of these strategies becomes even more pronounced. The rise of container orchestration platforms has further transformed deployment practices, introducing new possibilities for automation and scaling while also presenting new challenges to be addressed.

Looking ahead, organizations must continue to adapt their deployment strategies as technologies evolve. The future points toward increased automation, more sophisticated monitoring capabilities, and even greater integration of AI in deployment decision-making. Success will depend not just on implementing these technologies, but on building robust processes that can evolve with changing requirements while maintaining unwavering focus on system reliability and user experience.

Index